Keeping
the Church
Catholic
with
John Paul II

Msgr. George A. Kelly

IGNATIUS PRESS   SAN FRANCISCO

Originally published by
Doubleday, a division of
Bantam Doubleday Dell Publishing Group, Inc., New York
© 1990 George A. Kelly

Reprinted 1993, Ignatius Press, San Francisco
ISBN 0-89870-413-8
Library of Congress catalogue number 92-75069
Printed in the United States of America

Dedicated
to
The Vincentian Fathers at St. John's University
New York City

Especially

JOSEPH T. CAHILL, C.M.
University President (1965–89)
AND
JOSEPH I. DIRVIN, C.M.
Vice President

Who have imbued their university with
the faith and spirit of their founder

Contents

CONTENTS

Commission. The Second Session and
the Fallout. Majority-Minority
Opinions. Charles Curran. The
Christian Family Movement. Incidental
Fallout. The Last Word.

CONTENTS

1989 Meeting in Seton Hall. The
Remarkable Address of Archbishop
May. The 1989 Meeting with the
Pope.

Introduction

Keeping the Church Catholic with John Paul II is a follow-up to *Inside My Father's House*, the book published by Doubleday in 1989. It continues the story of my reflections on the present doings of the Catholic Church in the United States. After fifty years as a Catholic cleric I have a few things left to say.

This book differs from the other. It deals with matters far beyond the previously related experiences with parochial and diocesan matters. Whereas *Inside My Father's House* touched issues of universal import only incidentally, I will deal here almost exclusively with those larger subjects as they impinge on the conduct of Catholic affairs in the United States. Whereas the first book covered the administration of the Church in the United States as it concerned me personally, my role in the Church of New York and elsewhere whenever those duties carried me into neighboring Catholic worlds, *Keeping the Church Catholic* focuses on events and controversies that have affected not only the lives of my parishioners and their children, but those of many other Catholics in similar circumstances throughout the country.

Proclaimed experience is, of course, a two-edged sword. On the one hand, it is, by definition, a personal account and only a slice of reality. The reporting of it makes public very personal judgments. On the other hand, it is testimony based on long and careful reflection; and when joined to the testimony of others whose experience has led them to similar conclusions, it can challenge and perhaps refute the views of those in the Church today who have made their personal research or wisdom the basis for a new ecclesiology, a new sacramentology, and a new morality. I speak of such views, of course, only insofar as they are in partial or total contradiction to the Word of God as understood in the Church and interpreted by the Church over many centuries.

Whatever one thinks of any one person's experience as a reliable source for evaluating what has happened in the Church, such experience can make a claim to be heard only if it is thoroughly rooted in and reflects the experience of Jesus Christ with His Father and the Holy Spirit. Ironically, however, it is precisely and principally the contemporary passion for the *self*-fulfillment of personalities that has led Church authorities into conflict with a significant number of other persons in various Church leadership positions—some bureaucrats, some college and university personnel, some scholars, some journalists, and some religious superiors. Church historian John Tracy Ellis calls this development a religious revolution, with uncertainty in high and low ecclesiastical places as to how to evaluate the many changes critics demand and how to deal with the conflict, mistrust, and polarization that these debates over change have spawned.

Yet you cannot cure a condition admitted to be irregular, if not pathological, unless you diagnose its causes properly. And even if the reasons for our current institutional distress or breakdown (call it what you will) cannot be identified with the certainty of a medical examiner, symptoms of dissatisfaction within the Church can be identified. These call for immediate relief.

I happen to be one of those priests who think that our nineteenth-century bishops bequeathed to U.S. Catholics a first-rate twentieth-century Church, one of the finest in the history of Christianity. Leading into the 1960's, the U.S. Church was a strong, faithful, joyful Church, where faith was known, believed, supported internally, and defended in the public forum. Not even the Church of France in its heyday, when it was touted as the "eldest daughter of the Church," was the equal of the Church of my early lifetime in faith, piety, and religious works. I was ordained (1942) into a remarkable priestly fraternity and pious lay community whose commitment, behavior, and productivity were as fine as the universal Church has ever experienced anywhere.

Then came the revolution, which I experienced first hand as a pastor and diocesan official. Shortly thereafter I began to notice the downturn by American Catholics, including clergy, in the commitment, behavior, and productivity for which we were universally respected. It was not simply external pressures that led Catholics to drift away from or question articles of faith and morals. Few informed observers—from John Paul II to Hans Küng—deny the existence and severity of the crisis that ensued, although conflicting parties obviously disagree about its nature and its ultimate resolution. People who share my convictions and/or have been shaped by my kind of experience believe that "the crisis," if left to follow the direction in which it is heading, bodes ill for the U.S. Church of the twenty-first century, when those who at this point still regularly occupy most of the pews at Sunday Mass throughout the country will have gone to God. No one, least of all I, can foretell the ultimate outcome of the post-Vatican upheavals, but every serious student of Church affairs can contribute his or her views in an effort to specify and clarify the long-range significance of these upheavals.

Whatever full and final implementation of Vatican II brings, it remains necessary to admit today that we are in the midst of a revolution. During the last quarter century broad leeway has been given by ecclesiastical authority to the Church's centrifugal forces, at least enough leeway for those persons and movements to deny in practice some of what is explicitly and regularly affirmed in binding Church teaching statements, including those of the Second Vatican Council. *Inside My Father's House* touched lightly on some of the doings that presently enfeeble the Catholic body, some of which would have been unthinkable even a generation ago. *Keeping the Church Catholic* examines these events in greater detail with specific reference to my personal relationships with the people worldwide who have been engaged in the battle for and against the institutional Church.

I do not wish to wallow in the unpleasant aspects of present-day controversies. On the other hand, neither do I wish, after the manner of so many political leaders, to cover up wrongdoings of commission or omission that deserve frank exposure. It is important, therefore, to achieve an understanding of how the present revolutionary situation in the Church came about and how the Church, which canonizes faith, obedience and holiness, may regain some kind of sanity and order.

Granted that from afar—Paris, for example—the U.S. Church looks better at the moment than anything to be found in the parish life of older Christian lands. Yet, few would deny that we too have fallen from grace, not from their grace, but from ours. Parents see their growing children not only absent from Mass, but also uninformed abut their faith or unbelieving. Since the Church is not a political democracy, it would be useless and indecent to inflict on Catholics a Watergate-type investigation of our present ills. Nor can we place responsibility for our recent downturns on an apathetic voting public. Within the Church the buck of responsibility for effective or ineffective evangelization stops at the doors of bishops, especially the ordinaries of dioceses. And here we speak mostly of good men, often arguably holy men, whose governing wisdom or ability is only indirectly related to goodness or holiness.

What we must address are the ecclesial policies and procedures currently followed by the Church's highest authorities in institutionalizing the principles and norms of post-Vatican II Catholicism. And these subjects, it seems to me, must be discussed not abstractly, as if we were engaged in a college debate or in an academic exercise of little practical import, but in terms of the thoughts and feelings of those on both sides of a shaky ecclesiastical fence, in Rome and elsewhere, who have responsibility for the eternal salvation of believers. This is what the present book will attempt to do—from my point of view.

I will begin by describing the state of the U.S. Church, past and present, and the beginnings of our contemporary problems —problems that are associated with Vatican II (1962–65) and the Papal Birth Control Commissions (1963–66). One of my theses is that Church authorities let both these institutions get away not only from their intentions, but from their direct supervision. Popular folklore in some quarters would blame the Council itself, or certainly *Humanae Vitae* (1968), for the subsequent doctrinal conflicts and institutional weakness within the Church. In fact, a multitude of events, movements, actions, and writings during the years 1962–1968, between the opening of the Council and the promulgation of Birth Control Encyclical, set the stage for the revolution that developed. The Faith has always lived in the midst of the world's greatest disorders, but in the end the Church does not compromise what may not be compromised. Vatican II was a great grace for the Church, providing precious guidance for the future of its varied apostolates. Trouble, which began first at the edges of the Council, later ate its way into the heart of the Church. Regrettably, during this period and especially after the Council's close, Rome and the national hierarchies mulled over controverted issues as if they had all the time in the world to declare the authentic meaning of Council documents. There is a story here worth reviewing.

After the Council, evidence started to appear that important prelates in various hierarchies were pursuing policies that were at odds with the Council's own implementing directives vis-à-vis administration of the sacraments, imprimaturs, annulments, catechetical instruction, etc. The Council itself clearly provided a debating experience for bishops about new courses and new priorities for the Church. But the very process of the Council also came to be interpreted by some as a foundation to justify dissent from binding Church teaching and disobedience to Church law. Indeed, by 1976 a noted theologian in his presidential address to the Catholic Theological Society of America felt sure enough on this point to say: "By its actual practice of revisionism the Council implicitly taught the legitimacy and value of dissent." Popes Paul VI and John Paul II did not see it that way. Catholic tradition was challenged to its roots by what went on, and the faithful, who were used to a coherent Catholic identity were offended. Neither were Roman cardinals (with whom I began to deal on a regular basis) happy with the turn of events. Among these would be Amleto Cicognani, John Wright, Gabriel Garrone, Egidio Vagnozzi, and Silvio Oddi, to name a few. The new leaders of the national conferences of Catholic bishops world-wide (initially Detroit's Archbishop John Dearden, in the U.S.) faced virulent dissent almost immediately. And so did Dearden's successors, Archbishops John Krol, Joseph Bernardin, John Quinn, John Roach, James Malone, and John May. How all these prelates reacted in theory and in practice to this dissent, especially as I saw them at work, is a story somewhat different from and perhaps of more permanent significance than the doings of Council Fathers from 1962–1965. How the performances of prelates on both sides of the ocean are to be evaluated will vary, naturally, with the reader's expectations of what the future, and the Church's comprehensiveness of dissent, ought to be. This is fair enough, as long as those making judgments realize we are not dealing with a secular political entity, but with the Living Body of Christ, whose form, meaning, and direction—along with the holiness of Catholic people—is entrusted to the Catholic bishops in union with the Pope.

In recent years, Roman cardinals have disagreed with cardinals of various national conferences. Joseph Cardinal Ratzinger, the Holy See's top doctrinal officer, is not concerned about national conferences of bishops per se. St. Irenaeus, and a host of ecumenical councils, insist that "every Church must be in agreement." The German prelate does worry, however, about the ability of episcopal bureaucracies to overwhelm the freedom of diocesan bishops who are trying to govern their own "portion of God's people," because in fact they are only part-time members of their own conferences. Even their freedom to make independent decisions in national assemblies is at risk. In turn, some bishops in the United States, France, and elsewhere think that Rome tries to micromanage local Churches. They resent the interference. NCCB president John May opined after a 1989 meeting with John Paul II that relations between the Holy See and the U.S. hierarchy are "stronger" than ever. This is not exactly clear, if one talks to enough bishops on both sides of the ocean.

Here is what *Keeping the Church Catholic with John Paul II* is all about, a discussion of the contemporary post-Vatican II revolution in the Church from my perspective, taking into account my relationship with key prelates I have known and the actions of episcopal conferences. These have changed the course of Catholic history as Vatican II directed, but not necessarily or consistently, in my view, to the benefit of the Church's eternal mission. Some episcopal decisions that have been made in Rome and in the various nunciatures throughout the world would not need rethinking or reevaluation if our communion of local Churches throughout the world evidenced the same unity within and among themselves and the same vitality as they exhibited earlier in this century. Persons at all points along the ecclesiological spectrum express dissatisfaction with the controversies and polarization now enfeebling the Church. What follows is one priest's view of the crisis and the actions needed to overcome it.

A final word. Dissenters, and those who argue that "freedom" is what Vatican II was all about, have controlled the rhetoric of the ongoing debate about changes in the Church. With support from masters of the secular media, they have succeeded in having the controversies described in this book evaluated as battles over opinion, not about truth. The onlooker and the reader are thus conditioned to choose the side of the argument that favors freedom over authority. This seems to be not only the American way, but to make sense. If we are dealing with personal opinion, why not make the individual, the scholar or the person in the pew, the final judge of the merits of the case? Inevitably, then, he is asked to choose between theologians, between pre-Vatican and post-Vatican II afficianados, between ultraconservative and ultraradical extremists, between standpatters and reformers. This parlance of the American political game is so much a part of our thinking apparatus that applying it to ecclesiastical differences seems to be the right and proper thing to do. The trouble is that in the present Catholic controversies the common rules of district politics do not apply. We are discussing here the substance of God's Word and what He has revealed about Jesus Christ and the Catholic Church. The declarations of the Church are not just any man's opinion. Magisterium is not simply another debater. The everlasting "good of souls" is not determined by consensus. While individual Catholics in the United States, as in Equatorial Africa, have as much right as anyone to their personal tastes in matters of religious practice, the bottom line for their choices is what the Church teaches in Christ's name as Catholic truth. And the truth of Catholic teaching and Church support for that teaching or its lack is what the post-Vatican II controversies are all about.

Many contemporaries contributed to the thinking and the experience reflected in this book—from unwashed altar boys to pious Rosarians; from good priest friends to hardworking pastors, including three archbishops; from lay apostles in many walks of life to the popes who have held office in my lifetime—as fine a run of popes as the Church has reason to hope for in any century. For all of these gifts I am thankful. And in a special way I am grateful to Miss Alice Patricia Hand, who readied this manuscript for publication from day one with great attention and editorial insight, and to Doubleday's bubbly senior editor, Miss Patricia Kossmann, who is publishing the end product. Finally, may we all thank God for the fathers and mothers who raised us and for the Catholic faith which sustains us.

GEORGE A. KELLY

PART ONE

The Mystery of the Church

PROLOGUE

The Mystery

"MOTHER, can we possibly experience greater evils than these?"

This was the question put to St. Catherine of Siena slightly over six hundred years ago by her spiritual director, Friar Raymond of Capua. The priest, distressed by the lack of loyalty to the Church and by the apostates he saw in the Church of 1375, went to his Dominican protégé for consolation.

Catherine's answer was hardly comforting: "Father, what is being done now is being done by lay people; but it will not be long till you see clergy doing worse still."

"Do you mean to say," continued the priest, "that the very clergy will rebel against the Roman Pontiff?"

Catherine answered with a prediction: "You will see them do it with your own eyes the moment he takes on to reform their evil conduct. They will raise a universal scandal throughout the holy Church of God, that will rend it and ravish it like the pest of heresy itself."

What makes anyone think that the life of the Catholic Church should be serene? Or that a member of this Church should lead an untroubled life? Certainly such equanimity was not character-istic of that religious body which came into existence only after the death of its founder, an execution brought on by the betrayal of one of his closest associates. Over two millennia the Church has managed some great moments, and on balance the world owes a great deal to Catholic parents, saints, popes, intellectuals, mis-sionaries, holy women, and just plain pastors. What other church can be found in every nook and cranny of the earth?

And yet the Church experiences as many "deaths" as it does "resurrections," a recurring phenomenon which always seems to catch the faithful by surprise, those who seemingly forget that Easter Sunday saved Christ from being a total failure. On Good Friday the founder of Christianity was abandoned by everyone except His mother, a few women, and a scrawny young disciple named John. Even Peter, the rock upon which He was to build His Church, abandoned Him. But He rose from the dead by the mysterious power of the God that was in Him. And the Church was on her way.

If mystery surrounds the birth of Christianity, as it does the origins of the universe, why are we surprised about the ebb and flow of "death" and "resurrection" that has marked the history of the Church ever since? Why do we expect in this life to compre-hend the mystery of God, Who we know by faith reveals Himself to His people, but always in His own way, and never fully?

It is not surprising, therefore, that the Catholic Church de-scribes herself first and above all as "mystery." In Vatican II's document on the Church (*Lumen Gentium* No. 8), the Council Fathers, drawing on St. Augustine, described her role as follows:

> The Church, like a stranger in a foreign land, presses forward amid the persecutions of the world and the consolations of God, announc-ing the cross and death of the Lord until He comes.[1] But by the power of the risen Lord she is given strength to overcome, in pa-tience and in love, her sorrows and her difficulties, both those that

4

are from within and those that are from without, so that she may reveal in this world, faithfully, however darkly, the mystery of the Lord until, in the consummation, it shall be manifested in full light.

The Church by definition is called upon in every generation to act as a stand-in for Christ, to keep God's presence alive among sinners who would rather worship idols of their own making, to announce the Good News of salvation, and to bring God's grace to His people. These works she is expected to perform through the instrumentality of weak and foolish men and women[2] whose failures are as noticeable as their successes. Christ Himself defined the norm earlier—only when the grain of mustard seed dies does it bring forth fruit.[3] This parable almost describes the natural history of the Church. St. Catherine of Siena, for example, who in 1377 helped Rome recapture the papacy from France after an exile of seventy years, was only one saint in a long history of sanctity who became the "hand of God" reaching down to clean up one of the many socio-political or ecclesiastical messes in which the Church has regularly found herself enmired.

NOTES

1. Cf. 1 Corinthians 11:26.
2. 1 Corinthians 1:27.
3. John 12:24.

ONE

The State
of the U.S. Church:
Past and Present

THE U.S. CHURCH IN THE MAKING

THOSE OF US baptized into the Catholic Church during the early part of the twentieth century became members overnight of one of the finest Christian bodies any nation was ever privileged to see. How the U.S. bishops transformed a once faithless and often disobedient American Catholic community during the period 1800–1900 is a saga in itself, an accomplishment few particular churches can claim in so short a period. All modern popes have admired the accomplishment, not the least of whom is John Paul II. He left the United States in 1987 with "an unforgettable memory of a country that God has richly blessed from the beginning until now." He was thinking as much of the patrimony left by John Carroll to the Church as of that bequeathed by George Washington to the nation.

Six months after George Washington took his presidential oath Rome appointed John Carroll (November 6, 1789) as its first bishop in the United States, partly because the twenty-five thousand Catholics here then were not very good and the twenty-four priests serving them were not much better. Church historian Peter Guilday described this infant Church as "sadly hampered by the presence of priests who knew not how to obey and of laity who were interpreting their share in Catholic life by non-Catholic Church systems."[1] Guilday's judgment has a modern ring to it. Those early priests were often old men, and not a few of them had already scandalized the little Catholic community with their public behavior. Yet these were only part of the problem facing the struggling Church. Everywhere in the colonies Catholics experienced hostility, that prejudice which historian Arthur Schlesinger, Sr., has called "the deepest bias in the history of the American people." Catholics enjoyed civil rights only in five states in early America. New York and New Jersey barred them from public office.

The growth of Catholic life in the United States was slow. A few Catholics were prominent in the American Revolution, mostly from Philadelphia and Baltimore. In New York there was hardly any significant development beyond the Portugese woman and the young Irishman whom the Jesuit priest, Isaac Jogues, discovered there in 1643. As late as 1825 there were only two Catholic churches in that city. Then, shortly afterwards, the rush of Irish immigrants into the country began, to be followed later by Germans, Slavs, and Italians pouring in by the millions. By 1900, almost twenty million immigrants, most of them speaking in foreign tongues or with a distinctly foreign English accent, filled the port cities of the United States. At one time bishops on the East Coast were asked to absorb forty thousand new Catholics per annum.

Sheer numbers were not the only challenge. The greatest pain for the clergy was the people's poverty and their tenuous connection with the Church. When John Hughes took over as New York's bishop in 1842, for example, fifty three thousand New Yorkers were applying for public aid; three out of four of these were Catholics. Catholics, only 10 per cent of the city's popula-

8

tion, contributed 40 per cent of the bodies to Potter's Field. Hughes looked out on his transplanted countrymen and called them "the scattered debris of the Irish nation," "the poorest and most wretched population that can be found in the world." And to compound his efforts at evangelization, they were not a pious or law-abiding lot. Historian Emmet Larkin claims that most of the Irish immigrants between 1847 and 1860 "were part of the pre-famine generation of non-practicing Catholics, if indeed they were Catholics at all."[2]

It is important to recall these early beginnings, if only to appraise adequately the scope of the bishops' later accomplishments, which must be measured not only by the growth in Catholic numbers but also by the intensity of the Catholic commitment that the bishops nourished in those numbers. As Guilday himself explained: "Uniformity, when it did come . . . came quickly after the promulgation of legislation."

In many ways, the quality of religious life was more phenomenal than the growth in numbers. By 1938, there were twenty million Catholics in the United States; at the opening of the Second Vatican Council in 1962, only one generation later, the Catholic population had doubled to forty million. The number of priests had doubled, too, while the number of religious women had tripled! By this time five million Catholic youth attended Catholic schools, and they came out better Catholics than they went in. In 1960 George Bull, speaking from his base at Fordham about the then typical Catholic college, said boastfully: "It has, thank God, sent forth from its halls generations of men and women who know their faith."[3] The best practicing Catholics in those years were college graduates! Two thirds of all Catholics in 1962 observed Church norms on contraception. These Catholic data underscored a situation which was exactly the reverse of what was to be found in the ranks of non-Catholic Americans customarily: the higher the social and educational status, the smaller the family size and the lower the rates of religious observance.

The remarkable thing about this Catholic success is that very few people have written to explain how it was accomplished. Church historian John Talbot Smith, speaking at the turn of the 20th century, credits the American parish, which he called "the highest achievement of the American priest." Of priests, he said:

> The records show them to have been strong men, though not culti-vated on the average, as both time and means were wanting to secure a thorough education. The people supported them handsomely. Con-fidence was not misplaced or betrayed. While the faith of the people edified their Protestant neighbors, the devotion of the priests to their people edified still more; it was seen that the plague had no terror for the priest, nor the poverty of his people, nor any distressing condi-tion. The virtue of the clergy and the people a half century ago was like sweet incense in the Republic.[4]

The push for parochial schools after the Third Council of Balti-more (1884) brought religious communities to the forefront of the Church's efforts, especially communities of religious women. Within fifty years, and specifically between, during, and after the two great world wars, American Catholicism ripened to maturity. Still, it is difficult to find a writer or a group of writers who in describing the phenomenon of Catholic growth have done full justice to the overarching role of bishops in the nineteenth and early twentieth centuries. Those bishops fostered a live faith among the almost forty million poor immigrants who crossed our boundaries between 1830 and 1930.[5]

Ordained a priest in 1942, I walked into the flourishing garden that was Catholic life in the U.S.A. When "our boys" returned a second time from making the world safe for democracy, the Church was in the secure possession of her faith and her faithful. Parish priests almost never received an argument about the faith from parishioners. When the pews talked back, they simply com-plained about the boring sermons on money or about getting their child into parochial schools. Contradictions of Church teaching were nonexistent. Things were far from perfect, of course, since at least one-quarter of the parish was nonpracticing. Still, even the sleeping Catholics usually closed their eyes in death with the blessing of the priest. As for sex, we rarely saw a pregnant teenager, and police of that day had no reason to come to rectory doors with news of pederasts "seeking whom (among our boys) they would devour." Routinely, Father preached and Sister taught, and in the end more of our young protégés made it through college or civil service exams than we ever thought possible.

In many ways it was the best of times for the Church, war or no. Like a wealthy family, the Church had begun to live off her patrimony, a rich endowment of faith amassed by nineteenth-century priests, increased by twentieth-century nuns, and guarded with great care by bishops. Cana and Pre-Cana Conferences were a breeze. Teachers never thought of "right wing" or "left wing" when they discussed probable opinions. *Theological Studies* was more popular with young curates than *The American Ecclesiastical Review* because it represented the less stuffy side of orthodoxy. Redemptorist "Frankie" Connell was a good theologian and a holy man, but most of us preferred Jesuits Gerry Kelly and John Ford, who seemed to respond better to the moral problems faced by parish priests. The faithful loved the radio talks of Fr. James Gillis and high school students relished Fr. Leonard Feeney's doggerel about the things you could buy for a penny.

Young seminarians, hardly out of their teens, mounted platforms in Columbus Circle on behalf of the Catholic Evidence Guild to explain to strangers why the pope was infallible. In every adult instruction class, and by the 1940's there were many, Fr. Smith regularly met a Mr. or Mrs. Jackson, and Frank Sheed's line of books could be found in every respectable Catholic library. Fr. Charles Coughlin had fallen out of favor for his intemperate attacks on FDR and the Jews, while Joe McCarthy divided the Catholic community with his vulgar crusade against real and alleged "Commies" in the State Department.

But on the streets where Catholics lived, you hardly ever found arguments about the Church, except in her favor. "Us" against "them" was commonplace. The Catholic weekly *Commonweal* picked on churchmen from time to time; but most of its editors were respectful of bishops and were themselves pious Catholics besides. The National Catholic Welfare Conference (NCWC) had its Social Action Department, mainly composed of Frs. John Cronin and George Higgins, and it looked dourly on the capitalistic tendencies of Notre Dame's Fr. Edward Keller. By modern standards, however, such disagreements over what was or was not consistent with Catholic social teaching were gentlemanly. Even the most serious intellectual fight in the early post–World War II era, between Frs. John Courtney Murray and Joseph Clifford Fenton over the Church's traditional stance on religious freedom in a civil society which professed no religion, was mild, considering the strong personalities on each side. Fenton even gave Murray space in *The American Ecclesiastical Review* to make his best case against the view staunchly held by the Holy Office's Cardinal Ottaviani. But labels like "liberal" and "conservative," "right wing" and "left wing" seemed more like Washington's words than Roman terminology. Such categories may have separated the New Dealers from the Hooverites, but hardly John Courtney Murray and Joseph Fenton or their likes.

Only a few were surprised when in 1960 The American Institute of Management issued a report in which it declared the Roman Catholic Church to be one of the most efficient management enterprises in the Western World. AIM saw the strength of the Church in three aspects of its everyday conduct: (1) doctrinal unity, (2) dedicated and industrious employees, (3) defensive capabilities. In other words, the reasons why the Church did so well century after century and was a source of inspiration for executives were, quite simply, the clarity of its mission (people knew what it stood for and were thus reinforced in their convictions); a staff of dedicated workers who had ability, integrity, and a good social sense; and the talent of the institutional Church to defend itself against internal and external enemies.

There are many ways to plumb the rich lode of Catholic piety regnant in those days, as well as to measure the gaping distance that separates the Catholic Church in the U.S. then from what it is now. I have already mentioned some. But there is one recollection of that period which left a deep impression on me—the kinds of Catholic magazines and books that enjoyed great popularity among rank and file Catholics. Would-be intellectuals had their *America,* but *The Sign* magazine (published by the Passionist Fathers), now extinct, was the magazine of popular choice. Catholic books on marriage and family life were best-sellers. No publisher who intended to make money on a marriage book would dare let it out to libraries or bookstores without an imprimatur, which was the sure guarantee by a bishop to Catholics that what they were to read was authentically Catholic. And this is what the people expected.

I found out personally how committed Catholics were to the truths of their Church on family life when Random House inveigled me during the period 1958–64 to publish five books—*The Catholic Marriage Manual* (1958), *The Catholic Family Handbook* (1959), *The Catholic Youth's Guide to Life and Love* (1960), *Your Child and Sex* (1964), and *The Catholic Guide to Expectant Motherhood* (1961). Here was a spectrum of subjects, subjects that are still very much alive in a culture that is not happy with Catholic answers. But at that time these books were bestsellers of a sort precisely because they offered Catholic answers.

The Catholic Marriage Manual was the most successful of that series. Its acceptance was seen not so much in the 300,000 copies Random House sold to Catholic couples, mothers mostly, but in the approval given the book by the reigning Catholic elite. Considering the routine nature of the content—Catholic doctrine as it is still being taught by John Paul II—the reviews in hindsight were remarkable. Donald Thorman, later a procontraception editor of the *National Catholic Reporter,* thought it was a great book. But, of course, in 1958 Thorman was working for the Christian Family Movement when it was fully Catholic. In November 1959, *Woodstock Letters,* then based in Maryland and years away from the Jesuit disasters in New York, described it as "a fine presentation of the Catholic case against birth control, abortion, divorce, mixed marriage," and as "a valuable tool for priests and Catholic married couples." Dr. John Marshall, at the time a leading Catholic physician with Westminster's Catholic Marriage Advisory Council, called it "an excellent book" with one major defect. The Manual, he said, did not make the most effective case against contraception that could be made. Writing in the October 1960 issue of London's *Catholic Medical Quarterly*, Marshall suggested how to improve the book: "The argument must start from the fact that the error of contraception lies in the fact that intercourse is performed in a way which is contrary to that designed by God. It is not, therefore, primarily concerned with the intention of avoiding children, contraception would be equally wrong if practised by a sterile couple." A simple and shocking aftermath to all this is provided by one fact that highlights the sudden change from flourishing Church to ailing Church in the sixties: Five years after penning those lines, Marshall, then a member of Paul VI's Birth Control Commission, voted in favor of contraception.

The *Catholic Family Handbook* received more of the same embarrassing praise. In an editorial, Notre Dame's popular magazine *Ave Maria* actually (November 28, 1959) called it "the complete book of practical guidance and inspiration on every aspect of family life." Four years later (September 1963) under Holy Cross Father John Reedy, the same magazine began to promote birth control and eventually went out of business. Kansas City's *The Catholic Reporter* called *The Catholic Youth's Guide* (May 27, 1960) the "outstanding book to date for Catholic youth." A short time later Bishop Charles Helmsing, the paper's founder, banished the paper from his diocese as no longer Catholic. *The National Catholic Reporter*, which was its offshoot, would describe the *Youth's Guide* as "nourishing fare" and call for it to "be on every priest's bookshelf."

Those five books sold over 500,000 trade copies and were published simultaneously in England for marketing in the British Commonwealth, later in French and Spanish. *The Catholic Marriage Manual* alone sold over 300,000 copies at $4.95. When the first check for $10,000 was presented to Cardinal Spellman, he was dumbfounded. Years later, he introduced me to a group as someone who had been very generous to the Foundling Hospital.

To which I replied: "If I knew I was going to be that generous I might not have been so generous."

There is a tendency these days to debunk "the good old days" of the Church. But the Catholicity of the U.S. Church was remarkable. Anyone who worked as a parish priest between, during, and after the two world wars can give ample testimony to what can only be called a Catholic miracle. It was a good and pleasant time to be a priest; and the memory of those days still warms the soul. It was a time when a priest could teach unadulterated Catholic doctrine without being hobbled and obstructed by divisive dissent, which merely would have confused the faithful and clogged the ongoing life of religious belief and customary piety.

THEN CAME VATICAN II

I am not one of those who blame the Council for the subsequent troubles of the Church in the Western World. Breaking the Church out of her Italian and European mold was a plus, as was the shaking up of dying particular churches like France and Brazil. Rome may not successfully confront the challenge of expanding Communist empires (that remains to be seen), but the Conciliar demand that a try be made was a step forward. Interchurch union, certainly with the Greek and Russian Orthodox churches and with whatever Protestant groups could make "the leap of faith," are potential historic by-products of the Vatican II impulse, as is the proper catechizing of the millions of neglected but baptized Spanish Catholics of several continents. Hilaire Belloc once predicted the re-Christianization of the West by missionaries from the Orient. Should this become necessary, the African Church more likely will supply the manpower, so strong and immediate is the impact of the Council on that region of Catholicism. Certainly the worldwide institutionalization of the justice and peace apostolates as necessary components of the Church's modern mission was long overdue, especially since Leo XIII began the process almost a century ago; and the poor, a majority of the world's population, will be its chief beneficiary. The internal reforms of Vatican II, which I believe were inspired of God, include the new liturgy, new procedures of Church administration, recognition of the important role of the laity in evangelization, the updating of religious communities, new Catholic apostolates to intensify love of God or to meet the pressing human needs, decentralization of the episcopacy, internationalization of the Curia, and regular Roman Synods.

Pius XII was said to have considered a council, but this cautious pontiff put the idea to the side, partly because of his own age, partly for its anticipated difficulties. Indeed, Pius warned about the very dissidence that eventually tore the Church apart after the Council. In 1943, in what is often called his magna carta for biblical scholars *(Divino Afflante Spiritu,* No. 24), he warned historicists about ignoring the Church's teaching authority in their exegesis. In 1950, his encyclical *Humani Generis* condemned false opinions which threatened to undermine the foundations of Catholic doctrine and the antimagisterial virus already infecting would-be modernizing academics. In 1957, the year before he died, he sent a chill through the thirtieth General Congregation of Jesuits by taking note of a tendency in their midst to forswear the basic principles of religious life and their well-known loyalty to the See of Peter. While these latter *monita* had European Jesuits in mind (the American company was remarkably faithful at the time), breaking ties with the Holy See became a trademark of many religious communities in the post-Council period.

Angelo Roncalli, as cardinal of Venice, once made the offhand remark, "If I were elected pope, I'd call a Council," but then there was no reason to believe he would ever be pope. Suddenly he was in Peter's Chair (on the twelfth ballot), and off the Church went on an adventure that seemed to fit no historic pattern. General councils have usually been called to remedy great ecclesiastical evils, to settle controversies, to deal with heresy, to define doctrine, or otherwise to legislate new liturgical or pastoral norms. But at the death of Pius in 1958, the Church was held in high esteem worldwide, and the trend of Catholic development by human standards was on the upgrade. The jolly Pope had different ideas, however, although his reasons are irrelevant to any assumption that Vatican II represents an act of God—especially since John XXIII offered at least seventeen different reasons for convoking a general council at a time of relative ecclesiastical peace.

Although Milan's Cardinal Montini (later Paul VI) thought three more years of preparation were required before the world's bishops would be ready for a general council, John, probably because of his advanced age (he was 81 at the time), went ahead anyway on October 11, 1962. The speculations of the media and subsequent events aside, John XXIII seemed to have had the idea that running an ecumenical council was as easy as doing his Roman Synod, which occupied one week of his time in 1960. This misapprehension was to create difficulties later. Apparently, the old Pope was giving the Council three months and expected it to complete its business in that period. Westminster's John Cardinal Heenan recalls how at the end of the first session (December 1962), the aging Pontiff called a few cardinals together and raised the question: "How can we call this off gracefully, without this thing going into more sessions?" According to Italian historian Giacomo Martina, the "three-month limit" had been the understanding of all of John's closest assistants. He certainly was not on a revolutionary course, not this Pontiff who on June 20, 1961, warned New Testament exegetes to observe caution, and who a year later (June 30, 1962) spelled out the dangers to the Church in the works of Teilhard de Chardin. John never really identified the specific ideas he wished to be institutionalized universally. When the French and German bishops sidetracked the two-year labors of his preparatory commissions, the Pope obviously had no backup plan. He surely would not need one, since God planned to call him home before the second Council session began (June 3, 1963). Paul VI instead was given the responsibility to bring Vatican II to its Catholic conclusion.

The story of the Council has been told often enough. The only thing worth remembering here is that the debates and politicking

17

among bishops, between curial and diocesan cardinals, too, became the basis of a presumption, carried over virulently into the post-Vatican II period, that dissent* from affirmed and reaffirmed Catholic teaching had somehow been legitimated. Marcel Lefebvre, the excommunicated archbishop, and Hans Küng, his ideological antagonist, used the Council's deliberations to justify their respective aberrant judgments that the Council either went too far or did not go far enough.

In any case the dysfunctions of the Council were not long in coming. The Church of Holland, hailed early as an exemplar of the new Vatican II Catholicism, rapidly came as close to schism as a particular Church can get and still remain within the fold. Weekly Mass attendance there fell from 75 percent to 20 percent; new priests dropped from three hundred to fifteen annually; the supply of Dutch missionaries, who were once great Church heroes in Africa and Asia, dried up; and ecclesiastical bureaucracies defied their bishops and the instructions originating in Rome. Holland's bishops today manage what has been called "an empty Catholic shell," one maintained by loving Catholics who are scorned by the power brokers who dominate the Dutch Church machinery. Other particular Churches, mostly those in affluent corners of the world also fell into crises of one kind or another, impelling John Paul II toward a traveling ministry to keep the authentic faith of the Church alive.

---

* In this book, when I use the word "dissent" I refer to contradictions or denials, express or implied, of doctrines considered by the Church's Magisterium to be divinely revealed, or of teachings on faith and morals which have been proposed definitively by the same authority, or of those which are enunciated by the Pope or the College of Bishops when they exercise their authentic Magisterium. I am not speaking of those disagreements which have to do with practical judgments of the Church's institutional leaders, certainly not their prudential judgments, nor their private opinions on the fine points of theology still legitimately debated by theologians.

REVOLT IN THE UNITED STATES

The full dimension of this revolt comes into sharp relief when you compare the condition of the Catholic Church in America of today with the conditions a generation ago.

By 1960, the 40,000,000 Catholics could be categorized as follows:

- 30,000,000 Catholics going to Mass every Sunday (75 percent).
- 34,000,000 Catholics making their Easter Duty annually. Over 85 percent of single Catholics 19 years and older, attended Mass weekly.
- 25,000 seminarians in training to join the fraternity of 60,000 priests, mostly U.S.-born and young.
- 160,000 religious sisters and brothers training 5,000,000 Catholic youth in Catholic schools and an equal number of children under catechetical instruction.

As Greeley and Rossi concluded in *The Education of Catholic Americans:*

> These (conditions of Catholic religious practice) are not only the apparent effects of Catholic education: they comprise as well what the American Church expected of its laity during the years it was still concentrating on the preservation of the faith of the immigrant and his children and grandchildren.

In contrast, by the 1980s the religious practice of the Catholic masses, now estimated to be over 50,000,000, fell sharply:

- Only 25,000,000 Catholics now attend Sunday Mass, a figure 17 percent lower than that of 1960, even though by virtue of natural increase the Catholic population today is 25 percent larger.
- Baptisms have declined by 500,000, indicating an unusually low Catholic birthrate.

19

- The Sacrament of Penance has virtually been wiped out, evidence of a lessened sense of sin.
- There are almost 75,000 fewer converts, the result of the loss of the unique status of the Catholic Church among Christians.
- The 5,000,000-student Catholic school system has been cut in half by attrition and leakage, with questions increasingly raised about the Catholic quality of what is left.
- Seminarians studying for the priesthood are below 6,000, one quarter of the 1960 number.

Defenders of the status quo tend to question the significance of these statistical downturns, choosing to emphasize instead the positive effects of the Council, previously mentioned. But even granting that all the new priorities will eventually work to the Church's advantage, the disaffections among the Catholic masses, amply reported everywhere, remains a serious worry, especially when an American Catholic community divided on doctrine is challenged today by an influx of twenty million Hispanics with a high birthrate. The extent to which the American Catholics are divided doctrinally is illustrated in the study of four thousand graduates of Notre Dame University, three-quarters of whom are over thirty years of age, which provides evidence that this supposedly *crème de la crème* body of educated Catholics questions papal infallibility, the Church's moral norms, and even her dogmatic definitions on the priesthood, and hardly ever goes to Confession.[6] It is into this Church that the Hispanic Catholics have come, 88 per cent of whom "are not actively involved in their parishes," whose "youth are estranged from the Church."[7]

According to pollsters George Gallup and Jim Castelli, "pick and choose religion" is as American as apple pie, even among Catholics. "What has not been appreciated," they say, "is that by sheer numbers they (the Catholics) have adopted this style of loyal opposition. They have forced American bishops to accept their new definition of Catholicism."[8] The only trouble with such an announcement is that John Paul II during his 1987 visit told

American bishops that dissent from Church teaching is totally incompatible with being a "good Catholic" and an obstacle to the reception of the sacraments.[9]

There is a basic question here waiting for an answer: Is the Catholic Church in the United States of the next century to reflect as essential elements of its nature the definitions and norms proclaimed by John Paul II, or is it to be a Church which officially accepts "pick-and-choose Catholicism" as an approved option for its constituency?

If the latter option is a possibility or a likelihood, then truly is *The Church in Anguish,* (the title of a book[10] coauthored, among others, by Bernard Häring, Charles Curran, Rosemary Reuther, David Tracy, Andrew Greeley, Richard McBrien, and Eugene Kennedy, which accuses the present pope by his repressive measures of betraying the recent Council).

If, on the other hand, the definitions and norms of John Paul II are normative but not controlling, then the Catholic Church is in the middle of a major institutional breakdown. Not only has pick-and-choose thinking led to widespread misbehavior and scandalous conduct in the Catholic community, not excluding the lives of priests and religious, but it means that the bishops are not governing or are not able to govern their own people according to the mind of the Church. It is widely recognized that they are at present unsuccessful in getting significant numbers of priests to teach as John Paul II does, and they seem to lack practical authority over colleges, religious orders, and theological groups which are in various stages of dissent from Church norms and from the requirements of canon law. Within their own diocesan machineries they face a powerful lobby on behalf of pick-and-choose Catholicism, hardly what one expects of a Church which still speaks of its teachings as true. The "outsiders" to this machinery, and the ones likely to be ignored, if not disciplined, by its leadership, are those who "believe all that the Church teaches" and those who think that Catholic law ought to be observed at least by those entrusted with its care.

The extent of the present Catholic revolution will become clear as the story of this book unfolds, relating the manner in which Roman prelates and American bishops have dealt with the revolution and with each other.

NOTES

1. *History of the Councils of Baltimore*, p. 185.
2. *American Catholic Historical Review*, June 1972, p. 651.
3. *America Press*.
4. *The Catholic Church in New York*, vol. 1, pp. 173–74.
5. Gerald P. Fogarty's 1985 book, *The Vatican and the American Hierarchy from 1870 to 1965*, was almost entirely given over to questions of internal and external Church politics. Jay Dolan, Notre Dame's expert on urban Catholicism, wrote *The American Catholic Experience* in which he almost sneers at the Church's early success with immigrants, their piety and adherence to Church authority.
6. *Notre Dame Magazine*, Summer 1987.
7. See a paper issued by the National Conference of Bishops (NCCB) on the occasion of John Paul II's 1987 visit to the U.S.
8. *The American Catholic People*, p. 178.
9. *Origins*, October 1, 1987, p. 261.
10. Harper & Row, 1987.

PART TWO

The Fall from Grace

Pope Paul VI:
The Man for Human Life

A Man for All Seasons was a Broadway hit in New York about the time Martin Luther King was leading his marches through Montgomery and Selma. What could be more exciting in an age of civil rights than a struggle to the death between a pious Catholic lawyer and a powerful Catholic king? Even though it was a sixteenth-century story, when well told four hundred years later for theatergoers, it remained high drama: person against state, religious principle against lust.

Here was Henry VIII craving a second wife whom the Church would not allow him but desirous, when he took her anyway, that his lord chancellor, Thomas More, should bless the union. If More, who known for his piety, did so, then perhaps Catholic people of the kingdom might follow suit. Thomas did not, and the contest began. All the King's wiles and all the King's men were arrayed against him—the Archbishop of Canterbury, Thomas Cranmer; Thomas Cardinal Wolsey, the Papal Legate; the Catholic Duke of Norfolk; Thomas Cromwell, the new Chancellor; and a character designated in the script as the Common Man, otherwise the personification of the sixteenth century itself. Robert Bolt, the playwright, even has More's wife and family unsympathetic to his uncompromising stand against his king.

As the play unfolds, the tension grows—between More, self-described as "the King's good servant but God's first," and Henry, no longer the "Defender of the Faith," a title given him by a pope for defending the Church against Martin Luther. Thomas first loses his friend, then his job, finally his head. Through it all he stands fast, neither "devoured" nor "deflowered," to use his own words. When asked to acknowledge Parliament's decree making Henry, not the Pope, the head of the Church in England, More responds: "This is directly repugnant to the law of God." Pressed by the Crown to avoid high treason, he cries: "It is not for the Supremacy you have sought my blood, but because I would not bend to the marriage."

At this moment in the drama, Bolt has Paul Scofield, majestically playing More, rise, move to the block—in the presence of leaders of Church and State—and lower his head. But not before telling the Axeman: "Friend, do not be afraid of your office. You send me to God." And when the kettledrums cease roaring, the Axeman proclaims: "Behold—the head of a traitor."

The play ends there, leaving Henry with Anne Boleyn. Cranmer became a Protestant, Cromwell was later to be deposed, while the infamous Cardinal Wolsey lived long enough to bemoan his craven conduct in words that have been immortalized by Shakespeare: "Had I but served my God with half the zeal I served my King, he would not in my old age have left me naked to mine enemies." Thomas More was canonized a Saint of the Church in 1935, exactly four hundred years after he was beheaded.

Of course, dramas about religion are as old as Adam, or at least Moses, with the longest theater run ever belonging to the Passion Play. Throughout the Christian era much of what is known by the "common people" about saints and sinners comes to them through actors or minstrels of one kind or another. A Peter, Paul, Aquinas, Becket, Francis Xavier, Pius XII continue to fascinate

26

playwrights who must decide whether to make them seem taller than they were or simply to destroy the myths built around them. I am waiting for someone to find theater in the pontificate of Paul VI. They have already dubbed him Hamlet, and so he may have been. Yet he is one modern Catholic who thus far has drawn little more than sympathy from those who watched him perform. But who knows? As yesterday's news turns into history, tale-tellers may give him a second look. Giovanni Montini, the lawyer's son who became Paul VI, looks like a man of God standing alone in a circus waiting to be crucified by the worldly power brokers of his time. Any play about him would reek of matters sexual, because with the world around him saturated with it, he, like Moses, offered his people commandments to obey, not idols to worship.

TWO

The Battle in Rome
over Contraception

PAUL VI will likely be remembered more for his encyclical *Humanae Vitae* than for having brought the Second Vatican Council to a decent conclusion. Some theologians think that, from a doctrinal point of view, it was better for a pope using his supreme authority to reaffirm the Church's teaching on contraception than to have the Birth Control Commission do it. Not only would this have been a bad theological precedent, but it would have been looked upon by the Catholic world, and by everyone else, as a contrived public relations gambit and so demeaning to the papal office. Those theologians are probably right.

Nonetheless, the Birth Control Commission helped bring on the very revolution he intended it to forestall. Not only was it badly conceived, but it was improperly administered. Only naiveté can explain how a pope would initiate a procedure which could be misused to propose that what the Church always considered evil might not be evil after all. The infighting which followed the Commission's creation became the platform for undermining popular belief in a firm Catholic doctrine.

For in 1963 when the commission was born, the doctrine was taught as true and recognized as such by Catholics. Pius XI saw to that with his famous encyclical (December 31, 1930) on Christian marriage:

> The Catholic Church, to whom God has entrusted the defense of the integrity and purity of morals, standing erect in the midst of the moral ruin around her, in order that she may preserve the chastity of the nuptial union from being defiled by this foul stain, raises her voice in token of her divine ambassadorship and through our mouth proclaims anew: Any use whatsoever of matrimony exercised in such a way that the act is deliberately frustrated in its natural power to generate life is an offense against the law of God and of nature, and those who indulge in such are branded with the guilt of grave sin.[1]

Casti Connubii, as the letter's official name, was the Church's immediate and solemn response to the Anglicans' Lambeth Conference which earlier in 1930 opened the door slightly to the use of contraception in hardship cases, the first time in two millennia this was permitted by a major Christian body. Even at Lambeth, the Anglican theologian and bishop Charles Gore, no friend of Rome, rose to warn his peers that from a Christian viewpoint the separation of sexuality from its God-given procreative reason for existence would free men and women from the need of marriage. If man and woman could legitimately engage in sexual relations for reasons of love and personal fulfillment (or for less worthy reasons, such as lust), they might rightly seek this boon if they were in love, but for a variety of reasons were unwilling or unable to marry. And, cautioned Gore, if heterosexuals could relish this freedom of sexual fulfillment, why not homosexuals, since procreation no longer was an essential function of sexuality?

Later developments in England and in Anglicanism proved Gore correct about the effects, personal and social, of abandoning a first principle of Judeo-Christian morality, namely, God's will. If a church in Christ's name could endorse contraception, it could be called upon later to endorse fornication, adultery, and pederasty. Henry VIII would have been vindicated on the dissolubility of Christian marriage and Thomas More made out to be a fool for the sacrifice of his life.

If the Catholic Church was so sure of its teaching, why a study commission?

THE "PILL" COMMISSION

By 1960 "the pill" was coming into wide use, and while it inhibited female ovulation, it did not denaturalize intercourse. Pope Pius XII saw no problem in using steroids for medical purposes, i.e., to treat pathological conditions. A long Catholic tradition justified such choices. But the pill also involved gray areas, many of which scientists had not fully explored. Was it a menacing drug if used indefinitely? Would it regulate menstrual cycles? Would steroids help to perfect natural family planning procedures which were fully endorsed by the Church?

By 1963, the first year into the Council, "birth control" had become a hot issue among Catholics. Pope John XXIII responded by nominating six experts, three scientists and three theologians, to study the pill, its usefulness and its possibly morally correct usage. Although Pius XII had clearly rejected it when used directly as a sterilizing agent, studying its medical mystery seemed a sensible thing to do. The panel of experts was small, the meetings were quasi-secret and removed from media pressures for immediate answers one way or another. The six experts eventually disagreed, but not before one medical wag reported (incorrectly, it would seem): "The scientists were against it because it was dangerous; the priests were for it because it was useful." Little noticed then was the fact that the group operated under no guidelines, an unusual procedure given the importance of the subject matter. This lacuna would later create major difficulties for the successor of John XXIII, who died before the six experts even met. It was an oversight neither Pius XI nor Pius XII would have allowed to occur. Institutional leaders who are conscious of their responsibility, whether chief executives or labor leaders, never allow outsiders to arbitrate issues intrinsically linked to their well-being or survival.

Faced with a deadlocked commission, Paul VI on his ascendancy reinstituted and enlarged it. Was there really any need to open wider the possibility for change in the public eye when it is clear in hindsight he never intended to alter Catholic doctrine at all? And if that was the case, why did he wait so long to promulgate the ancient teaching of the Church? (Especially, since during the commission's meeting, when Paul was asked by member John Ford, S.J., "Are you ready to say that Casti Connubii can be changed?", the Pope answered a vehement "No.")

The members of the Birth Control Commission included certain papalists, Jesuit theologians John Ford of the United States and Stanislaus de Lestapis of France; stout hearts such as Dr. and Mrs. Henri Rendu, French activists on behalf of natural family planning (NFP).

But the adversaries became more numerous as time wore on: no one was more determined to overturn Catholic teaching than Bishop Joseph Reuss, auxiliary bishop of Mainz, Redemptorist priest Bernard Haring, and Jesuit Joseph Fuchs, both of whom taught American seminarians. Other contraceptive-minded members of the commission were cast in less significant but by no means minor roles. They included the Dominican priest Henri di Reidmatten, secretary of the commission, who played the Cranmer role here, ostensibly standing for the Pope's interest but in fact working against him, and Msgr. Ferdinand Lambruschini, a theologian at the Pope's own Lateran University, who later appeared as an embarrassment to Paul VI's final decision. Then there would be Mr. and Mrs. Patrick Crowley, presidents of the Christian Family Movement–U.S.A.; their friend John Noonan, a Notre Dame lawyer, whose book *Contraception* was not yet published.

On the outside were the media ready to exploit the issue. Robert B. Kaiser, who reported for *Time* magazine, became an active partisan against the Pope. Today Rome is acutely aware of media power and, as can be discerned by its handling of recent Synods, is better equipped to control its own investigations. But during the 1960's, a certain naiveté about "openness" contributed to the unfortunate results that followed.

JOINING THE COMMISSION

No one was more surprised than I when one morning a letter arrived from Rome, dated February 25, 1965, signed by Amletto Cardinal Cicognani, Secretary of State, appointing me to Paul VI's Birth Control Commission.

My reactions to the Roman letter that morning were purely personal. Did Cardinal Spellman know of the appointment? Had he been consulted? A visit to his residence did not provide answers to either of these questions. The Cardinal was polite, interested, but noncommittal. For a prelate who was passionate about any public issue which affected the Church, he was uncharacteristically aloof on the birth control issue. This was partly a matter of age (he was 75), but also a reflection of what a low priority he and other bishops gave to Catholic family issues then in controversy, although by the opening of Vatican II in 1962 family breakdown was considered to be the country's prime social problem. On paper, the nation's Catholic bishops believed this to be a fact—they had already made a major statement on the subject as far back as 1949—but neither they nor the Cardinal ever moved to protect the Catholic family after World War II, as nineteenth-century bishops did after the Civil War in order to protect the children of poor immigrants. Parochial schools were the result of those efforts; nothing comparable for the family attracted the enthusiasm of twentieth-century bishops. The subsequent family movements were for the most part voluntary efforts.

In light of the Cardinal's seeming unconcern for the issues involved, there was only one thing to do and that was to call Fr. John Ford, S.J., former dean of theology at the Catholic Univer-

KEEPING THE CHURCH CATHOLIC

sity of America, the one prominent Commission member who came to mind. (Later it was discovered that the American members also included Archbishop Leo Binz of St. Paul-Minneapolis; Dr. John Cavanaugh, a Washington, D.C., psychiatrist; Thomas Burch, a demographer from Georgetown University; Mr. and Mrs. Patrick Crowley of Chicago's Christian Family Movement; Donald Barrett, a sociologist from Notre Dame; and gynecologist Dr. Andre Hellegers of Johns Hopkins. Another Notre Dame professor, John Noonan, had been named consultant to this enlarged Papal Birth Control Commission.)

Fr. Ford was sanguine about the possibilities. After all, the new papal body was basically an enlarged "pill committee"—struggling to understand whether and under what circumstances steroids could be used in good conscience, even if the indirect effect would be the prevention of conception. Nor was Ford concerned about a Catholic statement from the Commission on "responsible parenthood," about which he himself had written many times. Ford had been encouraged by John Noonan's unpublished manuscript on the history of the Church's teaching on contraception. The Notre Dame lawyer had not given the Jesuit his last chapters. But his report on the history of this Catholic teaching was definite: "Never had it been admitted by a Catholic theologian that complete sexual intercourse might be had in which by deliberation, procreation was excluded."[2] Noonan's research also established Pius XI's solemn statement in *Casti Connubii* as the capstone of a universal teaching of the church from the beginning.

We were further assured by the research of the French Jesuit, Stanislaus de Lestapis, whose *Family Planning and Modern Problems: A Catholic Analysis* demonstrated how from Malthus to Marx, from England to India, from wealth to poverty, the direct link between contraception, sterilization, and abortion was inexorable. Besides, de Lestapis had been a member of John XXIII's Commission from the beginning.

There were other assurances. Jesuits Marcellino Zalba, as early as 1951, and John Ford, by 1963, considered the Church's position to be infallibly true. Furthermore, their fellow Jesuit, Joseph

Fuchs had written two years before the Second Vatican Council began in 1960 that any Catholic who did not accept the teaching of *Casti Connubii* sinned against the Faith! The doctrine seemed secure. The only open question was the morality of using the pill.

There were storm warnings, to be sure, and in hindsight it is surprising that so few people in high authority moved to keep the deliberations within Catholic bounds. If some bishops during the Second Vatican Council were in doubt about the absolute truth of the Church's ban on contraception, what could one expect of journalists? Wrestling between the pro- and anticontraception forces broke out in earnest when the Council fathers began to compose the section on marriage for a document that was to be entitled *The Church in the Modern World*, usually referred to by its opening Latin words *Gaudium et Spes* (Joy and hope). The proposed draft on marriage had much to say on conjugal love but said nothing new on procreation or birth control. After some cloak-and-dagger activity of one kind or another, the text of *Gaudium et Spes* (No. 51) as finally approved by the Council Fathers read:

> In questions of birth regulation, the Sons of the Church, faithful to these principles, are forbidden to use methods disapproved by the teaching authority of the Church in its interpretation of Divine Law.[3]

Paul VI, not satisfied with what was going on about this grave matter within the Council, directed that a footnote be added in the appropriate place to the text of *Gaudium et Spes.*[4] It included this admonition:

> By order of the Holy Father, certain questions requiring further and more careful investigation have been given over to a commission for the study of population, the family, and births, in order that the Holy Father may pass judgment when its task is completed. With the teaching of the Magisterium as it is, the Council has no intention of proposing concrete solutions at this moment.

One question immediately comes to mind about the Pope's statement here: Solutions to what? To the problem of legitimate or illegitimate uses of the pill? Since the record shows that this was the only doubt he was entertaining at that time, why did the Pontiff not say as much? However, the Pope did place three references in that Footnote 14—all condemnations of contraception: one reference to a 1964 allocution of his own, and one each to Pius XI's *Casti Connubii* (1930) and Pius XII's famous *Address to Italian Midwives* (1951). The mind of Paul VI could not have been clearer.

Yet, even as the final printing of the last draft of *Gaudium et Spes* went into production on the early morning of December 3, 1965, three days before the Council's end, while the assembled bishops waited to see what they were to vote on, someone discovered during the printing process that Paul VI's references to the condemnations of contraception by Pius XI and Pius XII had been omitted. Was this a printer's oversight? Some thought not. In any event the presses were stopped and the error corrected, thus ensuring that the Council bishops knew what they were doing when they voted on December 4. The formulation of Catholic doctrine was open to restatement, even amplification, but not correction nor denial.

Naturally, this bickering within the Council between 1963 and 1965 spilled over into the public forum. Inevitably, members of the enlarged Papal Birth Control Commission were carried along by the tide. And while Monday morning quarterbacking is always infallible, it serves curiosity to ask what purpose did statisticians, social scientists, lay witnesses, even Family Life Directors serve on this commission since they could speak only about questions irrelevant to the moral determination the original Commission was called upon to make. This mixed assortment of theological amateurs turned Paul's Commission almost immediately into a debating society arrogating to itself the function of reformulating Catholic doctrine in political caucus.

Cardinal Cicognani told me before the Commission met that no change in doctrine was possible. He further expressed pique that any bishop should suggest otherwise. He indicated further, in 1965, that an encyclical letter from the Pope about contraception was in the offing. I had to ask myself what I was doing on the commission. I was no expert on the pill. Given this situation, by the time the commission met in Rome's Spanish College in March 1965, the stage was set for the coup that followed.

THE FIRST SESSION OF THE COMMISSION

Professor John Noonan's presentation at the first session of the papal commission now seems more like an opening gambit in a game of political persuasion than a clarification of the true and sacred Word of God revealed through the Church's teaching office. Noonan was a good man and a solid scholar. His book *Contraception* is a classic of its kind and deserves the praise it has received. Yet, at the same time, he was at Notre Dame University, which then housed some of the Church's leading contraceptionists. In commission sessions, he represented the advocacy camp, backing into contraception, as I later told him in a Washington, D.C., meeting. He knew the history of this subject better than anyone, but he sifted its meaning in the direction opposite to the source from which it came and against the unilinear development according to which the doctrine unfolded throughout the centuries. Despite the vagaries of circumstances of people's lives and the Church's pastoral practice, the Church always, consistently, without evasion had condemned contraception as evil. And even apart from the teaching authority of the Church—the Magisterium, as it is called—Noonan himself affirmed in 1965 that no Catholic theologian had ever approved contraception.

Noonan's brilliant two-hour lecture to the commission on the opening day highlighted the source of the Catholic teaching, which developed from Gospel thinking and in response to a Greco-Roman culture characterized by fragile marriage, sexual libertinism, exploitation of women, abortion, infanticide, and other ills. The Church's answer had many elements: marriage— holy and indissoluble; equality of the sexes in marriage; the sacredness of life and of the process of giving life; the value of children and the importance of their proper rearing; absolute opposition to divorce, family violence, abortion, contraception, and infanticide. Certainly, as Noonan indicated, the Church erected walls against the family evils of that day, high walls around the sacredness of indissoluble marriage and of the right to life, especially of the unborn. The absolute exclusion of contraception was one of those protective walls.

Noonan conceded that all those walls made sense as needed protectors of fundamental Christian values that had been clearly stated by Christ and the apostles. But, he asked, since the ban on contraception was not specifically treated in the New Testament, was this wall merely an outer wall, not absolutely necessary, and dispensable if the more central values of sacred marriage and sacred life could still be effectively protected? Noonan raised that question, leaving it to commission members to find the answer. However, the variables in his account of Church history, the variety of reasons given by Church fathers to justify the contraception ban, the diverse penitential practices of the Church toward contraceptive sinners, including silence when Church leaders knew that immoral birth prevention, usually by coitus interruptus, was widespread—all this left many aspects of the contraception question unanswered.

Once open discussions began within the Commission, the impetus for change took over. The makeup of the Commission made this easy for the procontraception forces to get going. The scientists were not sure how the pill worked or what its long-range effects might be; the theologians were unsure of its use in regulating monthly cycles; what then was there to discuss except doctrine? And there were enough pro-contraceptionists on the Commission to facilitate the process of discussing a doctrine already declared absolutely by the Church!

Auxiliary Bishop Joseph Reuss of Mainz and Redemptorist Bernard Haring began almost immediately to do precisely that. Whereas Reuss was direct, Haring was slippery. After Noonan's presentation, Redemptorist Haring made the case that even the patron saint of all Redemptorist moralists, Alphonsus Liguori, favored the interruption of sexual intercourse in marriage for just and sufficient cause. Haring's suggestion that there might be other and modern exceptions to the absolute veto on [contraception] was insinuated by example, not by argument. But no sooner had Haring finished than his superior, Redemptorist Jan Visser, then president of the Alphonsianum College where Haring taught, rose to agree that St. Alphonsus surely admitted that marital intercourse could be interrupted before its fruition. But he accused Haring of not giving the complete statement of Alphonsus: "For example," St. Alphonsus had added, "when thieves break into the house." The audience laughed at Haring's ruse. Obviously, to interrupt intercourse in such circumstances would be legitimate, but surely no argument in favor of theological justification for contraceptive intercourse!

Following the general assembly, the first meeting of the commission's theologians took place. By majority vote, they decided that the teaching of *Casti Connubii* was "reformable," without specifying what that meant. One theologian compared the Church's view of contraception to her approach to Friday abstinence from meat: common sense and free choice were called for, he averred, as circumstances required. The theological group, however, were not all high-quality experts in the field. I was assigned there, even though my specialty was sociology. Other groups meeting separately pored over medical views, population statistics, social surveys, and the testimony of lay witness. By the end of the four days allotted to the first session, the lines were drawn between opponents. A political process had begun. The delegates returned home with the full understanding that the issues raised during those four days in March-April 1965 went beyond traditional casuistry and touched fundamental questions: the nature of Divine revelation, the role of the teaching Church, and the nature of marriage itself. The U.S. delegates met briefly in June 1965 in Washington, D.C., in order to review the deliberations and to propose that input was needed from dogmatic theologians. During the interlude between the sessions, Bernard Haring and Belgium's Cardinal Suenens roamed the U.S. promoting

39

change. The supporters of Pope Paul and his teaching, especially the U.S. bishops, were as quiet as church-mice.

I have two poignant memories from that time. Archbishop Leo Binz of St. Paul-Minneapolis, the only episcopal representative of the U.S. hierarchy on the early papal commission and a favorite of Cardinal Cicognani, received a new auxiliary bishop in the person of James Shannon, president of St. Thomas College in St. Paul. Shannon was an attractive personality who at a relatively young age had acquired prestige in educational and ecclesiastical circles. Walking around the Spanish College one morning with me, Binz spoke quizzically about his new auxiliary without indicating any personal attachment: "Shannon has what it takes to go as far in the Church as he wants to go." As events developed that was not to be very far. Four years later, and one year after *Humanae Vitae* had been published, Shannon abandoned his priesthood, citing as his reason an inability to accept the encyclical. Weeks after making his public disavowal of the Church's teaching, he married outside the Church. Binz, who was not an aggressive member of the Commission, took the defection in stride.

The second memory is of how an ultimate champion of contraception was forced to face up to the importance of Catholic faith when he came to New York in July 1965, after the first session, to address 150 Cana and Pre-Cana directors gathered in the New York Chancery Office. We wanted him to discuss the Church's teaching on contraception. At the meeting's end about 9 p.m., Fr. Joseph Fuchs, S.J., asked to do a little sight-seeing. With several priests in his company, he walked across Madison Avenue into St. Patrick's Cathedral. The night was cool and beautiful, and it was World Fair time in New York. As Fr. Fuchs walked through the Cathedral's rear door, he encountered a half-filled church in various stages of pious observance. The sight of people at that time of night kneeling before the Blessed Sacrament or shrines saying the Rosary or just kneeling was impressive. Sightseers seemed to be caught up in the quiet hush which pervaded the center of New York's Catholic worship.

For many moments the German Jesuit stood in front of the

main altar in quiet wonderment. The diocesan priests, who normally would have no reason to be in their Cathedral on a summer night, were surprised at the large number of nightly visitors. At one point Fuchs turned and said: "Is this normal? Such piety I would not see in Germany." To which a humorous reply was given: "No, we knew you were coming, so we arranged this demonstration for your benefit."

When we walked out of the Cathedral's Fifth Avenue doors, Fuchs asked to see more. So we trotted him three blocks north to the famous St. Thomas Episcopal Church, an architectural beauty in its own right and in that year much better tended. It was empty. When Fuchs completed this visit he stood on those steps silently, then turned backward to look once more at St. Patrick's Cathedral. As if talking to himself, he mused aloud: "Down there where believers cannot use contraceptives, people pray; here where they have been allowed contraceptives for thirty years, no one prays. Hmm." Fr. Fuchs was not making a theological statement as much as allowing himself to be caught up in a spontaneous reaction to the piety of people who were living lives unaddicted to contraception or the contraceptive mentality. They believed.

THE SECOND SESSION AND THE FALLOUT

By 1966, when the second session of the papal commission took place, I had been appointed secretary for education to Cardinal Spellman. This prevented me from returning to Rome for the final meetings. I continued to provide input, however, and corresponded frequently with key figures in Rome. Paul VI decided to add sixteen cardinals and bishops to the Commission, hoping to bring the deliberations to a speedy conclusion. Two of these were Archbishops Dearden of Detroit and Sheehan of Baltimore.

Years later Sheehan would become an outspoken defender of the Church's teaching on birth control. But in 1966, when his argumentation would have counted, neither he nor the participating American bishops were of much help to Paul VI. The contraceptionists took full command of the second session—with notable help from Joseph Fuchs, who walked away from his previous public positions, and, of course, into the attention of the omnipresent media.

When the Commission ended its labors, the foreseeable results were of an earthquake potential. A majority were in favor of lifting the Church's ban on contraception. A minority held on to the traditional teaching and issued a minority report.

Once these results became known, and they did with the proverbial speed of lightning, the immediate effects on the general Catholic public were three: (1) doubts about the reliability of the Church's teaching authority; (2) ecclesiastical status and power for scholarly opinion independent of Magisterium; (3) the rise of conscience as the final arbiter of right and wrong, particularly when reinforced by popular opinion.

While freedom of conscience was a particularly attractive aspect of the questions raised in the second session, doubt is the more sinister theme for Catholics of any age. Once it was known that a majority of the Church's chosen advisers considered the Church's ban no longer tenable, the binding power traditionally attributed to Jesus' demands that Christians eschew lust, adultery, and dissoluble marriages was also in jeopardy.

Twenty years after the Council's end, efforts are still being made to prove that Paul VI in 1965, and *a fortiori* the Church, was in doubt. Because the Church was studying, it was in doubt. Even Jesuit Richard McCormick, who in 1965 was supportive of John Ford, wrote only a year later: "Only an authentic teaching statement is capable of dissipating a genuine doctrinal doubt." *Humanae Vitae* was intended to be such a document, but by then the doubts of McCormick and others were beyond dissipating. Such was the most serious fallout of Pope Paul's Birth Control Commission.

MAJORITY-MINORITY OPINIONS

When the majority of the Birth Control Commission voted against the Catholic position on contraception as proclaimed by an unbroken tradition of two millennia and reinforced in the twentieth century by Pius XI and Pius XII, they argued as follows:

> There is a certain change in the mind of contemporary man. He feels that he is more conformed to his rational nature, created by God with liberty and responsibility, when he uses his skill to intervene in the biological processes of nature so that he can achieve the ends of the institution of marriage in the conditions of actual life than if he would abandon himself to chance.[5]

Their position is simply stated: God made man the lord of his own universe, as of the outer world, and modern man is now asserting this essential control of his own life. Reason says nothing should be left to chance, if chance leads to pain and discomfort. And if, only in this century, humankind wishes to place greater value on the husband-wife relationship than on procreation, which in other times and cultures was more highly prized, all is still well and good. They do not say that anything goes, because they would hope that human decency, love, and a sense of responsibility for spouses and the general community would prevail against the forces of hedonism, excessive selfishness, or sexual exploitation. The papal commission's majority, in fact, went out of its way to reject such aberrations, and even to counsel against "the contraceptive mentality."

Events after 1968 demonstrated that such expressed limitations on a contraceptive lifestyle (confining it to married couples, for example) were at best a pious wish, written into the final report to make its procontraception recommendations more palatable to the Pope. Not only Charles Curran, Richard McCormick, and Joseph Fuchs, but the entire Catholic Theological Society of America and its Paulist Press publication *Human Sexuality* offer

43

abundant later evidence that sexual behavior, once loosed from its moorings in God's overarching moral law, floats wherever passion, not reason or right, takes it.

The majority on the Commission also tried to justify their case by alleging that periodic continence (natural family planning) is simply another form of contraception, since the intention is the same. Obviously, they misused language to make an objectionable view sound good. Lying is as different from not telling the truth as contraception is from abstinence during the fertile period. Granted, non-truth tellers and NFPers may sometimes have evil intentions, but their iniquities are different from the sins of lying and contraception—which are morally bad of themselves (apart from any good or bad intentions). One cannot make a bad act good by having a good reason for doing it.

Apart from any other considerations, the entire Christian tradition, beginning with St. Paul (Romans 3:8), asserts that we are not to do evil, even if good comes from it. For Christianity, at least up to modern times, the sexual ability to love and procreate, is seen as an unusual sharing in the life of God Himself, since the giving of life is God's power, of which men and women are stewards, not owners. If it is perfectly proper for man and woman to place effective obstacles in the way of God's role in the life-giving process even once, there is no sensible reason why God cannot be excluded entirely, since men and women have a large fund of motives, should they choose, to use for excluding God completely. In the Christian tradition this has often been done (an exercise of freedom), but just as often it has been declared sinful.

Asserting God's role in the life-giving process gives men and women ample room to exercise their own dominion, to use their freedom to copulate and bear children with sense, responsibility, and consideration of each other and the good of society. Christians must solve their personal problems and society its social difficulties within the framework permitted by their role as cooperators with God, but never against him.

Little attention in the public media has been paid to what the minority said to the papal commission[6]:

44

Why Cannot the Church Change Her Answer to This Central Question?

1. The church cannot change her answer *because this answer is true.* Whatever may pertain to a more perfect formulation of the teaching or its possible genuine development, the teaching itself cannot not be substantially true. It is true because the Catholic church, instituted by Christ to show men a secure way to eternal life, could not have so wrongly erred during all those centuries of its history. The church cannot substantially err in teaching doctrine which is most serious in its import for faith and morals, throughout all centuries or even one century, if it has been constantly and forcefully proposed as necessarily to be followed in order to obtain eternal salvation. The church could not have erred through so many centuries, even through one century, by imposing under serious obligation very grave burdens in the name of Jesus Christ, if Jesus Christ did not actually impose these burdens. The Catholic church could not have furnished in the name of Jesus Christ to so many of the faithful everywhere in the world, through so many centuries, the occasion for formal sin and spiritual ruin, because of a false doctrine promulgated in the name of Jesus Christ.

If the church could err in such a way, the authority of the ordinary magisterium in moral matters would be thrown into question. The faithful could not put their trust in the magisterium's presentation of moral teaching, especially in sexual matters . . .

New Notions of the Magisterium and Its Authority

1. What has been commonly held and handed down concerning the nature, function and authority of the magisterium does not seem to be accepted by everyone today. For among those who say that the teaching of *Casti Connubii* is reformable and who say that contraception is not always intrinsically evil, some seem to have a concept which is radically different about the nature and function of the magisterium, especially in moral matters.

Before assessing the effects of the Birth Control Commission's performance, and the long-term results, there are two other factors to be taken into account. One was supplied by the Reverend Charles Curran of the Catholic University; the other was the

45

Christian Family Movement (CFM). Both gave direction and impetus to the hostile reception accorded to *Humanae Vitae* from 1968 onwards.

CHARLES CURRAN

On a day that now seems long ago, April 24, 1967, a young priest, not ten years ordained, changed the course of Catholic development in the United States. He confronted American bishops and won. He challenged a pope and was promoted. He institutionalized private judgment over the teaching authority of the Church and received the backing of a majority of U.S. Catholics. On that date the American bishops "ate crow," words Washington, D.C.'s, Patrick O'Boyle used to describe their defeat to Rome's Apostolic Delegate Aegidio Vagnozzi. Charles Curran would never have succeeded in his 1967 onslaught on Church doctrine and on the U.S. hierarchy without the support of theologians and religious educators at the bishops' own Catholic University in Washington, and without the collapse of their own will. The U.S. hierarchy has not recovered since.

It must be noted that Charles Curran is not unique among Catholic theologians. By the time Vatican II ended in 1965, certain Catholics, mostly priests, were on their way to becoming sensations in college lecture halls, in seminaries, in convents, and even in chancery offices. The best known of them now, twenty years later, are Walter Burghardt, S.J., Roland Murphy, O.Carm., Bernard Haring, C.SS.R., Richard McBrien, Bernard Merthaler, Anthony Kosnik, Godfrey Diekmann, O.S.B., Christopher Mooney, S.J., Gabriel Moran, Alfred McBride, O.Praem., Luke Salm, F.S.C., David Thomas, David Tracy, and some others.

What gave these men prominence? They all became signers of Charles Curran's protest against *Humanae Vitae* when it appeared in the *National Catholic Reporter,* August 4, 1968. This veritable Who's Who Among Catholics roamed the Church's educational terrain as professors, editors, or officials of bishops' offices or the United States Catholic Conference (USCC). Not only did they encourage Catholics to use contraception, but without portfolio they undertook to redefine the Catholic Church and the authority of bishops as well.

Such was the general tone of Catholic academe long before *Humanae Vitae*, and surely by the time Paul VI decided on a Papal Birth Control Commission.

Strangely, the national body of bishops did not see Curran's defiance as undermining the authority of all bishops, even though effective authority depends on its proper exercise more than on assertions made on its behalf. At its November 1968 meeting, the National Conference of Catholic Bishops (NCCB) added to its own difficulties by publishing "Norms for Licit Theological Dissent" in their pastoral *Human Life in Our Day*. That statement would be rejected in 1984 by Archbishop James Hickey, O'Boyle's successor once removed, as impractical, when he supported Curran's removal from his theological post at CUA. Such dissent as his is impractical in an era of instantaneous media coverage, but as practiced by people like Curran, it is inherently illicit. John Paul II in 1987 would go further and tell U.S. bishops during his Los Angeles visit that such dissent undermines bishops' teaching authority everywhere and can be an obstacle to the reception of the Sacraments by Catholics.

THE CHRISTIAN FAMILY MOVEMENT

The Patrick and Patty Crowley who participated in the Papal Commission were not the same people who fifteen years earlier were the favorite, some would say handpicked, leaders of a family movement spawned out of war-time retreats for married couples. These retreats, later conferences, were couple-oriented, child-oriented, Catholic in doctrine. They provided theological, psychological, and social uplift for Catholic spouses already awash with the antimarriage, antilife, antireligious forces in U.S. society. When those conferences became organized nationally around Cana, Msgr. Reynold Hillenbrand, a Chicago activist pastor, seized on

47

the couple concept as the basis for his own Chicago-directed Christian Family Movement. The Hillenbrand-dominated CFM, through the fifteen years that preceded the papal commission, chose the Crowleys as his chief organizers and his lay voice. They were good people and they were good at what they did. They believed with Hillenbrand in the Church's teaching on marriage, no less than in the Catholic Social Gospel, in large part because he taught both with equal conviction.

When they returned from the deliberations of the papal commission, Msgr. Hillenbrand, their spiritual father, "refused to have anything to do with them." So said Rupert Kaiser in his book *The Politics of Sex and Religion*. But the story of the Crowley dismissal is not so simply explained as the result (in the Kaiser view) of Hillenbrand's being "a fine priest whose training was preconciliar." The Chicago pastor was thirty years ahead of most of the Papal Commission members in his appreciation of the social encyclicals, but he was also a Catholic. Nevertheless, his CFM, the Crowleys, and the "Hilly" priests he trained got away from him and from the Church. Those Chicago priests were the ones who "stole" the Crowleys away from their master, and from the teaching of the Church on marriage. Yet it did not occur to him even then that he had a monster of his own making.

CFM collapsed with a bang. Some of its leaders became notorious dissenters on many other aspects of Catholic Life beside contraception. Donald Thorman went on to become editor of the *National Catholic Reporter*. CFM couples, once the pride of many dioceses, began to drift away from close association with the institutional Church, once their most cherished identification.

INCIDENTAL FALLOUT

The first result was bitterness. Patricia Crowley's latest word (1988) is: "I'll never forgive the Church for *Humanae Vitae.*" Robert Kaiser recalls those days with bitterness. He makes no bones about his hostility toward the Catholic tradition and toward

48

Rome. The contraceptionists were heroes, the supporters of the Church teaching were pre-Vatican II reactionaries or clericalists. Bernard Haring was an "eminent and top theologian," Joseph Fuchs was "the most highly regarded moral theologian on the Commission," Charles Davis was "brilliant," Leo Cardinal Suenens was "a man of vision and courage" and Patrick Crowley, "a good lawyer who could cut to the heart of things." On the other side were "the Ottavani Crowd" and people like Stanislaus de Lestapis, "a French intellectual full of grand abstractions." After hearing arguments that the wishes of married couples must prevail, de Lestapis is quoted as saying: "The couple has become a state of grace and contraception their sacrament . . . and the result is a sort of intoxification, a practical obliteration of the sense of God." Msgr. George A. Kelly was a "well-tailored monsignor from New York," who testified as if he were appearing before a congressional committee. Unfortunately, J. C. Penney did not receive credit for the impression made by Kelly's thirty-five dollar suit.

Kaiser identifies John Ford as "a villain of the Council's last days," because he and his allies were not crusading for a cause, so much as "for their own vindication, for a vindication of the ideas they have been teaching all these years. They obey the Pope when the Pope obeys them." When during the last session Ford objects to a medical doctor's going beyond his competence, Kaiser has him "fuming" and "lashing back." Ford "whines" and is "miffed" when he is ignored. Finally, Kaiser reports John Ford's leaving Rome a defeated man, assigned to teach in Weston College, where he found himself scorned by young scholastics who, having heard from other Jesuits of the positions Ford had taken in Rome, refused to attend his classes. What Kaiser does not mention is that those same young Jesuits did not wish either to listen to John Courtney Murray at Woodstock. Murray, like Ford, though an entirely distinct theological specialist, still believed in objective moral norms. And as time would tell, the rising Jesuit elite no longer did.

There were other dysfunctions worth noting. Dr. John Cavanaugh, who as the first session ended was handing out his latest book *The Pope, The People, and The Pill,* in support of the Church, returned for the second session the author of a study purporting to show that women were at their sexual peak at ovulation time, just when "rhythm" said they must abstain. John Marshall, the English doctor who a few years earlier was fortifying Msgr. Kelly's weak argument against contraception, overnight became an avid contraceptionist.

John Noonan, the detached scholar of 1964, by 1966 was a central figure in marshalling political forces against *Casti Connubii.* His little book the following year, *Church and Contraception,* left the question open, although he no longer was. Indeed, after *Humanae Vitae* he called a press conference (October 1, 1968) to express the opinion of lay members of the papal commission that Paul VI's opinion was his personal opinion, nothing more. Although Noonan is an ardent Right-to-Lifer today and the author of an excellent book on abortion *(A Private Choice: Abortion in the Seventies),* he continues to reinterpret *Humanae Vitae* against the mind of the Church and the Pope who wrote that encyclical. In a 1980 article for the *American Journal of Jurisprudence,* he argues that Paul VI was simply forbidding contraceptive acts by married couples only during the fertile phase of the monthly period (about four days), leaving the rest of the month open to contraceptive or sterilizing use. The fact is that Paul said "each and every marriage act must be open to the transmission of life," that the moral law forbids "every action which, either in anticipation of the conjugal act or in its accomplishment or in the development of its natural consequences, proposes, whether as an end or as a means, to render procreation impossible."[7]

Perhaps Kaiser focused on the heart of the matter when he suggested that the issue was not simply contraception but the Church herself. Kaiser resents the power the Church has asserted and exercised in determining the boundaries between right and wrong and making people confess their sins when they passed those boundaries. When the battle over birth control was over, he said, "the balance of power had shifted away from priest (and pope) and toward the people. For them it was not a question of seizing power, but opting for something which liberationists of all stripes call 'empowerment,' a fashionable word that means nothing more than what we used to call growing up." In his lexicon, "growing up" means "growing away" from the Catholic Church.

THE LAST WORD

The Papal Birth Control Commission solved nothing for Catholic couples when it proposed a change in Church teaching. But faced with the clear moral affirmations of several popes since 1968, the various national conferences of bishops have done little or nothing to train believers in the secrets of NFP. Not surprisingly, the people have chosen contraception. And in this sense the papal commission's majority has prevailed.

NOTES

1. *Casti Connubii*, December 31, 1930, No. 56.
2. John Noonan, *Contraception*, p. 438.
3. Austin Flannery, O.P., ed., *Vatican II Documents* (St. Paul editions, 1981), No. 51.
4. Footnote No. 14 (added to No. 51 of the text).
5. Cited by Robert Hoyt, *The Birth Control Debate*, p. 71.
6. Cited by Robert Hoyt, op. cit., *passim*.
7. *Humanae Vitae*, Nos. 11, 14.

PART THREE

Rome,
the Catholic Revolution,
and the U.S. Church

PROLOGUE

The Issues to Be Resolved

IN THE COURSE of writing this book I consulted many academics, and not a few pastors. The latter, after all, are the ultimate judges of what works in any parish that authentically claims the name Catholic. One priest, described by a seminary professor as "the finest theological mind I ever had in class," responded with a long letter which said, in part:

> In these critical days for the Church, any listing of intellectual currents, doctrinal controversies, and (mistaken) pastoral initiatives should include the following:
>
> **1.** The dissent first over the anovulant pill and then over all forms of artificial contraception; the widespread promotion of dissenting opinions on this subject by church teachers and the implementation in pastoral practice of these opinions with no effective counteraction by church authorities—from the mid-sixties onward and into our own day—with the result that misinformation on this subject contin-

ues to be presented within the Church, which, in practice, has no unified pastoral approach to this problem.

2. The widespread liturgical experimentation that occurred from the late sixties onward and which, in some contexts, made the liturgy a free-wheeling self-fulfillment service that turned many people off, led to a loss of the sense of the sacred and transcendent in the liturgy.

3. The movement, based on debatable psychological theories, to discourage children from receiving the Sacrament of Penance at an early age sometime before their First Communion, beginning in the mid to late sixties and extending through the seventies and eighties in some places, with the effect of discouraging and impeding the use or the regular use of this sacrament by children and by the teenagers and adults they eventually become.

4. New theories regarding the nature of the presence of Christ in the Eucharistic Sacrament—transsignification/transfinalization vs. transsubstantiation—leading some persons to make significant changes in Eucharistic practice, especially regarding the reservation and adoration of the reserved sacrament and the practice of Eucharistic devotions.

5. New theories about the ministerial priesthood, which, in Reformation fashion, conceived the ordained bishop or priest as a baptized lay person commissioned by a special ceremony for specific functions in the Church community, but not as a person consecrated by a special sacrament, leading to a continuing crisis of priestly "identity"—what is a priest and what should be the conditions of his ecclesial life?

6. The crusade against celibacy and "clericalism," which at base argues against any special state of life for the priest, further contributing to the confusion over the nature and role of the ministerial priesthood and discouraging priestly vocations.

7. The debates over the nature of original sin and whether we are talking really about an originating sin of two individual first parents, and its consequences for the human race, or only the "sin of the world," the sum total of the sins of all individuals, which they commit by reason of the evil atmosphere around them, leading to a basic misunderstanding of fallen/redeemed humanity and of the nature of Christ's saving work.

8. The new theories about the indissolubility of sacramental, consummated marriage, about tolerance of remarriage after divorce in such instances, and a host of related questions leading to contradictory pastoral practices on internal forum solutions, the admission of divorced and invalidly remarried persons to the sacraments, and the growth of a perception that in some instances Church marriage tribunals were actually divorcing persons who had entered valid, sacramental, and consummated marriages.

9. Substantial catechetical deficiencies and/or confusion in Catholic high schools and other Catholic institutions of learning, together with the presentation of trendy new opinions to persons not equipped to evaluate them, leading to misunderstandings of the faith, fostering a pick-and-choose attitude toward key elements of the faith and broad religious ignorance among a whole generation.

10. The appearance and rapid spread in moral theology of the proportionalist theory, now being applied to all actions, including all forms of sexual activity, as evidenced in the 1977 report of the Catholic Theological Society and in the debates over in vitro fertilization and abortion, leading to confusion about what is morally right and morally wrong and mistrust of, even disdain for, the Church's teaching office, which has repeatedly disallowed conclusions of the proportionalist theory in its present form.

11. A too exclusivistic application of the historical-critical method to the New Testament, leading to doubts concerning the biblical foundation of various Catholic dogmas such as the sacrament of orders, the papacy, the Church's charism to teach infallibly, etc. Are these perhaps only historical accretions not based in God's revealed Word?

12. The "intercommunion" craze among some Catholic ecumenists (and most Reformation Church ecumenists), resulting in efforts to broaden as far as possible the admission of non-Catholic Christians to Holy Communion in the Catholic Church and blurring the important distinction between "partial communion" and "full communion," and the need for the recipients of Communion to embrace at least implicitly all that the Catholic Church is and teaches.

13. The debate over the proper interpretation of Vatican II's teaching that "the Church of Christ subsists in the Catholic Church," although elements of the Church can be found in other Christian churches and communities, with the effect that all churches are per-ceived as more or less the same: Then why be a Catholic or enter into communion with the Catholic Church?

14. The "general absolution" movement, which at base questions the Church's binding teaching that by the will of Christ grave sins need to be confessed in the Sacrament of Penance, a movement assisting the decline of individual, personal confession.

15. The insistent call in some quarters for the priestly and episco-pal ordination of women, despite the Church's repeated, authorita-tive teaching that by the will of Christ the ministerial priesthood can be conferred only on men; the continued attacks by some feminists on the so-called patriarchal church—leading to increased tension and confusion over ordained ministry in the Church.

16. In some cases, the radical transformation—in the sense of *opposed to the authoritative teaching of Vatican II*—of the religious life so that it bears little similarity to that described in the authentic teaching of the Church, leading to more confusion, loss of identity by religious, and few vocations.

17. The substantial departures from the active priesthood and the religious life and the scandalous conduct of a few priests and reli-gious, leading to lesser esteem for, even suspicion of, the priesthood and the religious state, fewer vocations, doubts among some of those who remain faithful.

18. The frequent, considerable changes in the format and content of priestly education/formation from the conclusion of the Council until now and the closure of many seminaries; the dramatic decline in vocations to the priesthood and the religious life in North America and Western Europe—all leading to a very unsettled and unsettling atmosphere in the Church, a malaise, a drifting, a loss of nerve, a capitulation to self-fulfilling prophecies.

19. The growth and spread of dissenting opinions, sometimes in books intended as textbooks, over the entire area of binding Church teaching—the faith as it is to be believed or lived—and the presenta-tion of such opinions as a foundation for belief or action, leading to a perception that much is uncertain; almost everything can be ques-tioned, debated, doubted.

20. The strong anti-papal and anti-Roman sentiment among some Catholic intellectuals over the last decade and more; the attempt to peg and isolate the Pope (John Paul II) as a leftover from a past age of the Church; leading to mistrust of Church authority, hostility to the Pope and his congregations.

21. The effective secularization of many Catholic colleges and universities and their consequent inability to preserve, safeguard, promote and encourage the Catholic identity and Catholic practice of their Catholic students, thus facilitating the weakening of fidelity to the Church among the young.

22. The continuing steep decline of the Catholic school system on the elementary and secondary levels, facilitating broad religious ignorance, depriving the Church, also, of the best context for nurturing the faith of the young and of promoting vocations to the priesthood and the religious life.

23. The more or less consistent failure of the bishops effectively to confute and refute (which is not the same thing as *punish)* well-known dissenters who roam throughout the U.S. Church spreading their dissenting opinions, leading to acceptance of erroneous doctrinal views and confusion over "who is right."

24. The debate over the salvific role of other religions—e.g., Islam: Is there any need to preach the Gospel to these "Gentiles"? Do we just dialogue with them? Are all religions equally vehicles of salvation?—leading to religious relativism and a weakening of the missionary enterprise.

25. The very recent debate over the relationship of the Mosaic Covenant and the Covenant of Christ, the New Covenant: are these parallel covenants—one for the Jews and the other for the Gentiles only? Do we only dialogue with Jews and never invite them to believe in Jesus Christ, Savior of the world?—leading to religious relativism and confusion.

26. The continued decline in active affiliation (of Catholics) with the worshipping community; growth of nominal, cultural or communal Catholics who are nonpracticing and often religiously ignorant, whose beliefs, values, and practices are minimally distinguishable from those of other Americans who accept prevalent secularistic and relativistic standards, thus impeding within the broader Catholic community a unified adherence to those beliefs, values, and ideals identifiable as those of the Catholic Church of all ages or of the Apostolic Tradition.

During the same period that these currents, controversies, and pastoral initiatives arose and developed, our whole Western society was undergoing a cultural change, not least of all in moral values respecting wealth and the good life, marriage and family life, the relationship of the sexes and sexual conduct both within and apart from the marital union. The abuse of drugs became widespread; and in the philosophical/psychological "shift to the subject," feeling, emotion, and self-fulfillment came to be valued high above reason, evidence, logic, duty, and self-sacrifice. The Church community could not be immune to the effects of these other currents within the whole of Western society, though many Church leaders did not muster the wisdom and the courage to deal effectively with the conflicts arising within the Church itself, some of which were undoubtedly heightened by the broader cultural changes.

Sincerely yours

———

THREE

The Pope's First Team:
Roman Cardinals

THE PAPACY is Catholicism's first and foremost resource "in saving the Faith and the Church." I believe this to be true, but this pointed observation is unfortunately not mine. It belongs to San Francisco's Archbishop John Quinn. He made the statement in 1977 when he assumed the presidency of the National Conference of Catholic Bishops.

Now, as every informed Catholic knows, with human nature and national politics being what they are, the Holy See has not been uniformly successful, at all times and in all places, in accomplishing the Quinn objective. To cite an example, the dilly-dallying and procrastination of Clement VII (1523–34) in dealing with Henry VIII's divorce and with the Lutheranism moving at the time through Norway, Sweden, and Denmark eventually led to schism not only in England, but in Scandinavia. On the other hand, down through the centuries, especially in modern times, it is the papal office which has protected the Church from the internecine warfare that has splintered many other religious bodies or so watered down their message that little content has been left which can be called Christian. Indeed, the popes of the last century have been extraordinary vicars of Christ. Their quality explains in large part why the Catholic Church continues to grow in numbers and in influence, as other mainline Christian bodies wither. It was decisive action by Pius X (1903–1914) that halted the spread of Modernism and helped guarantee his place in history as a reforming pope.

Still, governing the Church is never an easy task for the Vatican, even with its two-thousand-year tradition. Harry Truman's well-known advisory applies more to a pope than to a president. At Dwight Eisenhower's inauguration in 1952, Truman allegedly told wife Bess: "Wait till he presses the button on his desk and finds that no one answers." That often happens to popes too. If Rome moves slowly at remedying Catholic defects, it is not without a semblance of reason. Looking at events from the viewpoint of eternity popes look upon evil within the Church, even religious crimes, with great forbearance. In spite of early fears to the contrary it looks as if Catholicism will bury Communism without having any of Stalin's legions under the Pope's generalship. On the other hand, delay by Rome in facing up to Gallicanism, a heresy going back at least to the sixteenth century that would give French bishops right of veto over Rome's universal decrees, helped disinherit the Church's eldest daughter of its substantial Catholic birthright.

The frustration in Rome over the dysfunctions of Vatican II will become clear, as we follow the response of the Holy See to the doings of the U.S. Church after 1965.

JOHN CARDINAL WRIGHT ON MAGISTERIUM

Bishop Wright had not been in Rome more than three years when he learned what it meant to be the Cardinal Prefect of the Congregation for the Clergy during a revolutionary period in the Church. An action committee of Spanish bishops, completing a provisional report for their national conference, solicited his unofficial evaluation, and he was only too happy to oblige. His criticisms were later leaked to the Madrid press by bishops at odds with their conference leadership. When the news broke in Spain that a Vatican cardinal objected to a course preprogrammed for the Church there, the cardinal president of the Spanish hierarchy vented his fury on Jean Cardinal Villot, Paul VI's secretary of state. Villot proceeded to chastise Wright publicly for failing to clear his commentary with his office.

Not long thereafter a lower-level Church official from the United States walked into Wright's office, apologetic for the intrusion but excusing himself by the need to unburden his local problem on someone. The American cardinal listened to a tale about pederasty among priests, catechetical instruction that was undermining the faith of Catholic teenagers, and women in diocesan office who were undermining the teaching of the Church on the priesthood. At the end of an hour of intense conversation, the priest apologized again: "I feel better. I don't know what to do about these problems, but I had to dump on someone." After a moment's silence, Wright looked at the young man and said: "Fine. But now who can I dump them on?"

John Wright was my first real Roman connection. The year was 1972 and the occasion was the International Congress of Catholic Universities in Rome. He may not yet have mastered the game of Vatican politics, but his brilliance and humanity made him a star in a center where normally only Italians shined. Defeat had done little to dampen his *joie de vivre.* When he learned later that John Cardinal Dearden, then the NCCB president, had ruled that Wright could no longer vote in U.S. episcopal councils, the ex-Bostonian, knowing that Cardinals of other nations were welcome in their national assemblies, laughed the exclusion off with the crack, "I'm no longer an American bishop." Less funny, however, was Paul VI's question about the phraseology Wright used in the document he issued bringing Cardinal O'Boyle's "Washington Case" to a conclusion. The Congregation's statement, published

63

April 26, 1971, summarized the Holy See's agreement with the offending priests about "the objective evil of the contraceptive act." The Pope wanted to know why the words "objective evil" were chosen rather than "intrinsic evil." Paul expressed unhappiness with the possibility that some theologian might think the contraceptive act was not evil per se. The explanation that no great harm was done by the use of the less precise description of the evil inherent in contraception since the Congregation for the Clergy was not a doctrinal body seemed to satisfy the pope. But the close supervision made Wright uncomfortable.

By 1972 he began to face up to the bad catechesis that was going on in the West. He had few illusions that the *General Catechetical Directory* which he had imposed on the universal Church the year before was the final solution to a serious problem in Catholic catechesis. Because he had lost confidence in the willingness of local hierarchies to control their wandering religious educators, he tinkered with chartering independent catechetical institutes in various parts of the world under the jurisdiction of his office. He lifted the idea from an obscure reference in the Vatican II document on the missions (No. 17) concerning the need of special training centers in missionary countries. Not for a moment did he look upon the U.S. as a missionary country, but he was determined to shake up the catechetical environment in his own country. Seven such centers in various American cities were authorized. Certain bishops, notably those close to the USCC apparatus, were unfriendly to the idea, believing that the existence of these pontifical institutes reflected on the authenticity of their own diocesan catechesis. They surely did. Other bishops simply saw it as an episcopal bypass, which it was. Still, John Wright was determined to go as far as he could to challenge what he called the substitution of "muddle-headed" theologies for the Church's faith. One such Institute for the Advanced Study of Catholic Doctrine was established in 1974 in New York at St. John's University by its president. A year later Fr. Joseph Cahill, C.M., asked me to take charge of the Institute.

Local religious educators almost immediately dubbed IASCD as reactionary, a put-down by which they sought to stifle any return to strict Catholic teaching. Even some of Cardinal Cooke's advisors suggested that he keep IASCD at arm's length. I cautioned him on November 27, 1974, to resist efforts to tarnish this institute before it even had a track record to criticize. It was not pleasant to take over an institute with a preordained right-wing reputation. Cardinal Cooke saw the problem as clearly as anyone. Two years later (1976) he established his own Archdiocesan Catechetical Institute at Dunwoodie Seminary. Due to the imaginative direction of Fr. Michael Wrenn, New York's Catechetical Institute became an instant success, and in 1986 at the request of Cardinal O'Connor, this institute received Roman approval.

By the time I met him, Cardinal Wright had begun to involve U.S. priests in his effort to enforce Rome's sacramental sequence for eight-year-olds—Confession before First Communion. When Pius X lowered the age for the reception of Holy Communion in 1910, Confession usually preceded Communion, even though no one argued that eight-year-olds were capable of mortal sin. The sequence took hold as a stage in Catholic formation and became an important element in developing among Catholics the habit of receiving both sacraments regularly. For seven decades the discipline worked. Confessional lines were as long as the lines at the parish altar rail, especially in the United States, a credit to training begun at an early age. If there were imperfections in the system, they were due to misuse of the sacramental discipline (by a priest or by the penitent himself) not to the discipline as such. All habit training in its early stages involves individual discomfort, but once learned, good behavior becomes routine. At the very moment academics were complaining about the Church's early childhood formation, the U.S. government was offering Head Start to prekindergarten children and prominent athletes in ghost-written best sellers were attributing their polished skills to preschool training. Almost overnight, however, a new brand of religious educator began to claim that an eight-year-old Catholic was too young to make his First Confession.

The substantive issue turned out to be not the private Confession of children, as such, but private Confession itself. Delaying the First Confession of children was merely one small step in the deconstruction of an ingrained habit of U.S. Catholic adults. As the controversy evolved, the omission of personal Confession in favor of general absolution would be proposed. But in the process, which began in 1965 and continued beyond the 1983 Code of Canon Law, the Catholic faithful were led to deem the customary penitential rite an expendable Catholic command.

John Wright felt strongly about the First Confession of children. In 1970, when he was readying his catechetical directory, a young lady from the staff of the USCC challenged him during a conference in Rome: "My children confess to me." To which the Cardinal replied: "I'd like to remind you of what Pius XII said about the human conscience—that it is a sanctuary in which a man meets God. Don't you ever invade that sanctuary, even of your children. That's a sacred territory."

About this time John Wright was also saying to me, as if in disbelief, "I know no reputable theologian or sane layman who thinks he is pope, yet religious educators are seeking to veto every new directive from Rome concerning First Confession." By 1975 almost one-half of 120 American bishops polled reported that most of their parishes were already postponing the First Confession of children. The complaints of parents that they were unable to obtain First Confession for their eight-year-olds began to increase. Parish priests often would refuse to hear such confessions, sometimes because the school's principal said "no." Fr. Howard Basler, Brooklyn's CCD director, by 1973 considered Rome's insistence on First Confession an affront to the American bishops, "a new exercise of ecclesiastical power." He called upon people "to talk back to the perpetrators of the affront." Two years later the Pope's secretary of state, Cardinal Villot, reaffirmed Rome's desire for First Confession first, prompting *Sign* magazine, hitherto recognized for its fidelity to Church teaching, to advise readers that the Roman decision need not be followed in practice. When challenged on this advice by a Roman spokesman, *Sign* defended itself by referring to the guidelines of the Newark Archdiocese. These regulations decreed that "first penance should follow, not precede, First Communion." Newark's director of religious education, Fr. Thomas F. Ivory, provided what was becoming a common exercise in doublespeak: "Our diocesan guidelines are consistent with the mind of the Church." Still, the fault did not lie simply with religious educators. At the November 1975 bishops' meeting, Archbishop William Borders, chairman of the NCCB's education committee, announced that Rome's decision did not bind American bishops wherever the practice was otherwise. When asked about this contradiction, Cardinal Cooke could not explain. In New York the Roman sequence prevailed for the young, but by then most adult American Catholics were neglecting the Sacrament of Penance.

Canon 914 of the 1983 Code reaffirms the responsibility of parents, teachers, and pastors to see that children reaching the use of reason are prepared for, and if disposed, receive, their First Communion "preceded by sacramental confession." But the damage has been done, damage foreseen by an experienced pastor in 1976. Asked what he thought the ultimate effect of the Church's new penitential practice would be, he wrote:

> . . . I suspect at least on the part of some it is a serious attempt to destroy private confession. The new rite with all its optional elements may be fine for a monastery where numbers are limited and time is not. But in a busy parish, especially at holidays when there are long lines of penitents, it will be impossible to do justice to the spirit of the rite and hear all the people. So bishops will be besieged with requests to grant communal absolutions for pastoral reasons. Unless great prudence is shown, what is now intended as a most rare exception could become standard procedure. It's happened elsewhere in the revised liturgy. Then the next step would be to abuse the communal absolution and include people in bad marriages and other irreconcilable situations. Sure, you can tell them to go to private confession within a year but will any private confessions be left?[1]

Cardinal Wright's last words on the subject were these:

Witness the reported ripping out of the confessionals in some places and the substitution of conference rooms, without regard for canonical cautions of long standing and great importance.

By the time the First Confession controversy had ripened, John Wright was wondering whether the theological community was setting itself up as a rival to the Papacy.

A conversation in Wright's Vatican office in November 1975 led to a discussion of countermeasures, one of which was an International Symposium on Magisterium. He wondered what the impact of such a meeting might be. He and I agreed that St. John's University in New York was a good place to assemble such a symposium, with Wright himself assuming the role of invitor. The symposium, scheduled for Easter Week 1977, was to be held in the chancery building of the New York Archdiocese. Nine major papers on Magisterium were to be presented—on its nature, history, scope, spokesmen, binding power, fallibility or infallibility, alleged past errors; and on modernism and the modern problem and on the doctrine of *Humanae Vitae* and *Humanae Personae*. The audience would consist of scholars. John Wright's contemplated speakers included: Bishops Jeremiah Newman (Limerick), Edward Gagnon (Rome); Archbishops John Whealon (Hartford), John Quinn (Oklahoma City), James F. Carney (Vancouver); Cardinals John Wright (Rome), John Krol (Philadelphia), Alfred Bensch (Berlin), Karol Wojtyla (Krakow), Lawrence Sheehan (Baltimore), Joseph Hoffner (Cologne), Basil Hume (Westminster). The person he chose to give the keynote address was Archbishop Jerome Hamer, O.P., then Secretary for the Congregation for Sacred Doctrine, Vatican City. (Cardinal Seper, Hamer's boss, could not speak English.)

By April 1976 the framework of the symposium was clearly established and practical decisions were necessary. The president of St. John's University, Fr. Joseph T. Cahill, C.M., was more than willing. Cardinal Cooke had already agreed on the date and place. The key to a successful symposium was the presence of Hamer, number two man in the reformed Holy Office. Cooke understood that he would invite Hamer, while responsibility for the symposium rested solely with St. John's University. This was to be a New York event, not something requiring national sponsorship or approval. A national body was not a place to go for a quick decision, and bishops closely tied to the NCCB machinery were unlikely to favor a symposium of this kind. Hamer had previously expressed satisfaction with a simple invitation from Cooke, who needed no one's approval to hold such an event in his own archdiocese.

On April 9, 1976, Cardinal Wright wrote urging that the invitation from Cooke to Hamer proceed. Cooke, who suddenly discovered he would be in Rome during July, said he would handle the matter personally. When Cardinal Cooke returned from Rome he telephoned me to say that everything looked in order, but then suggested that I fly to Cincinnati to discuss the matter with Archbishop Bernardin, who apparently had been informed about the project by Cooke in June during Philadelphia's Eucharistic Congress. My answer to that suggestion was a resolute no. St. John's University had been stonewalled once by Bernardin, and it was not about to let that happen a second time. It was clear, however, that Cooke, sensing that an international symposium with Wright's star cast had extradiocesan implications, did not feel up to acting independently of the NCCB leadership.

Within a week I informed Wright and Cooke that the symposium was canceled. Wright wrote: "You and your ordinary are in total agreement," but he agreed that there was no purpose in pursuing a course Cooke was hesitant to undertake on his own initiative. Then in a letter to me Wright added: "There is nothing I can do to initiate or spark it from this end without causing a tizzy."

John Wright died August 10, 1979, just as John Paul II was coming into his own: These two would have been good collaborators, offspring of devout common stock, both bright, both charismatic, both fully Catholic, and both realistic about the forces arrayed against them. As the degenerative disease which ultimately took him home to his Maker began to incapacitate him, Wright wrote me (April 13, 1977) following a two months' stay in the hospital: "I have been having trouble with my legs, but there is nothing the matter with my tongue." Then he zeroed in on the United States Catholic Conference as a focal point of the Church's contemporary difficulties:

> Massachusetts Avenue plays a principal role in this muddy picture. It is, of course, Middle Management copied from the Harvard Business School's replacement of all executives in the United States with efficiency experts and like *periti*. Any article or speech requested of a head of a department there (editor: read bishop) will be written by Middle Management, some of whom I had in class back in the good old days.

Speaking of the *National Catechetical Directory* then being prepared, Wright remarked: "I have not read the entire (draft) NCD. The parts I read sounded like a bad mixture of incomplete American history and incomplete (or erroneous) Catholic doctrine." His final line read: "I do not read Hans Küng's books nor reviews of them. I have my soul to save."

John Cardinal Wright died short of his seventieth birthday. His beliefs were considered "dangerous to the Church" by the *National Catholic Reporter,* but in the minds of those who worked with him he was a priest who surely saved his soul.

GABRIEL CARDINAL GARRONE
AND CATHOLIC COLLEGES

Cardinal Garrone brought to his oversight of Catholic higher education in the United States not only the mind of the Church, but a fine mind of his own. A one-time protégé of Jacques Maritain, he had a cultivated flair for the exact word to define a situation and a good pastor's sense (he had been Archbishop of Toulouse) of how to deal constructively with troublemakers.

70

Following the Council he came to Rome at the invitation of Paul VI to head up the Congregation for Catholic Education. From the moment he became a cardinal in 1967 until he retired in 1980 (to make way for Washington, D.C.'s William Cardinal Baum) he worked night and day to keep Catholic higher education within the Church's fold.

I did not come to know him until 1972, when he invited Fr. Joseph Dirvin, C.M., of St. John's University and me to attend the Congress of Catholic Universities in Rome, scheduled for November 20 of that year. There I watched him suffer impertinent remarks from some of the American delegates to that assembly, and unveiled threats besides, all the while admiring his tact. While facing hostility from those who were determined that no ecclesiastic at his level or above, certainly not below, would have anything to say in deciding how Catholic their schools were to be, or even to define for them what it meant to be a Catholic, he remained composed. He remained so even while discussing the misinterpretations and misconceptions of the intentions and directives of the Holy See that were being filtered to the Catholic people of the United States by American university leadership. Garrone's demand in 1973 that each institution unequivocally state its Catholic commitment in its statutes, and simultaneously create machinery to regulate the school's faith, morality, and discipline, was ignored almost absolutely in this country.

It is difficult to say which has been Rome's most critical battleground in the uncivil war that has gone on over papal authority since 1962. The college campus? The monastery and convent? The theological association? Whatever choice one makes, it certainly is true that the Catholic campus intersects those other two infrastructures of the Church. Practically all institutions of higher learning were founded by religious orders and most scholars of any quality are still being paid by these schools.

In recent years the story of the breakdown of the proper relationship between the Holy See and Catholic higher education in the United States has been told often in great detail. Many books and articles have extolled the independence of Catholic academe as evidence of the mature Catholicism that was designed in Vatican II. I have two books—*The Battle for the American Church* and *The Crisis of Authority*—which minutely explore how after 1965 the Catholic campus came to be a "rival Church" to that governed by hierarchy, as Cardinal Newman a century ago warned it would become if it was left unsupervised by bishops (or by Rome). Much of this detail does not bear repeating here, but the significance of the schism must not be underestimated.

In meeting after meeting Cardinal Garrone labored for more than a dozen years to turn Catholic college presidents around and failed. He did not succeed because the educators did most of the talking. Nor did they care to be contradicted by an authority figure who they decided did not dare exercise his authority. If he tried to, they were prepared not to obey. These college administrators were standing pat on the Land O'Lakes Declaration of Independence (June 23, 1967) which insisted that any effective Catholic university "must have a true autonomy and academic freedom in the face of authority of any kind, lay or clerical, external to the academic community itself." This particular declaration made no commitment to the doctrines of the faith or to the specific Catholic meaning of theology and its place in shaping the Catholic mind, nor was there a word about what the Church insists is a distinctive way of life expected of those trained under Catholic auspices. The institutional link between the Catholic university and the successors of Peter and the apostles was to be broken.

Now Cardinal Garrone, as a European intellectual, knew better than the Americans that the idea of autonomy and academic freedom they wished to follow was the product not of the Catholic tradition but of a period in nineteenth century German history when unbelieving academics wished freedom from all religious orthodoxies. The government of Otto von Bismarck (which owned all the German universities anyway) was only too happy to have academic institutions which excluded advocacy of the Catholic faith. Thus the so-called "neutral" university was born, chartered to promote unbelief or non-belief, but excluded from being faith-

72

fully Protestant or Catholic in the religious understanding of those terms. Garrone also knew that whatever social acceptance in the United States Land O'Lakes achieved for Notre Dame and Fordham, this would be gained at the expense of the Catholic commitment and of the faith itself. Garrone knew, too, that "university" was not an abstraction, but the topmost level of an educational system. If the system was secular, the results had to be secular, even if a Catholic patina—like a golden dome or a Jesuit president—remained tolerable. If the system was Catholic, however, the rules and the results, whatever their secular value, had to be Catholic. And in matters of faith, faculty, and student body makeup, way of life too, must needs be dominantly Catholic. The Catholic Church, through bishops or religious orders, need not manage the institutions. But if these schools were truly Catholic, then the president and the board of trustees, while fulfilling all civic and professional requirements, must also follow Catholic norms and obey canon law. Within the Church of Christ there cannot be a rival Church, and this is what the "Catholic university" that follows secular norms must necessarily become.

For the better part of a quarter of a century, Cardinals Garrone and Baum have tried to move the Americans toward acceptance of the Holy See's terms. Throughout these years the Association of Catholic Colleges and Universities in the United States has demanded that Rome either accept its own decisions as *faits accomplis* or issue norms so general as to leave ACCU free to continue making its own independent judgments. Americans remain unhappy with the requirements of the Revised Code of Canon Law (1983), particularly with Canon 808, which says: "Even if it be really Catholic no university may bear the name Catholic without the consent of the competent ecclesiastical authority"; and Canon 812, which directs that those who teach in theological disciplines at the college level must have a "mandate from the competent ecclesiastical authority." Americans would like this authority to be the university president, anyone but the ecclesiastical hierarchy. For the better part of the 1980s Cardinal Baum on behalf of John Paul II has been trying to publish a document on Catholic higher education. It is not certain at this time what the completed product will be, but American consultants seem determined that the final document must from their point of view be harmless. At present Cardinal Baum's office is attempting to accommodate the Americans' worst fears that papal norms will compromise their credibility with secular counterparts in the United States. On the other hand, Rome is well aware that the various drafts have been filled with ambiguous terminology, some of which dilutes the clear meaning of the Code of Canon Law, now only seven years old. A Roman document that fails to deal with the present realities will be as meaningless a solution to the problem of authentic Catholic identity on the college campus as was the 1980 statement of the U.S. bishops on the same subject.

On March 1, 1989, the Holy See on its own initiative upped the ante for dissenting Catholic college presidents and their professors by requiring new appointees to make a profession of faith and, on assuming any office to be exercised in the name of the Church, an oath of fidelity. The appropriate university personnel are expected to affirm their faith in what the Church teaches as divinely revealed, to accept all that is taught definitively concerning faith and morals, and to adhere to authentic hierarchical teaching, even when it is not proposed definitively. The oath of fidelity additionally calls on them to preserve the deposit of faith and to foster the discipline of the whole Church and Christian obedience to the Church's shepherds. In one place they are told to shun those who teach contrary to the faith.

The response of the American Catholic academic community— from important members of the Catholic University faculty to delegates of the Catholic Theological Society of America (CTSA) to university presidents—has generally been one of hostility. Notre Dame president Edward Molloy simply says no. It would serve no purpose, he avers, because a university is a center of debate, not a catechetical center. The excuse for most of the other negative votes is that these oaths are not clear and are therefore inapplicable. Since the tactic has worked before, they expect to stonewall any effort by Rome to enforce its simply worded purpose in

74

the United States. Canon lawyer Msgr. Frederick McManus is even alarmed that pastors may be forced by the oaths to take a stricter view of the Church's sexual ethics, as if the pastor in Rome, Georgia, is really free to be less Catholic than the Church's pastor in Rome, Italy.[2]

There is another view, of course, one not shared by the Church's academic leadership. Ralph McInerney, Notre Dame's most prominent philosopher, asks and answers the key question: "Why in the name of God should a Roman Catholic theologian have trouble declaring himself loyal to the Vicar of Christ on earth? He is ashamed to because—here is the tragic truth—to do so would be a lie."[3] Dominican theologian Benedict Ashley phrased the question differently for the Catholic Theological Society. Mindful of the fact that prominent members of CTSA have been insisting for years that theologians are partners with bishops in the double Magisterium of the Church, Ashley described the oath of fidelity for their 1989 convention in these terms: "It is inconsistent for theologians to maintain, as a lot of them are doing here, that they participate in the Magisterium (teaching authority) and refuse to take an oath of office."[4] Here is the sticking point. As McManus in his interview indicated, theologians in U.S. Catholic colleges see themselves as acting out of professional competence, not in the name of the Church. By their self-definition they exclude hierarchy from the right to evaluate their work.[5]

Once upon a time Catholic college educators were proud of the double commitment of their institutions, to fashion souls as well as minds. Today the emphasis is chiefly on autonomy and academic freedom.[6]

Throughout this debate little attention has been paid to the complaints of students who come to Catholic colleges as believing Catholics and write later about how shocked they are at what they experience in an environment no longer fashioned by an institutional commitment to a specifically Catholic way of life. They provide abundant horror tales of professors who deny that Christ ever intended a Church, certainly not an hierarchical Church;

75

denigrate indissoluble marriage; ridicule students' inherited views of original sin, purgatory, angels, and transubstantiation; present the New Testament words of Christ as largely post-Resurrection fiction; and allow the Church's moral norms to be set by Charles Curran, not John Paul II. Such students report coming face-to-face with a vicious antihierarchical ecclesiology taught with evident conviction and a biting antipapal ideology as well. Trendy causes are reinforced in and out of the classroom, as if these were the new dogmas of the people's church—contraception, women's ordination, liberation theology, etc. What scandalizes innocent matriculants even more is the conduct of many priests and nuns, practically all out of religious garb. The bitterness of nuns who deride their own religious formation is especially disturbing to those who experience it in large doses. Students who think with the Church or who support John Paul II's policies are ridiculed. As one student said, reporting his reactions to me: "The student who naively sits through the perverted theology will unwittingly begin to doubt all that he once held dear and true."

These are the substantive issues with which Cardinal Baum and the U.S. hierarchy must wrestle. They are already twenty-five years late. Their special difficulty is not the privileges of Catholic academe but the state of soul of the young whom they turn over to a professional caste which rejects their right to evaluate the process or the product. And bishops (and Rome) do the "turning over," because such colleges would lose most of their credibility and large amounts of their benefactions and student body (to say nothing of faculty) if hierarchy ever said in whole or in part that such and such schools do not pass scrutiny on Catholic grounds. The special difficulty for Cardinal Baum and the U.S. episcopal leadership is not the power that Catholic academe has asserted against the hierarchy (and the willingness of the hierarchy so far to tolerate or even accept the status quo), but that the academic elite has set the terms of the debate. For vast numbers of educated Catholics, products of their system, these academics represent Vatican II. Anyone who resists them or who proposes the recapture of the genuine Catholic tradition or who insists that canon law become more than a dead letter, up to and including the Pope himself, is reflexively labeled reactionary, pre-Vatican II or anti-Vatican II. Since the elite has successfully rendered ambiguous what used to be called Catholic truth or Catholic principle, the only reference point for debate is opinion, and in the context of this rhetoric academics have as much right to their opinion as the Pope.

In essence, the critical matter for the Church of the twenty-first century is not the nature of a Catholic university, but the nature of the Catholic Church. And since the Church is not a political democracy, only the Pope and the bishops in union with him can settle the controversy definitively. The stakes are higher than the authors of Land O'Lakes contemplated.

SILVIO CARDINAL ODDI AND CATECHETICS

Cardinal Oddi came to St. John's University at my invitation on May 15, 1981, to give a major address on catechetics. At the time he was an unknown name in the United States, and some would say not a familiar figure in Rome either. Anonymity, however, was not this "little man's" style. Once he bounced in on any scene, you knew he was there—a person not likely to be forgotten. His coming to the Vincentian Fathers in New York was pure happenstance, since few of us over here knew that Oddi had been trained by Vincentians, considered them to be the great inspiration of his life, and attributed some of his diplomatic accomplishments to the training he received from a Vincentian apostolic delegate in Egypt. At the time, as director of The Institute for Advanced Studies in Catholic Doctrine, I was looking for a speaker to enthrall a 1981 symposium. "Would Wright's successor be a good speaker?" I asked. No one there that day knew much about Oddi, not even his first name. "He must be a somebody simply by virtue of his office," I was told.

Silvio Oddi today is a retired prefect of the important Congregation for the Clergy, but he remains an active Roman cardinal, a member of the congregation that nominates bishops, for one thing. Although his beginnings were promising, he almost did not make it to the top of the ecclesiastical ladder. Young Oddi's bishop in Piacenza had a penchant for sending bright young priests to the Diplomatic Academy in Rome, which had turned out luminaries like Pius XII. Indeed, in 1981 four Piacenza priests were functioning cardinals, including the present Secretary of State, Agostino Casaroli. But, in those early years on the diplomatic trail, Fr. Oddi bounced from one minor post to another until he was sent to the Middle East, a Vatican hot spot then as now, and then into Yugoslavia where he served as nuncio during Marshall Tito's lifetime. Oddi managed to outmaneuver the dictator once too often while protecting the Church's cause there and was banned forever from Yugoslavia. He was then named nuncio to Belgium. Later he was brought to Rome by Paul VI, who made him a cardinal in 1969, along with Terry Cooke. He was 59 years of age, a prelate without a job, a red hat on his head but with little to do of world-wide importance, until John Paul II named him to succeed John Wright in 1979.

Even so, no one knew just what Oddi had to offer on Catholic catechetics, which by then was a matter of grave concern to many pastors and most parents, and to Oddi's predecessor. The faculty of IASCD had first-hand evidence of the U.S. problem from the research I compiled and published in a volume entitled *Catholics and The Practice of The Faith: 1967 and 1971.* This study reported the radical changes that occurred in attitudes and behavior during that four-year period among Catholic high school and college students and their parents. Cardinal Oddi did not need to know "the American experience" first hand to give an address. He had been friendly with John Wright and knew from him that the teaching of the Faith was being compromised for the young (and the old) by their exposure to too little of the one true Faith and too many contradictory theologies. Furthermore, Oddi already had behind him a year of reading one hundred letters and memos a day from all over the world, and he had participated in the writing of John Paul II's *Catechesi Tradendae* two years before. The chances were that if his English was good and his personality appealing, the Italian-born cardinal might just be the right man to invite. His English proved to be good and, as we learned, he had a wow of a personality.

THE ODDI SYMPOSIUM

Cardinal Oddi's three days in New York were more symbolic than productive, except for the 300 religious educators who were encouraged, charmed, and electrified by this well-informed and funny little man. He presented the Holy See's concern about catechesis going back to the latter days of John XXIII. And, though his visit would encompass various catechetical centers in the United States, he was sensitive to the fact that he was a visitor, with no particular charge from John Paul II except to speak at St. John's. That did not mean, however, he could not be his entertaining self while making points he had cleared with the Pope prior to coming. And he *was* funny. Once when Allentown's Bishop Joseph McShea was engaging the audience, the question was asked of him whether he personally read the catechetical texts used in his schools. Assured that he did, the questioner pursued the Bishop further: "How do you have time for that?" To which McShea responded playfully: "I've been around so long that in one quick reading I can smell a rat." At which point Oddi, speaking to no one in particular over an open microphone, with his nice Italian drawl making it funny, asked aloud: "What-sa dis smell-a da rat?" The audience broke up and the mood was set. He learned what smelling a rat meant in the United States. A few moments later, following a discussion of the contemporary situation, a theologian asked McShea: "Don't you think in view of all this confusion it would be a good idea if the U.S. bishops got together with the Roman cardinals?" Before the Bishop could utter a word, Oddi chimed in from the sidelines: "It would be better first if the Roman cardinals got together." The audience howled, even though the Cardinal was exposing a sensitive eccle-

79

siastical issue, namely, the divisions in Rome itself about how to deal with a bad catechetical situation.

Cardinal Oddi's keynote address was anything but funny. He brought the norms and message of John Paul II's *Catechesi Tradendae* to New York. That 1979 papal exhortation, he said, might seem fundamental to some "until one realizes that not a few of today's attacks on the Church are going for the jugular, the very fundamentals of our faith." Oddi also took cognizance of the popular error of trying to exhaust all Christian doctrine in concerns about social justice. The major segment of his address, however, concerned the content of catechesis. And hardly any aspect of this controversial subject escaped Oddi's touch. Pluralism did not exempt teachers or pupils from the precepts of the divine and natural law. The catechist is obliged to teach what the Church teaches, not his own speculative views. If in so acting he is accused of being divisive, so be it. So was Christ. A catechist steps out of his role when he poses as an expert in matters of temporal progress. Nor may the catechist dilute the Church's teaching to gain goodwill. As he drew close to the end, the Cardinal insisted on the Church's norms for First Confession for eight-year-olds and on "the importance of memory in religious formation, which is no less than [its importance] in other disciplines." His final word was one of caution "against discarding all the successful operations of the past and starting from the beginning as if experience had taught nothing."

One of Oddi's most poignant paragraphs was the following:

My beloved predecessor, John Cardinal Wright, enjoyed recalling, with a twinkle in his eye, that he never put foot as a student in a Boston parish school. He explained that he learned his prayers from his parents, his doctrine from the local pastor as well as from a devout Protestant teacher in the local public school, who took it upon herself to drill him in the Baltimore Catechism, which at that time was not on the Index of Prohibited Books! The great Cardinal was fond of saying that his higher theological studies never succeeded in opening to him much more about the mystery of the Triune God than

80

he learned from that remarkable Protestant lady in Boston, namely, that there are Three Persons in One God.

The principal charm of Cardinal Oddi was his bubbly personality. A close second was his forthright manner of speech. He was always the Cardinal and never indiscreet, but if you asked him a direct question, you were likely to receive a direct answer. Throughout two days he joined in open discussion with bishops, educators, and parents. New York's Auxiliary Bishop Vaughan, a well-known theologian in his own right, focused on "pluralism," which he called the "critical theological problem of our time." He saw the reigning pluralism as unhelpful to catechesis because it meant a vague relationship with anything Christ stood for and because it permitted the existence within the Church of contradictory expositions of the Faith. In either case the Christian message was too vague to take seriously. Brooklyn's Bishop Anthony Bevilacqua (now of Philadelphia) related for Oddi's audience how "fuzzy pupils are about the meaning of the Church, especially as an institution; and they have a poor knowledge of scripture. They are also confused about many doctrines of the Church." Bevilacqua cited studies showing that "religious doubts among school children now begin as early as thirteen."

A layman, psychology professor Paul Vitz of NYU, filled out the picture by telling his audience that psychologists hardly have the last word on religious education or the moral training of Christians. He pointed out that experimental psychology has been cut off from religion and philosophy for more than a century, rendering its conclusions tentative as to alleged "facts" and perilous as to "theories"; and that secular theories of moral development and values clarification no longer are considered satisfactory by *secular* scholars. Vitz was particularly distressed that this secular psychology has been dominating Catholic textbooks and diocesan workshops for more than a decade. With such books in hand, Catholic teachers began to follow secular theories of human goodness more than their own religious tradition about tainted human nature. As a result, post-Vatican II Catholic education has es-

81

chewed indoctrination, especially about God's law and sin, memory training and discipline. Meanwhile, secular educators were seeking to recapture such basics.

Cardinal Oddi faced tough questions on all these subjects and unflinchingly gave equally tough answers. In general he supported the right of parents to have a major role in the religious education of their children. When one theologian suggested that diocesan education officers exceeded their authority in blacklisting books with Catholic content, thus interfering with the rights of pastors, Oddi told offended parties to feel free to communicate their grievances to him. When pressed further about the ongoing abuses, he refused to encourage the idea that the Holy See would intervene, except in the most outrageous cases. "What can we do? We have no prisons, you know," he added. At which many in the audience laughed. Then, the Cardinal announced (four years before the 1985 Synod) that he had in preparation a universal catechetical handbook which contained the basic teachings of the Church to be included in the catechisms or catechetical directories of all hierarchies. This unpublicized initiative grew out of Rome's unhappiness with local catechisms beginning in 1967 with the one published with the approval of Holland's hierarchy. Oddi's announcement did not make headlines at the time, but when he repeated it in 1985, there was an outcry of concern from religious education establishments. The last thing they wanted was an Oddi catechism. Actually, he did not have a catechism in the works as much as a compilation of Catholic doctrinal statements on matters of faith and morals. The "universal catechism" is still only an idea whose time is overdue, but publishers of catechetical series, with an eye on the future, began to reconcile their texts more closely with approved directories following Oddi's 1981 visit.

THE ODDI AFTERMATH

Cardinal Oddi made three return visits to the United States after 1981. Having proved himself to be a feisty ecclesiastic, hardly what audiences usually experienced, the Prefect of the Clergy Congregation found himself the center of a great deal of American attention (except on the pages of *Origins).* Much of this was friendly, of course, because he did offer support and consolation to all those who were unhappy with the contemporary condition of the Church. He was unique in the sense that he spoke his mind wherever he went—Boston, Detroit, Arlington, Washington, D.C., Birmingham, Nashville, Philadelphia. In Arlington he spoke on truth, reminding religious educators of Catholic people's right to hear that truth convincingly from their teachers. It was a theme John Paul II made his own. In Detroit he told Catholics United for the Faith to work with their bishops. While Lyman and Madeline Stebbins, CUF's founders and national leaders, were people of sophistication and good sense, local officers sometimes acted as if their role was to war on the Bishop. Oddi heard complaints about CUF as he did from CUF, and typically he spoke directly to what was a sore point with many bishops. It was one thing to bring certain abuses to the attention of a bishop, quite another to badger him or to treat him with disrespect. Oddi made it clear where he stood on this subject.

One of his early visits was to Birmingham and to Mother Angelica's Eternal Word Television Network. Here in the heart of Dixie Poor Clare nuns had launched the first, and thus far most successful, Catholic television network in the United States. However, foundress Angelica was in trouble, even with some bishops. She had upstaged everyone by being first. She chose to be independent. There was a question, too, of her financial stability in the face of widened outreach and creeping inflation, something about which bishops rightfully are concerned. What may have rankled most was that Poor Clares, cloistered nuns committed to perpetual adoration of the Blessed Sacrament, were becoming TV stars and public entrepreneurs in the electronic field. Cardinal Oddi's support softened some of the opposition, but it was his influence which helped to obtain the necessary permissions from Rome for her to continue the new apostolate, while still a member of a cloistered community.

Mother Angelica had proven herself by 1981 to be quite a lady, and she hit it off with Cardinal Oddi immediately. They were two of a kind. Asked what a contemplative was doing in the television business, her quick wit brought the reply: "The patron saint of television is St. Clare, declared so by Pius XII thirty years ago." The implication was clear. When Washington officials began to dub her as "too conservative," she jabbed back: "Is being orthodox all that much of a crime these days?" After the Oddi visit she and her twelve nuns faced further scrutiny but were left alone enough to provide 1,000,000 devotional booklets a month distributed free all over the world and to run their TV station without interrupting the five hours of prayer and contemplation they devoted each day to the Lord.

In another Southern city, Nashville this time, Cardinal Oddi made a different impression. There to join in the celebration of the one hundredth anniversary of the Dominican Sisters, an event which attracted 1,500 Catholic and non-Catholic Southerners, Oddi repaired to the house after the ceremony, only to be told that crowds were milling outside waiting for a look at the dignitaries, with no bishop in attendance. Out Oddi went into the heat, moving from circle to circle, listening, chatting, joking, even signing autographs for those who never met an Italian cardinal before. He was King for the Day, as much among the non-Catholics as with Mother Assumpta's nuns.

Informality may be the wrong word to describe his approach to people, since no one would dare slap him on the back or call him "Silvio." But friendly he is, and available too, especially to priests who are the direct object of his Congregation's concern. The canard that Curial officials are heartless bureaucrats, out of touch with real people or local circumstances, has been well sold, sometimes by some very mean local pundits. Cardinal Oddi was a hard man on which to pin such a label. He took his universal care of priests seriously. No priest coming to Rome with or without a problem was denied access to him. When they had complaints, he took them seriously and, if validated, supported their cause. What many outsiders forget is that Rome, certainly in modern times, protects the rights of priests, very often against bishops. Oddi used to call attention to the proper title of his Congregation: "Congregation *for* the Clergy."

Following Vatican II strange things began to take place in some dioceses. Priests who criticized local liturgical abuses publicly, or who refused to use a catechism they considered doctrinally defective, or who were forced to retire early against their will, were threatened at times with ecclesiastical sanction. These priests found a friend in Oddi. One of the strangest cases to come before him was the priest who under an official threat was told to undergo therapy or at least counseling because he was "out of it." What was his offense, you ask? Continuing the public recitation of the Rosary in his parish, believe it or not! Most of the priests' "victories" in Rome, however, were pyrrhic. Investigations took a long time, and a priest could hardly be restored three or four years after his wrongful removal. Few priests even made an appeal. On the other hand, Oddi did persuade some bishops to back away from their efforts to remove pastors, who have substantial rights in canon law.

The "little man" from Piacenza also maintained a close watch on catechisms, unafraid to ask a local bishop to explain his imprimatur on a book of dubious Catholic content. If the matter was serious enough, he would pass it on to the Congregation for the Doctrine of the Faith. Diocesan bishops, on the other hand, were loathe to seek Roman intervention even when it might help, for example, when religious communities began to deteriorate before their very eyes. One important bishop told a Roman congregation to keep its hands off "his" nuns, lest they leave "his" schools. They abandoned the school system just the same. The same bishops resented being told what they could not do, which Oddi sometimes told them. However, problems tended to outrun solutions and bishops allowed many outrageous situations to run their course without redress in the hope that they would go away or go elsewhere. Some of them, like deteriorating seminaries and novitiates, only became worse.

Cardinal Oddi, as long as he was coming to the United States, had one further interest—to coordinate the pontifical catechetical institutes which had been established by Cardinal Wright and were now responsible to him. The ultimate guarantor of authenticity of these institutes was the Clergy Congregation, which conferred a certificate assuring the reader that the graduate fulfilled the Holy See's norms as catechist. At St. John's University this was granted whenever a master's degree in Catholic doctrine was earned. There were ten other institutes, some with a university or seminary base, some tied in to the diocesan catechetical machinery without college accreditation. John Wright's idea was that eventually these institutes would tie in to parish parent organizations, thus extending their influence. This never came to be. The eleven such foundations, in Arlington, Buffalo, Cleveland, Erie, Dallas, Gary, New York, St. Louis, Philadelphia, Portland (Oregon), and New Orleans, were not even connected or related to each other. Oddi wished to change this, but he did not know how to proceed. He hoped to expand their influence in the United States but was handicapped by the fact some of these institutes had been "bootlegged" into certain dioceses by Wright without a by-your-leave to the local bishop. Others came into existence at the bishop's request to bypass his catechetical machinery without any guarantee that his successor would provide the same endorsement. Cardinal Oddi could not order the confederation of these institutes, but he could recognize a body organized by their directors. But in 1981 only Arlington, Erie, New York, Philadelphia, and Gary looked viable, and some of these, like Philadelphia, had no interest in working together. While he was in New York Cardinal Oddi met with the directors, but it was soon clear that John Wright's institutes were to remain a Roman symbol more than American reality. American bishops generally were not prepared

86

to have catechetics taught as Rome wished it taught. Oddi had tried once before by empowering two directors to organize the established institutes and promote new ones. That effort failed. Oddi had hoped that a national association would help his role in U.S. catechetics, but when he failed this second time, he abandoned the plan.

The long-range effect of Cardinal Oddi's American adventure was something no one expected: he gained instant personal recognition throughout the English-speaking Catholic world. His press generally had been good, and his message rapidly spread to Canada, England, and as far away as Australia. He became the focal point of interest among all those religious educators who were unhappy with the way their young were being catechized. Letters poured into his office from all over that world, with invitations to go here and there to see for himself. He became more and more convinced that things had gotten out of hand, far beyond the world of CCD classes. Hardly a matter of concern on three continents failed to cross his desk. Issues which went far beyond the province of the Clergy Congregation—the condition of seminaries, sex education courses, the various Roman investigations of religious houses and seminaries, the state of the Catholic press, the appointment of bishops, the internal condition of dioceses whose bishops gave free play to dissenting theologians, appointments to Roman offices, and so forth. The dissenting press tried to make Oddi out to be some sort of Neanderthal, a typical tactic intended to limit his effectiveness. And surely in Rome there would be other cardinals who were uncomfortable with Oddi's direct speech and his surprising popularity. But the Clergy Prefect was a Vatican II prelate to the core and fully Catholic. He also spoke freely to John Paul II and was a strong supporter of the Pope's policies. He had his own sphere of influence, although he was a realist about the conflicting forces that vied for the Pope's attention. Oddi was conscious of the opposition John Paul II encountered even in his own household and admitted that some episcopal appointments were weak enough to dilute the Pope's strength world-wide. Oddi was a member of the Bishops' Congregation but he realized that many of those appointments were reasonably prepackaged by the time they left the office of the local nuncio. Good arguments might and often did ensue in Rome over sees like New York and Chicago, and cardinals at the highest levels did not always agree on the best appointment. Even so, Cardinal Oddi was not without influence, and when he had formed a definite opinion, he made it known in unmistakable language. By the end of his fourth journey to the United States, he had formed a well-rounded judgment of the problems facing John Paul II. In a letter to me dated January 4, 1984, he summed up the situation as follows:

> It is finally out in the open the fact that there are doctrinal interpretations in different countries not entirely in accord with magisterium. Up until recently many priests and bishops might have considered some of these legitimate manifestations of theological pluralism, but it is becoming clearer to virtually all that some of these interpretations run into head-on conflict with Catholic doctrine and are therefore unacceptable. You and others have helped to clarify this, and I foresee that more and more right-minded people will publicly assert their adherence to the doctrine of the Faith.

There could be no better hope than this for a good priest and Silvio Oddi surely is that.

THE CATECHETICAL TEXTS

You cannot speak of Cardinal Oddi without mentioning the textbooks on catechetics that the Clergy Prefect was asked to review by priests and parents throughout the Catholic world. Many years later New York's John Cardinal O'Connor would mention textbook publishers as a source of difficulty for the Church, only to be contested by Minnesota's Bishop of New Ulm, Raymond Lucker, once the chief of the USCC's Department of Education. This in-house tiff merely symbolizes the depth, and the heat, of the controversies which have surrounded these books since the Council.

Catechetical leadership defended the commonly used texts by saying that books were not the real teachers, which is true enough, but there is enough evidence to suggest that teachers and texts were often slanted away from the content material required by the nature of Catholic catechesis itself. Catechetical reformers early made the mistake of patronizing parents, and they compounded their error by trying to ride roughshod over parental (and important priestly) objections, at the very time they were proclaiming in professional quarters that this was the age of the laity. Frustrated and angered by opposition from run-of-the-mill laity, the experts in experiential catechesis badmouthed their critics and found an occasional bishop to attribute withdrawal of imprimaturs by Rome to "extreme right-wing groups."

To avoid being lost in the quagmire of arguments over religious books, to learn why the catechetical controversy has generated so much passion, it is necessary to appreciate the groups competing for dominance. They are three: (1) those who argue that Vatican II changed Catholic doctrine or at least reduced Catholic claims; (2) theologians and religious educators who no longer believe in many doctrinal positions or in their obligatory force; (3) those who accept modern psychological theories as an appropriate mechanism for forming Vatican II Catholics.

The catechetical series, which regularly receive high marks from the National Conference of Diocesan Directors of Religious Education, have three characteristics that worry their Catholic critics: (1) they lay extreme stress on humanist concerns and psychological well-being; (2) they are imprecise in defining Catholic terms, failing to teach doctrines required to be taught by Rome's *General Catechetical Directory* and the U.S. Bishops' *National Catechetical Directory;* and (3) they contain unnecessary negative asides in texts intended for elementary school children supposedly still learning the basics of their faith.

The books' defenders usually think such objections are unfair, because the criticized segments are allegedly taken out of context or because the critics fail to consider the totality of a given series, that is, subjects treated lightly in lower grades are covered fully later on or in the parent/teacher manuals. It cannot be denied that some critics would distort printed material to make ideological points. Yet it must also be said that under the new catechetics the Church is turning out a large proportion of religious illiterates; and others, however well informed, often do not attend Sunday Mass after twelve years of Catholic schooling. Texts are not the sole source of alienation of Catholic youngsters, of course, but when badly structured they contribute to negative feelings about the Church.

The impartial observer must recognize the "values clarification" influence almost everywhere in these texts, especially in their repeated insistence on "ask questions," "seek," "search"— this in books that ought to impart with authority God's word as made known through Jesus Christ. Building up the child's ego, or his or her appreciation of the human situation, is not a vital component of catechesis. And when ego-development is combined with undue emphasis on humanist concerns, the final product may not be the God-centered instruction one is entitled to expect in a Catholic catechism class. For example, in Grade 1 of *In Christ Jesus* (Benziger) the opening lines read: "Who am I?" To which the answer is: "I am me. There are things I can do and say. See the gifts I have. I am me. I can talk and run and hug. I am special." Grade 4 of the same series tells the child: "You must like yourself for what you are." When the reader notices, too, that the text lays stress on the human and the natural aspects of Jesus and not the religious faith which ensued from his ministry, a parent is entitled to ask questions about what kind of catechesis this is.

Grade 6 of *Growing in Faith* (Silver-Burdette) explains "growth in spirit" as a human process of developing the art of being free: "What is for freedom is good—if laws and rules are *for* freedom, they're good. If they're *against* freedom, they're bad." This statement is made during a discussion of the Ten Commandments. Even Jesus is presented as having come to help us to grow in freedom, the same Jesus who said: "Not my will, but thine be done."[7] This text to the contrary notwithstanding, Christian

90

growth is not directed toward freedom from fears or discrimination, but toward the piety expressed in the Pater Noster, "Thy will be done."

Grade 7 of *The Lord of Life Program* (Sadlier) invites students to make decisions about God's dominion: "Take a stand on what you believe by choosing one of the answers below. In the column on the right give the reasons for your choice." Among the choices offered are these two extremes: "I believe God created the universe," "I believe God had nothing to do with creation." This is pure values clarification at work. Although the text later speaks of God's law, the very methodology lays more stress on personal opinion than on the truth of God's creative act handed on by the teacher who, in the classroom at least, stands for the Church.

Modern educators look down on the Baltimore Catechism for its simplistic reduction of the Catholic faith to black and white answers. Yet the old results were the inevitable by-product of a method and a philosophy. Newcomers do not seem to realize that today's results are related to a different method and philosophy. The method is inductive (search) and the philosophy inverts the traditional God-centered approach in favor of humanist priorities developed from other than Catholic sources. Those aspects of traditional Catholic learning which "science" considers to be mythological, or merely the Church's "cultural baggage," are no longer considered necessary to catechesis, even if the Magisterium of the Church says otherwise.

Christian thinking about human destiny in Christ develops from mankind's fall from grace with our first parents. From that point on, the elements of the Church's "deposit of faith" come together in the promise of a Redeemer, the Old Testament convenant, including the Ten Commandments, Christ's birth, his sacrificial death and resurrection, as these were celebrated in apostolic preaching and in the sacrifice of the Mass, with the Church leading the faithful to choices which shape their final end, death surely, and judgment, heaven, hell, or purgatory. This body of doctrine covering mankind's transit from creation onward lays great stress on God's continuing intervention in the process of

91

salvation, normally through the Church to whom Christ gave "all power in heaven and on earth—[to] make disciples of all nations —[to] baptize them—[to] teach them to carry out everything I have commanded." The same body of Catholic teaching also requires that believers become involved in their own salvation with active encouragement and support from the Church beginning at an early age.

Both the *General Catechetical Directory* and the *National Catechetical Directory* were promulgated to ensure that this world view is internalized by Catholic youth. Both directories require teachers and textbooks to include specific teachings, the most important of which are the following:

1. God's public revelation to the world closed with the end of the apostolic age. This revelation is to be distinguished from all other forms of communication by which God continues to make himself known.

2. God created the universe, angels, and finally man. In Adam all human beings sinned and fell from grace. From that moment human beings were injured in their natural powers and subjected to punishment and death. Original sin is transmitted to all men by generation. Fallen man is so weakened that he is unable for long to keep the natural law without God's help.

3. The sacraments are remedies for our sins and are sources of grace, beginning with Baptism which cleanses from original sin, and culminating with the Eucharist which is Christ's sacrifice on the Cross re-presented in an unbloody manner. Under the appearances of bread and wine Christ really is present.

4. The Church was founded by Christ, and in the Catholic Church may be found the deposit of faith, the sacraments, and the ministries inherited from the apostles. The Church is essentially a hierarchical society, headed by the Pope and bishops who are infallible, when they speak definitively and absolutely on matters of faith and morals. The Magisterium is responsible for interpreting the moral law, and its teaching demands religious submission of mind and will. Conscience must be taught absolute norms. The reality of sin as an offense against God and Christ's "work of justice" must be taught as one of the principal points of Christian faith. Sins can be mortal or venial, the former of which must be confessed to a priest.

5. The final end of mankind goes beyond death to include individual and collective judgment by God, with reward and punishment in heaven, hell, or purgatory.

The above brief summary of catechetical requirements represents only part of what textbooks are supposed to contain. The fact is, however, that many of these concepts are not taught or are inadequately taught in the most commonly used texts. This is not surprising. When the focus is on the child's essential goodness, on his unlimited potential for self-direction and growth, it is methodologically difficult for a course to speak of anything the child is obligated to accept as true simply because it is alleged to come from revelation.

As one reads from series to series, one finds that Catholic identity is consistently underplayed. If youngsters are to learn to believe that their road to Christ is through the Church, not just by being part of God's people, they will find little reason for so believing in some of these books. Some teachers today actually hold that Vatican II gave up the notion that the Catholic Church is the "one true Church of Christ." Such descriptions of the Church as "the house of God's family," "one way of worshipping and believing God," "the people of God," "a group of people called together by Jesus," or "a group of people who believe the same things about Jesus," are inadequate. In some series the few uses of the word "Catholic" ("Christian" being the common word) hardly reinforces the religious identity of the people being taught. How far these authors sometimes go to underplay the Church's true identity is evident in one Grade 7 book where we read, "Jesus founded the Church to be characterized by unity, holiness, *openness,* and the tradition of the apostles." The fourth mark of the Church actually is catholicity (or universality) and that word does not translate into "openness."

The failure in fully explaining the Church as the Living Body of Christ is deepened when the linkage between Jesus, the authority of pope and bishops, and the formation of a Catholic conscience is also weakly drawn. Jesus' mission was somewhat more (as in one Grade 8 book) than "to remind people that they were good and special, that they were loved and trusted by God, and that they had their own way of revealing God to others." The roles of pope and bishop are poorly explained, the latter being called in one place, "the leader of a group of parishes." "Church leaders are not bosses," we are told elsewhere. The ordinary infallibility of the Church and the pope in interpreting God's law and the necessity of submission to this teaching would not be convincingly understood from these books.

The authors consistently have difficulty with sin. In the normal course of eight years of Catholic schooling one would expect youngsters to come away with some understanding that they live in a world with an objective moral order, and that by sinning they violate this order and offend God, that God punishes sinners, and that Christ died on the Cross because of our sins. Very frequently, however, sin is defined as a poor choice, as selfishness, as harmful to others without reference to God. Original sin and the distinction between mortal and venial sin are often improperly defined, making it hard for children to fully grasp the significance of the Cross and the Sacrifice of the Mass. When the Ten Commandments are introduced, one Grade 5 text tells the students that Jesus wants them "to be more interested in the *spirit* of God's rules than in the *letter.*" Then when "examination of conscience" comes to the fore, the children are told not to "think of sins you have committed," but "look at your life. See the choices you have made."

The imperfect catechesis continues from grade to grade. One looks in vain for good descriptions of the Mass as a re-presentation of Calvary's sacrificial and redemptive act. Merely "Remembering" Christ's death will not do. There is little emphasis on the Real Presence. Sanctifying grace is either not defined satisfactorily or sometimes not mentioned in connection with the Sacrament. Concepts that are unpopular with dissenters are not mentioned at all, even though some are *de fide,* for example, the existence of angels, the institution of the Sacrament by Christ, purgatory, hell, transubstantiation. One book recounts the Annunciation scene without mentioning Gabriel. Another page dealing with Holy Orders has the picture of a woman minister.

Now it is possible to nitpick contemporary catechisms to the point of making them or their critics, or both, look ridiculous. Denials are frequent and heated when catechisms, old or new, are challenged. Yet the fact remains that our young Catholics are undercatechized and undercommitted to the Catholic faith. Not only are texts part of that undereducation, but, those who coauthor the books, or grant the nihil obstat, or review criticisms for the bishops who grant imprimaturs operate out of a world view that is irreconcilable with Rome's view of what the Second Vatican Council was and what the Church is. Not long ago the National Conference of Diocesan Directors of Religious Education published a booklet entitled *The Relationship between Evangelization and Catechesis,* whose introduction (p. 1) maintains (among other things) that after Vatican II "we found out that the Catholic Church is not the sole possessor of truth," and "we discovered anew that our Romanized form of Catholicism did not satisfy the spiritual needs of all cultures." Well, Rome, the final judge of catechesis, made one of its many final efforts to restore sanity to catechesis through *Catechesi Tradendae* (1979). In that document's ecumenical section (No. 32) John Paul made it clear that catechesis, even while respecting others' religion, must unceasingly "teach that the fullness of the revealed truths and of salvation instituted by Christ is found in the Catholic Church."

Such was the confusion in the post-Vatican II catechesis which Cardinal Oddi came to clear up when he arrived at St. John's University on May 15, 1981.

NOTES

1. *Our Sunday Visitor,* April 25, 1976, p. 15.
2. *NC News,* March 23, 1989.
3. *Crisis,* May 1989, p. 2.
4. *St. Louis Review,* June 16, 1989, p. 8.
5. Ibid.
6. Two years before Vatican II, Fr. George Bull, S.J., speaking out of a Fordham background, an institution that a few years later declared itself non-denominational: "If the Catholic college in this country has neglected even partially either of its two functions, it has not neglected the first. It has, thank God, sent forth from its halls generations of men and women who know the faith." Cf. *Why a Catholic College?* America Press, 1960, p. 14.
7. Matthew 26:39.

FOUR

The Pope's Second Team: Curial Officers

THE ROMAN ROTA AND MARRIAGE TRIBUNALS

I BACKED INTO INVOLVEMENT with the jurisdiction of the Roman Rota through lay people who felt that they received a raw deal from one or the other of their diocesan tribunals. Unlike my other "Roman connections," which were somewhat direct, this one was indirect, placing aggrieved Catholics in contact with canon lawyers in Vatican City who could assist them in their appeals to the Roman Rota. This is the Holy See's court of appeals for the review of important or contested annulment cases. The petitioners usually were Catholics who wished to defend the indissolubility of their sacramental marriage after a local diocesan court had declared it null. For me, this connection was more issue-oriented than personal, except when the aggrieved parties became my friends.

Once a priest gets away from day-to-day parish work, he rarely runs into many Catholics who seek to marry a second time with

Church blessing and thus need to have their first marriage annulled. Whereas divorce dissolves a real marriage, nullity (literally "to make a nothing") is a decree that a real marriage never existed, even though it looked real enough in its outward appearances. If, for example, an already married Catholic man managed to wangle a second Church wedding by keeping secret the existence of a first wife, the second marriage would obviously be invalid. The wife in the second case would have to prove her case before a marriage tribunal, of course, but the decision would be called a "declaration of nullity," not a divorce. (The word *annulment* is also used in American civil parlance, but because of the fraud so commonplace in civil annulments, the Church's word is more precise.) The distinction between divorce and nullity is not arbitrary. The mind of the Church from the time of Christ considers a consummated sacramental marriage as indissoluble—"until death do us part"—one that cannot be broken even by the Church. Since what a person does in making any contract under public law, especially one as important as marriage, is presumed to have been done correctly, the only choice left to the conscientious Catholic seeking a second marriage when a first spouse is still living is to have the Church look for factors—fraud, defects of consent, existing marriage, insanity, compulsion, and so forth—that would invalidate the first marriage at its very inception.

The Church has been fussy on this matter. Other churches search scripture for exceptions, notably Protestants and Greek Orthodox, and, like Moses of old, they grant both divorces and annulments. But the ancient Church, basing Catholic teaching on her own tradition and on the earliest patristic understanding of biblical texts, holds fast to Christ's absolute ban. "What God has united, man must not divide."[1] Christ foresaw man's difficult choices, yet he proclaimed as the word of God that indissoluble marriage was necessary for the good of all, for spouses as well as for children. The modern trend, of course, is in an entirely different direction—toward temporary unions and permanency only if personal happiness on both sides has already been secured. Children are incidental to the basic decision to dissolve an unsatisfactory union. Contrariwise for the true believer, bearing with difficulty, even suffering, is looked upon as a Christian virtue. "Anyone who does not take his cross and follow in my footsteps is not worthy of me."[2] Severe burdens are alleviated by the approved separation of spouses, and a certain compassion is shown by the Church to those who marry a second time without ecclesial sanction. But the norm remains—one sacramental marriage as long as both spouses live.

Rome has also been particular about her tribunals, partly because incompetent judges usually do not know enough canon law to free people who should be freed, partly because of the danger of collusion and conspiracy when demands for freedom run headlong into established law. Pius XII, on ascending the Papacy in 1939, was not satisfied with the American tribunal system and gave the new archbishop of New York the responsibility of setting up a "model" tribunal, which he did. His first chief judges were Bishop Edward Dargin, Msgr. James Kelly, and Msgr. John Costello, among the finest canon lawyers in the nation, with a host of first-rate assistants as backups, all trained doctors in canon law. Tribunal work was vital to parish priests who were closest to the sufferings of Catholics who had made bad marriage choices before, during, and after the war. Once civil divorce began to rub off on the Catholic faithful (today estimates of five million divorced Catholics are commonplace), rectory and chancery offices became dreary listening centers. Canonical consultants and tribunal judges sat day by day listening to pathetic tales of woe from pious Catholics, as well as a large amount of deceit from imposters who thought that money or fraud could win them another try at Catholic marriage. It is not surprising that many of those priests lost their judicial balance or opted out of tribunal work for the more satisfying life of a parish priest.

Although there may be a heartless priest here and there, most working pastors "feel" for divorced people, some of whom can be found in their own families. There are spouses who must go on alone, raise children alone, and, if they believe in the truth of the Church's message, do this even as they observe Catholic friends taking a second spouse without anyone's blessing but their own. Still, the paramount issue for the Church relative to marriage is God's truths revealed to us through Jesus Christ, one of which is the indissolubility of a marriage raised to a sacrament by Christ. This Catholic truth is important not only for the stability of normal family life everywhere, however unhappy some marriages become, but for the settled place of the "domestic Church" in Christ's overarching plan of salvation. The home is the primary training center of Christians and must not be allowed to disintegrate because of neglect by the Church or the weakness of people. Christ did not promise money, success, health, or happiness in this life to any of his followers, only eternal life to all of them who kept his commandments.

Few will gainsay that the Church, at various stages of Christian history, has been alternately lax and stern in her treatment of those who give up their religious commitment in or out of marriage. In the pre-Vatican II period, the Church held fast to her marital norms; no divorces were allowed, and fewer than two hundred U.S. marriages were nullified in a given year. But today we hear about forty thousand and more nullities per annum in the United States, six to ten times the rate in neighboring Mexico or Canada. Granted that the old procedures for examining "marriage cases" were often unwieldy and decisions (usually negative) came too slowly and that it was sensible for U.S. bishops to request Rome for permission to experiment with "American norms"—speedy trials, fewer judges, simple appeals, and greater use of experts in the psychological and humane sciences to help determine whether or not a given couple or one of the parties had the psychic capacity to consent freely to marriage. The new norms did facilitate speedier solutions, and many couples were delighted with "annulments" they did not expect.

Then, suddenly, a new type of complaint began to be heard from the pews. How could the Church dissolve a marriage of long standing, people ask, often with many children, when one of the spouses or the local parish community thinks the reason for the "annulment" alleged by the diocesan tribunal to be unbelievable?

Suspicions began to grow that some of the grounds being advanced by diocesan courts lacked solid basis in Catholic law. One university professor appealed to the Roman Rota because her local tribunal suggested she change her petition from the husband's refusal to have children to psychic incapacity for marriage. She was told it was easier to get an annulment that way. Her answer was blunt: "But your suggestion is a lie. There is nothing wrong with my husband's sanity or his personality. He just does not want children." Another university professor provided his tribunal with a diary to show that his wife was fully conscious of what marriage was all about and very much in love with him at the time of the wedding and thereafter for many years until she met someone else. Even so, she received her annulment. The wife in question also worked for the diocese.

What began to occur, of course, is that "marital consent," the basis of marriage, was broadened to include some guarantee of happiness as well as the right to sexual relations and a common household. After Vatican II, Church courts in the U.S. almost immediately (using American norms) began to annul marriages that most Catholics considered sacramentally established. The Church's reputation for integrity came under suspicion when a TV personality or a prominent politician boasted about or paraded his new spouse whom he acquired after a Church annulment had dispatched the mother of his five children. Years earlier a few Catholics believed money or influence could "buy" an annulment. Indeed, some of the true-to-life stories were funnier than fiction. One Broadway character tried to marry an Irish chorus girl in New York only to be told no by a chancery priest. A first marriage stood in the way. He knew Jim Farley, he said, would that help? Assured by his canon lawyer that Farley might help, the 42nd Street hot-shot then asked: "How?" Because Farley was a close friend of Cardinal Spellman, and with that kind of influence New York's archbishop was bound to intervene, he was told. What would Spellman do, the man asked, confident that he had found the keys to a new kingdom. "He would call my boss,

Bishop Dargin, who would call me," said the canonist, "and I would tell Dargin you have no case."

After 1968, annulments became quite commonplace so that when the New Code of Canon Law was promulgated in 1983, the tribunals found in Canon 1095—which declared as incapable of marriage those who suffered from grave lack of discretion or a "psychic" impediment—ample room to continue their generosity to aggrieved spouses. As one canon lawyer summarized the justification: "[Psychological incapacity] was the main grounds for nullity of marriage in many tribunals of much of the English speaking world."[3] How such incapacity could be "proved" twenty or more years after the wedding and after many children (whose legitimacy was cast into doubt) remained a puzzle to many Catholic couples who carried more serious marital crosses of their own.

Rome certainly knew what was going on during these years of easy annulments. Did Church officials, then, approve of the backdoor undermining of the indissolubility of marriage, permitting in practice what they could not afford to admit doctrinally? Dissenters maintained Rome always accepts change this way, and only this way. American bishops certainly knew what was going on, and were informed at high levels that what their courts were doing was wrong and scandalous. At the 1980 Roman Synod on the Family, Cardinal Pericle Felici, prefect of the Church's supreme court (called the Apostolic Signature), told the bishops assembled that "the non-observance or neglect of juridical norms in marriage cases would bring on divorce, even if it came under another name." He reported a 5,000 percent increase in the number of declarations of marital nullity in ten years, which concerned him less than the "levity with which these cases are often proposed and resolved," almost always for "psychological immaturity, incapacity for assuming responsibility in married life especially in interpersonal relations." Felici went so far as to tell the world's episcopal leaders of the game-playing that was going on within the Church, the flight of cases from one country's tribunals to another's, from one continent to another (from Europe to Africa, for example), in Felici's words, to the "easier tribunals."

"Case hijackers," he called them.[4] During this Synod Aurelio Cardinal Sabattini, prefect at the time of the Roman Rota, chastised the American bishops with the charge that the American courts, then granting most of the annulments, were in the hands of incompetent jurists. He did not mention that some ecclesiastics on both sides of the Atlantic were preventing appeals from a U.S. diocesan court reaching the Roman Rota, an unheard of interference with the administration of justice.

The questions still remain years later: Who at high levels knew what was going on? What were they doing to redress obvious evils? The matter was serious. Was the indissolubility of Catholic matrimony to fall into desuetude?

Complaints from some bishops and certainly from offended parties began to reach Rome, or so Cardinal Felici said. Although the machinery there always grinds slowly, the process in defense of the faith is inexorable, as Henry VIII once discovered. We can only cite here a few Rota determinations that overturned American decisions and provided evidence of judicial malpractice.

On December 18, 1986, for example, the Rota overturned an annulment that had been granted in the diocese in the Northwest to a Mr. A ten years earlier, after 38 years of marriage to a baptized Protestant lady. The grounds included "an absence of serious intent and total commitment on the part of both parties due to immaturity." Mrs. A, denied a copy of the file, protested to Rome that she did not hear of the annulment's existence until 1978, two years after its granting, and that she considered her marriage perfectly valid. One year after her appeal the Rota upset that decision.

A much more interesting case involves a West Coast couple, Mr. and Mrs. B, whose twenty-one-year marriage was declared null and void by the diocesan tribunal on January 3, 1980, because of "psychological factors" in both parties. Seven years later the Roman Rota, after examining the documents, decided to reopen the case. Three Rota judges provided a detailed glimpse of the practice of some American marriage tribunals.

The B annulment, first granted by a *single* diocesan judge, and upheld by three jurists from the Court of Second Instance, followed the presentation of these facts: After sixteen years of what was characterized as a "serene and happy marriage," the wife's mother moved in with the couple, and during the next eleven years marital conflict led to a civil divorce obtained in 1978 by the wife. Mrs. B then sought an annulment alleging that Mr. B was unable to offer "a true love or to establish a relationship with me as a wife and was incapable of a minimal matrimonial relationship." She, too, had worked for the diocese in question and had help from a chancery official in drawing up the proper petition. On February 18, 1980, the original decree of nullity was upheld by the second tribunal.

Mr. B appealed his case to Rome on November 13, 1980 because, as the Rota itself had reason to note later, the original tribunal ignored his request for an appeal. He was already too late for Roman action because the law allowed him only thirty days for such a recourse, so his case was "abandoned" by Rome. But Mr. B persisted, and a new Rota judge reopened the case on February 10, 1987, five days after John Paul II, in an allocution to the Rota, warned against basing annulments on psychological theories which are incompatible with a Christian view of man.[5] This Roman jurist judge began by asking himself a series of questions: Did the West Coast tribunals err "in applying the law or interpreting the facts?" In the decision-making was there a violation of the principles linked with the institution of marriage?

The steps by which the Rota proceeded—from acceptance of the case to upsetting a diocesan tribunal—is a story in itself, recounted in the decision of the Roman judges.

1. The Rota quickly decided (a) that the first and second tribunals erred in applying the law and interpreting the facts, and, more significantly, that they erred in explaining Catholic doctrine on indissolubility; (b) that Mr. B's accusations against both tribunals were "precise and accurate"; (c) that Mrs. B had been a diocesan employee with diocesan "connections."

2. The new Roman judges considered "astounding" the way

the Court of Second Instance handled the first appeal. Two psychiatric experts appointed to review the evidence never subjected either party to a diagnostic examination. However, upon interviewing Mr. and Mrs. B *together,* they each decided that Mr. B was a paranoid personality—a defect "of sufficient gravity to interfere with the intention and maintenance of a valid matrimonial contract" (entered into twenty-eight years earlier). One expert attributed Mr. B's inflexibility and stubbornness to the fact that *"he sees his marriage by its nature as a permanent commitment until death,"* evidence by itself of a *paranoid personality.* The second expert claimed that Mr. B's rigid adherence *"to the idea of a commitment for his entire life"* and *"his absolute determination to preserve the marriage is typical of the paranoid personality."* On this basis both experts recommended annulment.

3. The final determination of the Roman Rota read as follows:

(a) The first judge "uncritically and carelessly accepted the conclusions of the experts and made them his own," even though they were as uncertain and undefined as they could be."

(b) The second tribunal hardly made a canonical case when it offered as evidence against Mr. B the fact that "he chose to participate, taking advantage of every opportunity offered to him of affirming and repeating a religious and exaggerated preoccupation with the sacramentality of marriage and its indissolubility."

(c) The Rota's final estimate of the procedure: "This manner of proceeding by the Appellate Tribunal is hardly at the service of truth. It reeks with discrimination and the favoring of persons. Consequently, there arises a legitimate suspicion about the correct administration of justice, and more particularly confirms everything that the Respondent [Mr. B] explained in his letter of November 30, 1980."

(d) On October 28, 1988, the Rota set aside the original decision, declaring that the nullity of the B marriage was not established. After eight years Mr. B's defense of his original marriage was vindicated by the Holy See.

During its 1987 adjudication, the Rota's three-judge panel warned of the real difference between breaking a bond (divorce) and declaring that no bond ever existed (nullity). However, a year before Mrs. B sued to free herself canonically from Mr. B, the diocesan newspaper featured the following headline: "Tribunal frees people to remarry in Church."[6]

An Adrian Dominican sister named Marie Wiedner had recently been appointed coordinator of the Apostolate to Divorced Catholics by the bishop. In an interview with the paper she explained how today "the Church is really trying to free people to marry again in the Church." She explained: "A permanent commitment is still the ideal. But maybe people don't always reach that ideal. Do they have to live out their failure for the rest of their lives?" Her rationale for the unprecedented number of annulments being granted at the time was the following: "Previously the Church said that if you had a ceremony with a priest and if you had a physical consummation, you had a sacramentally consecrated marriage. Divorced persons are saying, 'No, there should be more present in marriage for it to be a sacrament.' A lot of re-education for both laity and clergy was in order."[7]

Many people think that secrecy contributes to the proliferation of annulments in recent years. The Church is not the State, of course, and normally has a greater concern for privacy and public reputations. Annulment procedures are often adversary with charges and countercharges, which when made public unnecessarily add little to the judicial process or to people's peace of mind. Yet canon law does provide for the "defense" to have access to the "acta" (Cn. 1598). For purposes of appeal the *Code* also entitles a party to a copy of the sentence, when he or she would like to challenge the original decision (Cn. 1634). Yet complaints persist that first and second tribunals resist those who wish to appeal, especially to Rome, withhold or delay proper notifications of nullity decrees and information about the basis of the nullity; and judges go so far at times as to manifest hostility toward those who insist on their right to appeal, even if they only seek to protect their reputation or their marriage. Diocesan court officials allege

106

the need to safeguard the "experts," many of whom would be reluctant to have their psychological judgments publicized.

Americans have become accustomed to almost a million divorces a year, the largest number of divorces in the civilized world. Nearly one-third of our school children are no longer living with their own parents, one family in five is headed by one parent, illegitimate births have more than tripled in twenty years, most mothers work outside the home, family size has dropped below the replacement rate, and cohabitation without benefit of marriage is considered normal, as is homosexuality. The Catholic Church, once the bulwark of family stability, now has its share of instant divorces, divorces by private decision, and divorces going by the name of annulment; and two out of every three Catholics are already demanding that the Church change her teaching and allow divorced Catholics to remarry within the Church.[8]

The recent practice of U.S. tribunals is often defended by appeals to psychiatric breakthroughs, which allegedly provide special insights in determining psychic incapacity for marriage years after the event took place. Professionals often offer judgments about "psychic incapacity" in marriage cases as "certain" which they would not be able to express with equal surety if the cases were criminal. (District attorneys can be devastating adversaries.) Surely, psychological experts may reach a morally certain conclusion in obvious and extreme cases. But few of them walk out on a limb any more to decide what a defendant's state of mind was when he committed a crime. They are less sure today when they are asked whether a given criminal has been sufficiently rehabilitated to merit release from prison. It must therefore be asked how, in all but extraordinary cases, a mental health expert can pontificate with moral certainty about the psychological capacity of a person to enter a valid marriage twenty or ten or five years later, especially when the relationship has had a history of stability. We should also ask—as John Paul II has asked marriage tribunals—why Catholic judges should permit therapists of one kind or another to dominate the nullity process.

The problem goes beyond the canonical issues involved, surely beyond the vagaries of experimental psychology. The Catholic Church has a well-defined teaching, considered to be the Word of God, well-grounded in Scripture, sustained in a long tradition at times against attempts of other Christians to change Christ's clear meaning, one that is considered by many to be an infallible moral directive, which at times has cost the Church principalities and kingdoms. How can the Church walk away from such an important truth? The controversy goes still further, much beyond the present practice of marriage tribunals. Some priests today freely "annul" marriages on their own initiative through a device called "the internal forum solution," whereby a priest, not a tribunal, judges a first marriage invalid, though unprovably so, and gives his blessing to a couple living together in a second marriage with the privilege of receiving Holy Communion.

The condition is serious. Forty thousand plus "annulled" marriages year after year, as they pass through the gossip lines of parish life, can undo the Church's marital discipline more surely than anything civil governments can do. In spite of official explanations that justify the reasons for and the frequency of such nullities, John Paul II, taking a second look at possible abuses, has taken to alerting his judges to restore some sense of sanity to the Rota, which is, after all, his own tribunal machinery. What else is possible for a Pope who wrote the *Exhortation on the Christian Family (Familiaris Consortio,* 1981), one of whose major points was the following (No. 20):

> It is a fundamental duty of the Church to reaffirm strongly, as the Synod Fathers did, the doctrine of the indissolubility of marriage. To all those who in our times consider it too difficult or indeed impossible to be bound to one person for the whole of life, and to those caught up in a culture that rejects the indissolubility of marriage and openly mocks the commitment of spouses to fidelity, it is necessary to reconfirm the good news of the definitive nature of that conjugal love that has in Christ its foundation and strength.

John Paul II's most difficult task remaining is to see to it that his tribunal jurists follow the lead of the Church's Chief Judge.

ARCHBISHOP PIO LAGHI AND THE AMERICAN SCENE

The first one to mention the name of Pio Laghi to me was Aegidio Cardinal Vagnozzi, the Apostolic Delegate to the United States from 1958 to 1967. I had known Vagnozzi slightly during my Spellman period, but got to know him better later on walking the beach at Rockaway, N.Y., where he was frequently a guest of Msgr. Edward Mitty, nephew of San Francisco's late Archbishop John Mitty. He was in New York in September 1979 waiting for John Paul II's first visit to Boston, and as befits a senior prelate he was talking about the U.S. Church. He wondered why Apostolic Delegate Jean Jadot had not been recalled to Rome long before this. Jadot's days had been numbered a year before, he said, because Vatican officials blamed him for some of the troubles the U.S. Church was experiencing. Vagnozzi predicted that the recall was at hand, and that Pio Laghi, then in Argentina, would be brought up to Washington with sailing orders to clean up the U.S. Church—and be given five years to do it.

Cardinal Vagnozzi, at the time the prelate in charge of the Vatican's temporal affairs, was a bulldog of a man, not as popular with bishops as his predecessor in the nation's capitol, A. G. Cicognani, had been. Still, he was an experienced Churchman. Once, in 1961, he criticized Catholic intellectuals for their growing predilection to think more as seculars than as Catholics, for which he was accused of interfering in the internal affairs of U.S. Church business. The Church's academe was not pleased. Not even Cardinal Spellman bought the entire criticism of the United States, although Roman prelates were already becoming uneasy about the new breed of scholars in Europe.

Whether popular or not, Vagnozzi continued his interest in the U.S. Church long after he had departed Washington. During his tenure there his constant bugbear (he said) was Spellman, who he thought interfered too often in Apostolic Delegate's business, especially in the naming of bishops. Vagnozzi confessed his difficulty he had getting John Krol into Philadelphia's archepiscopal chair. In 1951 Spellman's choice for the City of Brotherly Love, John Cardinal O'Hara, won out. When the latter lay dying in 1960, Vagnozzi polled U.S. archbishops for a reading on a best possible successor, and Cleveland's John Krol proved to be their choice. Still, when the actual time came for Philadelphia to be filled months later, Vagnozzi found that Spellman once more had already nominated his own man for the see. This time, however, the Apostolic Delegate was ready. Having established good relations with Spelly over the years, he had no difficulty in talking the New Yorker into accepting Krol. But Vagnozzi admitted that the "little man" was tenacious in backing his own choices.

Cardinal Vagnozzi never lived to see his prediction about Laghi come true. He reached Boston to greet John Paul II, and on his return home during the Christmas holidays, death came to him without warning.

Pio Laghi left Argentina early in 1980 to become Rome's tenth apostolic delegate to the United States, not knowing that within five years he would become the Church's first pro-nuncio to the U.S. government. It was a far cry from the days of anti-Catholic hatred when American nativists stoned the original papal visitor in 1853, far removed, too, from the oppostion in 1893 of all the archbishops, save one, to any apostolic delegate at all. When Rome finally insisted and sent Archbishop Francesco Satolli, the U.S. hierarchy went through the motions of celebrating the event but continued to fear for the loss of their independence. In time everyone became accustomed to the arrangement. Following Vatican II, when the National Conference of Catholic Bishops was established (1966), misgivings were again aroused in certain segments of the Church about the continued value of a delegate. Still, the Holy See, responsible for the universal Church, remained wary of national Church bodies, and so the institution of apostolic delegate remained.

The role of apostolic delegate, however, did not remain exactly the same once the NCCB came into existence. Historically, delegates have always been sensitive to leading spokesmen of the

American hierarchy. Today even more so, Archbishop Laghi walks a finer line in carrying out Rome's instructions to the American hierarchy. He could not do today, at least readily, what Archbishop Cicognani did in 1939, when on orders from Rome he and he alone investigated major U.S. seminaries. At the time and as a result, Dunwoodie Seminary lost one rector and one professor, not because of complaints made by diocesan officials, but as a result of criticisms by students! Speedy and unilateral action of this kind would not be likely today, even if conditions called for such a remedy.

Pio Laghi, mentioned as a future secretary of state, a post for which his long diplomatic service in vital Church centers would qualify him, served in the U.S. delegation after World War II under Vagnozzi. In 1980 he was plucked out of Argentina ahead of time by the new Pope to deal with distressing American ecclesial situations which in Roman eyes had been compounded by Archbishop Jean Jadot. Delegate Jadot, the first non-Italian in Washington, was a protégé of Belgium's Cardinal Leo Suenens, a maverick intimate of the Pope, who persuaded Paul to send Jadot to the U.S. Jadot quickly allied himself with what is sometimes called "the American party" among U.S. bishops, those who were somewhat anti-Roman and were prepared to be creative in matters of Catholic doctrine and discipline. During his tenure the Belgian appointed well over a hundred bishops, many of whom were willing experimenters with the Catholic tradition. Years later Archbishop Laghi would find himself in heated controversy for his role in the disciplining of Seattle's Raymond Hunthausen, but Jadot was not so victimized when he chastised Baton Rouge's Bishop Joseph Sullivan for refusing Charles Curran permission to speak at one of the bishop's diocesan facilities!

The Sullivan case was a good example of what was wrong with Jadot. Under normal Church conditions Sullivan would have been praised for exercising his episcopal office properly and supported by his fellow bishops. Instead, like Cardinal O'Boyle before him, he came out of the fracas looking like the offender. This letdown occurred not long after Jadot had privately lectured American

111

bishops on the importance of defending Magisterium, going so far as to instruct U.S. bishops to appoint a vicar for doctrine if they had no time personally to supervise what went on doctrinally within their dioceses. The double standard in the Sullivan case amounted to institutional doublespeak and became a lost opportunity to shore up Catholic opinion against dissent. I raised this very question with Jadot (October 30, 1975): "Has Catholic leadership lost among its own membership its power to form public opinion on faith and morals?" The Baton Rouge case left Rome without much visible episcopal support ten years later when Cardinal Ratzinger decided the time had come to move against Curran.

Jadot's policy set the stage for his removal and the takeover by Laghi. Indeed, Andrew Greeley anticipated the Belgian's likely fate. On September 30, 1976, Greeley wrote in Brooklyn's *Tablet:*

> The work of Archbishop Jadot in reforming the American hierarchy has been rapid and dramatic, at times almost breathtaking. If his enemies do not succeed in removing Jadot and if his health continues to be good, I suspect that in five years from now, the American hierarchy will be one of the best in the world.

Within five years Jadot was out; the high marks he received on Greeley's sociology scale were no match for the failing grade he received in Rome. Recalled, then retired, Jadot became the first U.S. Delegate to end his career without a Cardinal's hat.

Pio Laghi's appointment was the first major diplomatic move by the new Polish Pope, although in reality the prime mover for the appointment was Agostino Cardinal Casaroli, the Pope's secretary of state. Such appointments carry ecclesiastical risks. Archbishop Cicognani was sent to the United States in 1933 directly by Pius XI, even though Secretary of State Pacelli had someone else in mind, an oversight not to be forgotten by that Secretary once he became Pius XII. Pacelli permitted Cicognani to rest in Washington for a quarter of a century. It was John XXIII who finally brought Cicognani home in 1958, made him Secretary of State, and gave him the Cardinal's hat. Pio Laghi's diplomatic skills would also be put to their ultimate test, although from the beginning of his tenure he had the Pope on his side.

Future historians poring over once-secret documents will have their own estimate of Laghi's influence on the course of U.S. Church history. But once ensconced behind his Washington desk, the new Delegate knew that "bishops" were to be his most important concern. If the U.S. Church was in trouble, bishops had to be involved, even though the first troublemakers appeared elsewhere. Still, bishops were the solution. As was Rome itself. On the American scene Laghi was Rome. Leaks of his meetings and conversations made for good gossip, especially since the present Apostolic Pro-Nuncio, in friendly circles, is a frank talker. But those friendly to his interests are the least likely to break confidences or betray trusts.

Archbishop Laghi regularly felt pressure from all sides of the political controversies plaguing the U.S. Church, especially since the U.S. bishops' machinery was often involved more in secular than ecclesial politics. It is a good educated guess, however, that the Nuncio's day-to-day labors still involve him mostly in internal Church affairs—theological dissent, controversies over religious life, the internal condition of dioceses, Vatican documents, the conduct of priests, the naming and governing ability of bishops, and bridging the gap that sometimes seemed to exist between the U.S. Bishops' Chancery Office (the USCC) and that belonging to John Paul II (the Roman Curia).

The Apostolic Pro-Nuncio perforce deals regularly with bizarre statements by clergy out of synch with Church teaching, and with the transfer of good priests from important posts, especially by religious orders, simply because they oppose the policies of their provincial offices, which they consider anti-Magisterium. He is an appeals court for groups like the Catholic Hospital Association and others that are debilitated by internal conflict. His headquarters is bombarded with rationalizations, not infrequently from Jesuit sources, justifying the secularization of Catholic education and with threats against attempts at Roman intervention. He also has been overrun with a plenitude of complaints from Catholics who feel outrage at what they deem to be offenses against the faith or the good order they expect in the Church. Some of those missives reaching the Nuncio's desk are diatribes. Others are simple reports of derring-do or expressions of opinion.

Although my first meeting with Archbishop Laghi was due to our having a bishop-friend in common, most of our conversations over the years have dealt with the state of the Church. When my *Battle for the American Church* came out in 1979, he had his staff read it, although the archbishop himself was puzzled by the Celtic battle symbol which appeared on the book's cover. He seemed relieved to hear that I had nothing to do with it. I find him a good conversationalist, open to any discussion and in spite of his direct speech very diplomatic. He places high value on diplomacy, prompting me on one occasion that diplomacy sometimes leads to wrongdoing and coverup. As an example, I reminded him that after World War II all of Eastern Europe was ceded to Joe Stalin, not by generals but by the influence of diplomats on heads of state.

It has always been somewhat amazing to me how the more sensitive Catholics, even the well-informed, are reluctant to communicate personally with the Church's highest authorities. I say this in spite of the compulsive letter-writers who haunt me and everyone else. Reports come to me, for example, which I suggest to an intervenor properly belong on a bishop's desk, or even on that of Archbishop Laghi, only to find out that the person or group in question did not feel entitled to correspond directly with such a high official. This explains why at times I have passed on to Laghi information or views that were really intended for him. In late 1985, during the period of uncertainty about how far John Paul II was willing to go in restraining the Jesuits, I had reason to pass on a concern of one of that company, who had suffered at the hands of his superiors. This afforded me the opportunity to add a caution of my own: "Careful thought must be given about where and when the line is to be drawn." The hostility of the Jesuit infrastructure to Rome's authority at the time was somewhat unseemly. Another Jesuit veteran commenting on Malachi Martin's bitter criticism in his book *The Jesuits* said: "Things aren't as bad as Martin says they are; they're worse." A mother general of a women's community relating the Jesuit problem to the world of her own congregation, and that of women religious generally, said: "Short of a miracle the Community is finished."

Archbishop Laghi is a realist on such questions, even if some U.S. bishops are not. He also knows where the long-range interests of the Church lie, even if he cannot control its destiny. One letter of mine to Laghi (April 3, 1986) suggested what steps might be necessary for the restoration of wholesome religious life: "isolate those known for their dissent and disobedience"; "correct and reprove those who continue to rebel"; "sanction the contumacious offender for serious violations of the New Code." The lack of a strategy for dealing with dissent within religious communities is what debilitated the Catholic system in the first place.

Because combatants on all sides of today's ecclesiastical squabbles have no respect for the sacredness of the authority that guards the life of the Church, the Apostolic Pro-Nuncio finds himself situated in the middle of all controversies. And because the ongoing situations are volatile, he must insulate himself from media attention. A low profile shields him from public abuse by those intent on bringing Church authority down, or at least embarrassing it every chance they get. "This is our Church," they aver, and they know the prurience of the media, which have no sensitivity toward the sacred yet love the theatrical value of a brawl. Apostolic nuncios cannot afford too many fights, even those occasionally forced upon them. Nevertheless, to save the Church they must at times join a particular fray, especially when diplomacy does not work, or when diplomacy is patently leading to disaster.

In the *affaire Hunthausen* Archbishop Laghi was forced to fight back. Seattle had become the darling of dissidents for the reason that it was aggressively involved in widespread violations of Church norms in liturgy, sexual ethics, and general Catholic discipline. To ease the pain of overdue correction, Laghi decided to give Seattle a young auxiliary bishop, one not chosen by Archbishop Raymond Hunthausen, but who by mutual agreement with the Archbishop would share authority in those areas where Hunthausen's administration was weak or deformed. The diplomatic agreement might have worked, if the Archbishop had abided by the understanding. But Hunthausen proved difficult, violated his agreements, and even hired a public relations firm to promote his willful course. So it was that Laghi found himself in a "little war" he did not contemplate, learning that some bishops no longer play by Catholic rules.

When Hunthausen responded in essence, "Why pick on me?", he was only echoing Charles Curran. Seattle was not the only diocese in the United States where a bishop was violating norms he had sworn to uphold. If Laghi picked on Hunthausen, it because Rome had to begin its cleanup of the Church debris somewhere. Whereas other bishops made Laghi's reforms easy, sometimes by retiring, sometimes by accepting a "coadjutor" formally or informally, sometimes by undertaking reform themselves, Hunthausen balked, thus raising the ante for Rome. The final solution—a coadjutor and oversight by three bishops for a year and subsequent restoration to full power—will prove its worth, or its lack thereof, in due course.

The evils Laghi faced in some dioceses were serious; sometimes the local ordinary, by design or carelessness, was part of Rome's problem. By 1986 Pio Laghi had a good idea which bishops were out of step personally with John Paul II (and with Paul VI earlier), and which bishops were so permissive as to have dissenters regularly roaming their dioceses at will. In one diocese dissent was bootlegged, in another it was delivered openly in the chancery store. In either case the effect on the faithful was the same. If one "believed all that the Catholic Church teaches," he could find himself out of a job, his books banned by school offices. Criticisms reached Washington eventually about un-Catholic seminary training, inadequate catechesis, or the persecution of otherwise good priests and religious—criticisms that Archbishop Laghi could not ignore. His investigations led him to believe that as often as not the complaints were valid. At one point (March 29,

116

1985) I asked the Pro-Nuncio whether new bishops received any sailing orders concerning the *de facto* conditions of the diocese they were inheriting, concluding: "I realize the delicacy of these matters but we cannot allow things to remain the same."

The buck always came back to bishops, who normally have measured up to their responsibilities, as often at least as they are blamed for the Church's failures. Perhaps their past successes left some contemporary bishops ill-prepared for the recent onslaughts on Catholic faith from within their precincts. Usually a council cleans up an ecclesiastical mess, and Vatican II certainly had an upbeat purpose. But dismantling the Church was not on anyone's agenda in 1962. While some experts think only a Vatican III will clear up the confusion to result from Vatican II, the chances are more likely that the reform and renewal will rather come from the ordinary efforts of John Paul II. This means John Paul II–type bishops. If Ralph Waldo Emerson is correct in his adage that "an institution is the lengthened shadow of a man," and he is surely close to the mark, then the present Pope has to be as successful as the three popes who made Trent work—Paul III, Paul IV, and Pius V. Their success is attributed to the choice of leading bishops and a few good religious orders. If radicals liked Jadot's bishops, it is important for Rome to choose a different kind of bishop.

Choosing bishops who will cast the right shadow over the Church is no simple task for the reason that new bishops are chosen by older bishops. Once more the Apostolic Pro-Nuncio is in the middle. He is too far from local scenes to invent candidates. He can only shuffle those who are proposed, unless he becomes so informed that he develops potential nominees of his own. This is not easy. First of all, powerful prelates who are not unhappy with the status quo obstruct the Nuncio's plans whenever they can (Spellman did it regularly). Secondly, the appropriate talent is not always evident or is not available in the region where important openings occur. Thirdly, collegiality calls for local consultations, and locals do not like to be bypassed, even if their recommendations are second-rate. Finally, there is always the Roman equation. If the President of the United States cannot be sure how his cabinet officers will play the game, the Pope with a world-wide Church to manage has even less surety that things he plans will go his way. There are always prelates who do not like other prelates, or who vie for their own place in the sun, or who are simply obstructionists, many who are willing to serve the Pope more on their terms than on his.

There is yet another unspoken question: What kind of priest best meets the modern needs of the Church? History tells tales of bishops being named in times of simony whose only qualification was their access to money, and in times of sexual deviance candidates who were lechers, and in times of impiety bishops who had little faith or piety. The tendency of established bureaucracy is to take the safe course by appointing safe bishops. If the worst thing a bank can do with a bankruptcy is to appoint a receiver who is good only at spending money, then the worst thing the Church can do is to name a bishop who never created, enhanced, or recovered a Christian community; or a bishop who does not comprehend the given issues or would not know how to deal with them even if he knew them.

No papal representative in recent memory has been more careful at wide consultation on episcopal appointments than Pio Laghi. A *New York Times* story has it that he is still fifty bishops shy of having an American hierarchy favorable to the Holy See. That may or may not be true. Be that as it may, compatibility with Roman teaching is in Laghi's view a number one qualification for the episcopacy today. Still, the Nuncio is forced to play politics with leading prelates of the NCCB, who are jealous of their consultative rights. He has a difficult time evading certain nominations which reach his desk, including the names of priests who are not well known for their papal loyalty. Some closet dissenters and others with a background of collaboration with dubious Catholic activities have made it to the hierarchy. What is also fascinating about the process is the way in which opposition coalesces against the priest (or the bishop up for promotion) who owns a notable record of strong support for Magisterium. The temptation for Laghi, as for anyone in the middle, is to move away from a strong candidate to an apparently safe one (he thinks), a neutral whose chief qualification for higher office is that he lacks enemies, and who perhaps also lacks strong convictions about how to deal with a real revolution.

Leading members of the Catholic community have been consulted over the years by Archbishop Laghi, and it is no violation of trust to describe the qualities many would like to see in new bishops, and in major appointees especially. The chief weakness in all proposals, however, is the impossiblity of predicting greatness in advance. James H. Griffiths, auxiliary to Cardinal Spellman, possessed talents rarely found in any priest and which were superior to the seemingly modest gifts with which New York's archbishop was endowed. Yet historians will never provide Griffiths with a footnote in their books, whereas Spellman will always walk tall in their midst.

Nonetheless, Churchmen by now ought to know the no-no's— no second men for first place, "no" to rewarding friendly bishops' secretaries whose leadership qualifications are untested, "no" to anyone whose only title to promotion is success at fund-raising or powerful patronage or facelessness. What we need are strong characters who have the capacity to stand pressure and to explain intelligently what it means to be Catholic and who know how to redirect our machinery to reflect our positions. One special recommendation might be that care be exercised in naming auxiliary bishops. Good aides are not necessarily good number one men, as the "Peter Principle" explains.

Firm convictions about the faith and *theological competency* are surely basic qualities for the episcopacy, yet one consecrated bishop was heard to say to a scholar, "I have an obligation as a bishop to see that dissenting theological opinion is treated side by side with Magisterium in our seminary." He meant more than reporting it. Enthusiasm for the Church and its mission is essential to running a successful diocese. Tommy Lasorda of Dodgers' fame once explained: "I love the game and when I walk into the locker room it shows. Some people don't like it, I'm sure, but most find it catching." Even so, the competent enthusiast should also be a proven artist at ruling, an art personified in the classic pastor of whom everyone was proud, who was tireless in his ability to serve, but whose people knew him as "the Church" and were happy that he was.

Choosing a bishop simply for his orthodoxy also has its difficult side. The prelate in question may vote with the Pope without having the ability to articulate or defend his position. Many bishops go to national meetings with evident good will for the Holy See's stated positions, but have no time or interest in detecting those nuances presented by bureaucracy which undercut the Holy See's carefully honed teaching. A certain sophistication in theological matters is required. As I wrote to Archbishop Laghi in a memorandum dated January 8, 1987: "There are within every diocese a handful of priests, fully committed Catholics, brainy, indeed learned, and known for their ability and willingness to teach, propose, and defend publicly the teaching and discipline of the Church, even as they are respected for their priestliness, experience, and leadership ability." Many of these are passed over because they are not part of the local bishop's "in-group," which sometimes consists of men with less ability.

Pio Laghi knows that many of these views are not universally applauded, even by some bishops. Indeed, on one occasion he made it clear that some bishops are downright unfriendly to them. Laghi himself has addressed audiences where he faced tough questions about Church discipline or its lack. The bottom line is always the episcopacy. Some bishops are consistent sideliners, and some are positively hostile to anything called "orthodox" in the public forum. One Midwestern bishop thought that the so-called papal loyalists might be doing some good, but he also thought that people like Jim Hitchcock and George Kelly are loose with the truth. A letter I wrote to Archbishop Laghi on November 24, 1986, zeroed in on this mentality:

Neither Paul VI nor John Paul II has received vigorous support from national hierarchies in the West. In some cases this became the problem.

That comment would of necessity be modified today with strong promagisterial voices in sees like Denver, Orange, Philadelphia, and sundry other places. Regardless of what dissenters think, this is the direction in which the Pro-Nuncio, present or future, must lead the Church.

NOTES

1. Matthew 19:6.
2. Matthew 10:38.
3. Rev. William H. Woestman, O.M.I., *Canonica* 21 (1987), p. 315.
4. *Origins*, October 30, 1980, pp. 314–315.
5. *L'Osservatore Romano*, February 6, 1985, p. 5, No. 2.
6. *The Catholic Voice*, July 10, 1979.
7. Ibid.
8. George Gallup and Jim Castelli, *The American Catholic People*, p. 182.

PART FOUR

The U.S. Church, the Catholic Revolution, and Rome

PROLOGUE

A Problem
Seeking a Solution

DIFFERENCES OF OPINION between Rome and national hierarchies became inevitable after 1965 once local Churches assumed that the creation of national conferences permitted them
leeway to determine how best to institutionalize the Catholic tradition in the given set of circumstances which they, not Rome,
know first hand. St. Paul and St. John in New Testament times
had difficulty maintaining unity with their own distant Churches.
If the Councils of Trent and Vatican I overcompensated by concentrating all authority in Rome, the Second Vatican Council set
in motion a decentralization process which holds both opportuni-
ties and dangers for any pope trying to keep Christ's Church both
unified and universal. The effort to shift some decision-making to
lower levels of hierarchy, to develop approaches to evangelization
better suited to the regional experience, and to allow for a certain
amount of experimentation in liturgy, religious lifestyles, marriage procedures, etc., was surely legitimate. Rome does not have
all the answers about the best evangelization procedures, and

does not, or at least in the pre-electronic era did not, always understand local situations. Forty years ago, for example, Vatican officials did not recognize Fordham University as Catholic simply because the school had no juridical tie with Church authority. Actually, even then, universities like Fordham were tied to Church authority informally through the Father General of the sponsoring religious community which owned the university. (When that tie was broken after 1967 many schools abandoned their Catholic commitment.) In those faraway days, there were other difficulties resulting from Rome's inflexibility in liturgy, in ecumenical relations, in adjudicating matrimonial procedures. French bishops reached the point of heresy in fighting the Pope as far back as the sixteenth and seventeenth centuries. Belgian and German bishops had conferences in the nineteenth century. In the United States following World War I, the National Catholic Welfare Conference represented a certain American community of episcopal interest, whose deliberations never "bound" anyone, especially powerful cardinals like Daugherty, Hayes, O'Connell, or Spellman. In sum, however, the NCWC was pro-Roman and, although the Vatican was ever vigilant about national bodies of bishops, modern popes gave the American conference high marks for its accomplishments and its fidelity.

Its post-Vatican II successor, the National Conference of Catholic Bishops, was a different breed of organization. For one thing, the founding leaders, headed by Detroit's John Dearden, learned "independence" during the Council. Secondly, not every bishop returning home from the Council was pro-Roman. Some became enamored with theologians of the newer persuasions and returned home overawed or at least prepared to provide them with living room in their dioceses. Thirdly, the year of NCCB's creation (1966) was the midpoint of another American civil uprising during which breaking the ties that bind institutional living became fashionable, with bishops unprepared for its effect on the Church. Almost immediately, as NCCB evolved into a day-to-day operation through its civil arm, the United States Catholic Conference, circumventing Roman guidelines became a regular pastime. Few in the public forum knew that in the last days of NCWC some of the staff were procontraception, and some of the bishops coming home from the Council, too. If Rome could be wrong on such a universally held teaching, the reasoning went, Rome could be wrong on other things. Older bishops growled about the new appointments in and some of the opinions coming out of Washington, but they felt helpless to do anything effective to change the new directions. These older bishops found it difficult to reconcile an episcopacy which in 1967 said "obedience to the teaching of the Church is an obedience required of all" with the episcopacy which a year later endorsed "general norms of licit dissent."

Dissenting scholars began to have easy access to the USCC machinery after 1967 under the rubric of "dialogue." "Dialogue" was never used by bishops to control or limit dissent, only to expand its influence. The disagreeable task of correcting defects in teaching, in priestly or religious life and in liturgy—abuses that were impossible to correct without the support of the national hierarchy—was left to Rome.

Joseph Cardinal Ratzinger, Prefect of the Congregation for Doctrine of The Faith in his famous "Ratzinger Report" summarized "the problem of episcopal conferences" as follows:

> The decisive new emphasis on the role of the bishops is in reality restrained or actually risks being smothered by the insertion of bishops into episcopal conferences that are ever more organized, often with burdensome bureaucratic structures. We must not forget that episcopal conferences have no theological basis, they do not belong to the structures of the Church, as willed by Christ, that cannot be eliminated; they have only a practical concrete function.

He said further that the Episcopal Conference, as such, has no teaching mission because the Catholic Church is a community of pope with bishops, not with federations of national churches. He called upon bishops to exercise their individual responsibility and not allow themselves to lapse into the anonymity of a national conference.

What Ratzinger has in mind, of course, is the fact that many bishops began to follow "the sense" of the Conference, rather than their own responsibility for Catholic truth. When the NCCB repeatedly opposed aid to the Contras in Nicaragua, few bishops felt free to contradict it publicly, unless one were a cardinal like Law or O'Connor. Ratzinger recalled how the reputation of the Church in Nazi Germany was saved not by a German Conference but by the Faulhabers and the Von Preysings, solitary bishops who dared to confront the Hitler menace. Cardinal Ratzinger may not have the last word on the usefulness or mission of episcopal conferences, but he does direct attention to their dysfunctions.

The 1985 Extraordinary Synod called for a study of the future role of national conferences. Those who seek independence from Roman oversight are content with the present course. They would have conferences legitimized on the well-known Catholic principle of subsidiarity, i.e. higher authority should not do what lower authority can do as well. Those opinions would change radically, of course, if suddenly the Conference under new leadership established strict rules for fast and abstinence, issued an officially approved list of Catholic colleges, tightened up lax annulment procedures, etc. If Rome is restive about the U.S. Church of 1988, it is because the "inner circle" which controls the agenda of the NCCB/USCC is more interested in peaceful relations with theologians who no longer believe in "the Catholic content whole and entire," than in working closely with Rome.

One measure of the failure of episcopal conferences worldwide is the decision by the 1985 Extraordinary Synod to proceed with a "Universal Catechism." The Fathers of Vatican II had bowed to the arguments of *periti* against a Catechism of the Second Vatican Council. Instead, the faithful received the Dutch Catechism, the American Catechism, and others which permitted to be taught in one school or class what was denied in another, with national conferences of bishops sitting on the sidelines.

On June 28, 1986, Pope John Paul II expressed the hope that the Universal Catechism would be ready in 1990, in time to mark the twenty-fifth anniversary of the end of the Council. What it will solve remains to be seen. But from 1967 to 1987 the NCCB engaged in consultations and made decisions which looked strange from the perspective of Rome.

FIVE

American Bishops and the Catholic Issues

THE NCCB'S PEACE PASTORAL

NO STATEMENT issued by the National Conference of Catholic Bishops in recent years has attracted so much attention as the one issued May 3, 1983, entitled *The Challenge of Peace.* Almost three years in the making, the pastoral was the most comprehensive effort by a national hierarchy to mold public opinion on a critical political question: How may nations avoid the holocaust associated with nuclear war? It was the latest effort by churchmen to explore old dilemmas about war and the place of war in a civilized world. No Catholic bishop was more anxious to face the issue the U.S. hierarchy contemplated in 1980 than was Bishop Ambrose of Milan from AD 395 onward, when Christianity was about to be declared the official religion of the Roman Empire. Ambrose was an optimist, allowing himself to hope that the Roman Empire, because of the Christian piety of its rulers, might reign in the world together with the Church, each with authority from God to

131

guarantee the safety and well-being of all men. Ambrose's optimism was quickly shattered by Alaric the Hun's sack of Rome in A.D. 410, leaving to Augustine, his protégé, to work out realistically how Christians can deal with the force of evil in the world, and still remain Christian.

Ever since Augustine's time, three traditions on war and peace have vied for the Church's attention. First, the ancient and respectable pacifist party, which rejects defenses of freedom and justice; then, the just war tradition, which attempts to identify the conditions under which force and military action is permissible; finally, what some authors call "the crusade current," which would justify offensive wars as a means of redeeming a sacred value or relieving an oppressed community.

Each of these positions can be presented in a way that accords with Catholic moral teaching. Though pacifism in its classical form, which claims that every military defense of human rights is immoral, has ordinarily been rejected by Catholic teachers, it can be restructured to mean chiefly an insistence on the duty to seek out alternatives to modern war. Moreover, the pacifist can draw heavily on the true Catholic teaching that one must never do evil that good may come of it. Meanwhile, the crusader may speak earnestly of the real duty to labor effectively to prevent international injustice, and be as nuanced and as firm as any other Catholic tradition in judging what in the contemporary context is really evil. Even the just war theory, so favored by theologians through the centuries, has its built-in difficulties. It is enormously difficult to apply. What is a just cause for using force? How can you tell if national leaders have the right intention or a good hope of success? And who is to decide whether the good to be accomplished is worth all the death and destruction? These judgments are made more difficult by the memories of Hiroshima and Nagasaki. To threaten to use the atom bomb, as Eisenhower did during the Korean war, raises serious questions of morality. Such threats may deter an enemy, but is it moral to make such a threat, when destruction must be intended if the threat is to be an effective deterrent?

The undertaking by Chicago's Joseph Cardinal Bernardin was not only a valid enterprise for a Catholic prelate (alone or with others), but a necessary and praiseworthy effort to form the consciences of Americans on a very vital social issue. What is more vital than the life and death of cities, perhaps of nations? Cardinal Bernardin's challenge—and he was the chief architect of the effort—faced the opposition of those who constitutionally rejected the Church's intervention in public affairs, perhaps with a "Mater si, Magistra, no." He also faced a unique difficulty, because dissenting theologians had by 1980 freed consciences, of Catholics particularly, from compliance with authentic Church teaching.

Yet Cardinal Bernardin pulled it off, and the final letter contained all that was clear about authentic Catholic teaching: Nations, no more than individuals, may not kill innocent human beings; nations, like people, may not "do evil as a means to good";[1] modern war, particularly nuclear war, is difficult to justify; large caches of nuclear bombs of their nature presuppose the existence of evil intent to destroy population centers, but they may be tolerated as "deterrents" to a first strike by a rival nation; and immediate, verifiable bilateral agreements are needed to halt the testing, production, and development of new nuclear weapons systems.

The salvific effect of the pastoral was likely to be long-term rather than short-term. The ongoing indoctrination of Catholic youth with the basic principles embedded in the pastoral guaranteed such an effect, but the short-term effects were not inconsequential either, since the U. S. government suddenly began to discuss American foreign and military policy in moral terms. There were disagreements, to be sure, partly because Catholics understand that there are more options in their answers to questions of war and peace than in their sexual preferences or in determining the meaning of Catholic doctrine. But the peace message was clear: No war, never again.

Many scholars outside normal NCCB channels became involved at several points: in providing input for bishops other than Cardinal Bernardin; in critiquing the most serious defect in the first

133

drafts of the pastoral, a defect so serious that it occasioned the intervention of Rome. The sentence that caused so much concern through two drafts was the following: "The *deterrence relationship* which prevails between the United States, the Soviet Union and other powers *is objectively a sinful situation* because of the threats implied in it and the consequences it has in the world" (italics added). The original drafts were willing to tolerate the evil situation because failure of deterrence would be worse.

This sentence brought certain outside theologians into the controversy (along with the Holy See): Germain Grisez, Ronald Lawler, O.F.M. Cap., William Smith, Joseph Mangan, S.J., Joseph Boyle, Richard Roach, S.J., Donald Keefe, S.J., William May, and political scientist Charles Dechert of the Catholic University.

Part of their problem was that the writing of the pastoral took place in a proverbial goldfish bowl. "Open covenants openly arrived at" may have been well-remembered Wilsonian political doctrine at Versailles, but not even the World War I President practiced what he preached. Negotiating the terms of their pastoral in the public forum subjected bishops to the vagaries of public criticism before most bishops knew what was being written in their name. Even the Atlantic Charter, which helped forge the U.S.-British alliance that led to Allied victory in World War II, was not subject to such scrutiny.

What was so bad about declaring deterrence objectively sinful but tolerable?

As Jesuit Donald Keefe indicated: "If American Catholics accept without discussion the notion that intrinsic evil can be tolerated to gain some good end, then the consequentialist theory is in place and, with it, the politicization of Catholic morality and worship." In other words, if one can do evil to gain some good, then pragmatism, not principle or doctrine, governs life, including Catholic life, no matter what Christ or the Church has to say about it.

During the past twenty-five years many theologians have adopted the position that there are no instrinsically evil acts in the sense the Church teaches there are. This theory was first advanced to justify the use of contraceptives by married couples, but later was extended to justify Christians performing any act, if in so doing they were choosing what they judged to be the lesser of two evils, even when the Church says what they are doing is sinful. Under this system not only contraception, but adultery and homosexual behavior have been justified.

What was at stake here is the reality of moral good and evil, indeed the reality of anything, including Christ and the Church. If evil can be turned into good simply because people say it is good, then they have power to turn their word into God's words. If people so decided, the Church itself, Christ, too, would be unnecessary to their needs or their salvation. The authority of the Catholic Bishop is essential to the Church because it is the Bishop, representing Christ, who conveys *the Word*, the word for all time, because it is God's word and God says you cannot do evil even if good comes out of it. To say otherwise is to put man at the center of the universe—not God. This is the significance of the rationalism which placed consequentialism into two drafts of *The Challenge of Peace.*

How could this be? The answer is not surprising. The USCC's staff choices of consultants, under Cardinal Bernardin's leadership, were mostly consequentialists. Charles E. Curran, if only by alphabetic priority, led all the rest. He thought "toleration (of evil) is an accepted concept in Catholic moral theology." Fr. Joseph Fuchs, S.J., denied that "there is such a problem as Christian ethics in the secular arena." He further argued: "Concrete ethical norms are not divine revelation; they do not become divine by virtue of traditional or offical teaching."[2] Jesuit Richard A. McCormick was also interviewed by the USCC staff, even though his name was not announced publicly. The task of writing the principal draft of the pastoral letter was given to Professor Martin Russett of Yale University, a non-Catholic. Not a single scholar outside of the favored Washington, D.C., complex was invited to make an original presentation, although many of them later were involved with bishops in proposing the correction of the early drafts.

The Challenge of Peace became a viable Catholic document by virtue of the zealous intervention of Bishop John J. O'Connor of New York's Military Ordinariate and that of Cardinal Ratzinger. By publication time the U.S. bishops had adopted the position enunciated by John Paul II: "In current conditions [deterrence] based on balance, certainly not an end in itself but as a step on the way toward a progressive disarmament may still be judged morally acceptable." The Pope made that statement in June 1982 to a special session of the United Nations, while the bishops' pastoral was moving toward its finalization. Those on the USCC staff and their consultants, with their supporting bishops, who want a more pacifist stance adopted, were thus overruled. Matthew Murphy in his book *Betraying Bishops,* which received a qualified endorsement from John Cardinal O'Connor, holds bishops to their duty "to make sure that those whom they charge with teaching their pastoral letters do so in accordance with the bishops' own instructions,"[3] especially since the NCCB allocated a half-million dollars for its faithful implementation.

(Even so, small errors crept into the final draft; for example, it identified St. Francis of Assisi with the pacifist cause, although the medieval saint marched off with soldiers during the Crusades, saying it was better "to go into the enemy's camp in order to preach the faith.")

THE ECONOMIC PASTORAL

No sooner was "the peace pastoral" approved and published, than the NCCB went to work on an "economic pastoral." The first draft, which had been in preparation since 1981, appeared in November 1984, with a third draft finished by June 1986, under the title *Economic Justice for All.* Several aspects of this effort made it a different experience for the bishops than the peace pastoral. For one thing, the media did not seem as interested in what bishops said on the U.S. economy. In the second place, leading Catholic laymen did not trust the bishops to say anything helpful to the cause of American prosperity. The fact, too, that the U.S. economy was moving ahead, in spite of dislocations, with inflation going down and the stock market going up, created a mood of disinterest among the voting public about the economy. Almost as soon as the bishops' ad hoc committee announced its intentions, a group of twenty-nine prominent Catholic laymen, led by William Simon, former treasury secretary, undertook to write their own economic pastoral. Strangely, they felt that the bishops would back a welfare-state program and more government interference with business than the lay committee wanted. Actually, the bishops' first two drafts turned out to be more complex and highly nuanced than the Simon group anticipated. There were highly debatable recommendations for sure, which caught the bishops in Democratic/Republican crossfires, but there were also announcements of sound moral principles. The principled preferential option on behalf of the poor was combined with concrete proposals for reshaping the American economy, leaving readers and politicians much to think about, much to accept or reject, as ideology and voting blocs would permit. Professor Charles Dechert (CUA) wrote a critique that was sympathetic but cautious, recognizing that the pastoral would be used as a rationale for more government, instead of less.

What had not changed since the peace pastoral was the charged atmosphere of public hearings, which placed the bishops in the role of legislators, clarifying the more or less social democrat point of view of their Washington-based staff.

By the completion of the second draft, Milwaukee's Archbishop Rembert Weakland, chairman of the committee, told the bishops assembled in Collegeville, "you have given us the assurance that we are on the right track." Weakland surely spoke for many bishops, but not for all. Some participants warned that specific prescriptions for public policy fall "outside the role of bishops." Fourteen of the thirty-two buzz groups (eight bishops each) said the pastoral should speak for bishops as moral teachers and avoid even the appearance of political partisanship. Twelve argued that the letter should explicitly acknowledge the achievements of the free enterprise system and the generosity of the middle class, something they felt was understated in the proposed draft. Six groups called for stronger criticism of the "inherent weaknesses of capitalism." It was clear that the bishops as an assembly would go along with the pastoral, but were uncomfortable with some of its provisions. Archbishop Weakland promised to take the reservations into account in the final writing.

The third draft incorporated a challenge to Third World countries to examine their own shortcomings as impediments to sustained economic growth, and added new material on family life and the importance of education, including Catholic education, to the upward mobility of the poor. These omissions in the earlier drafts surprised some bishops in view of the long Catholic tradition of emphasizing family and school in evangelization. Good family life was the important insulating force against the worst features of poverty. Often poor but well-integrated families did not know they were poor. Catholic schools, moreover, were the chief instruments for Americanizing the children of earlier immigrants. So it was important for the economic pastoral to recall this heritage, even if belatedly.

One section of the pastoral seemed to neglect Catholic doctrine and to contradict standard Catholic policy. The third draft read as follows:

No. 282—Hunger is often linked with the problem of population growth as effect to cause. While this thesis is sometimes presented in an oversimplified fashion, we cannot fail to recognize that the earth's resources are finite and that population tends to grow exponentially. Our concern, however, must be for the quality of human life as for the numbers of human lives. Whether the world can provide a truly human life for twice as many people or more as now live in it (many of whose lives are sadly deficient today) is a matter of urgent concern that cannot be ignored."

No. 283—Nevertheless, we do not believe that people are poor and hungry primarily because they have large families; rather, family size is

138

heavily dependent on levels of economic development, education, respect for women, availability of health care, and the cultural traditions
of communities. Therefore, in dealing with population growth we
strongly favor efforts to address these social and economic concerns.
Within this broader framework of integral development, the Church
also fully supports the need for all to exercise responsible parenthood.

There are two things to notice about these paragraphs. First,
they manifest confidence in standard population projections,
which are always of the doomsday variety. While propagandists
no longer speak of "population bomb" or "population zero,"
given the way so many demographic estimates are deflated by
subsequent facts, the Catholic bishops are made to say that "population tends to grow exponentially." This phrasing is deceptive
because it could be understood to mean that population grows
even faster than "the algebra of compound interest," which was
the expression contained in the second draft. Was the writer using
as a guide the classic Malthusian formulation? Church authorities
have traditionally been wary of that formula for obvious reasons.

The second thing to notice about No. 283 of the economic
pastoral (third draft) is that it suggests "responsible parenthood"
as a social responsibility for all. "Need for all" are the words
used.

The U.S. bishops ceased speaking of population questions after
1973, but up to that year they always treated population projections as the uncertainties they are. When they admitted the real
pressures of population on a given economy, bishops usually advised states (including governments) not to isolate population
questions from others of economic development, of migration,
and so forth. Episcopal judgments on population and development were never pessimistic. Governments, too, were always
warned not to do anything that appeared to be coercion in family
planning matters, although nations were granted the right to indicate or outline their national interests.

No. 282, in the third draft, is a subtle introduction of the
population question into a bishops' letter minus the cautions

found in earlier statements. This time it was also tied into "quality of life," the traditional code word for proposals either eugenic or contraceptive in purpose. In the proposed draft, "quality of life" became a backdrop for the introduction of the phrase "responsible parenthood," one phrase with a special history. The Church often takes over a secular term, but she baptizes it in order to serve better her own purpose, as she once did pagan feasts. "Responsible parenthood," like "academic freedom," was coined first to project a viewpoint inimical to the Gospel message. In the Planned Parenthood lexicon, from which "responsible parenthood" derived, the words mean the social obligation to have few babies and to use contraceptive techniques to further this end. Abortion was always part of the Planned Parenthood package. As the phrase "responsible parenthood" gained currency and filtered into Catholic conversation, it was always defined within a Catholic context, with Catholic cautions about "immoral means." When Paul VI used the term in *Humanae Vitae,* he wrote six paragraphs (in No. 10) to ensure that the term was "exactly understood" as stressing generosity as well as deliberation, right moral order as well as conscience, and the exclusion of contraception, contraceptive sterilization, and abortion.

What is equally important, "responsible parenthood," even when defined in Catholic terms, has always been offered in official Church documents as an "approved" option. It is never "recommended." In the first drafts of the pastoral on economic life, however, "responsible parenthood" is recommended as a need for all.

Unquestionably, there have been priests within the USCC who do not accept *Humanae Vitae,* and who prefer to keep its central doctrine in public policy limbo. A dozen years ago, J. Brian Hehir wrote an article for *Theological Studies*[4] that advocated silence by the Church on the contraception issue. His thesis was that the Church would fare better in public debates by concentrating her argument on the rights of the fetus, leaving "contraceptive practice as an issue of private morality which the Church continues to teach for its members, but not an issue of public morality." Who was Fr. Hehir? He was a staff writer for the bishops' 1986 economic pastoral.

The Church would not be true to herself if she permitted a recommendation of "responsible parenthood for all" to enter an episcopal document without explanation and distinction. Contraceptive intercourse is an intrinsically evil act. The Church cannot be silent on the subject, no matter what others say. Events since 1974 have demonstrated how wrong Hehir's political judgment was. Antiabortion arguments are not successful with people whose moral system already accepts contraception and with their assumed moral right to turn this evil into a good. In fact, abortion, sterilization, and contraception are linked philosophically, morally, industrially, and politically. What is more, John Paul II has gone out of his way (July 18, 1984) to speak of the Church's contraceptive norm as that which "belongs not only to the natural moral law but also to *the moral order revealed by God.*" This makes it inconceivable that the Church could remain silent on the subject, even though those who do not believe in that teaching or in the Church's authority to declare this teaching to be true prefer official silence to repeated ecclesial affirmations.

The above terminology stayed in the document through the third draft (June 5, 1986). When the pastoral was finally approved on November 13, certain changes were made, thanks to the intervention of Atlanta's Archbishop Thomas A. Donnellan. Some of the changes were subtle, but they were nonetheless meaningful. Hunger, linked in the earlier drafts with population growth, is described finally "often seen as being [so] linked." Population no longer grows "exponentially" but "rapidly." The "quality of life" argument (which is used to justify euthanasia) is eliminated. The Church's "full support for responsible parenthood" remains in, but this time with the addition of a long quotation of Paul VI on population policy—freedom of parents, avoidance of coercion, limits on state authority, and respect for moral law.

The final message on this subject in *Economic Justice For All* is not perfect, at least not as strong or precise as papal statements usually are. Still, it is consistent with Catholic thought.

Something certainly is wrong when bishops' pastorals are composed in the public forum incorrectly, leaving the responsible authors (hierarchy) needlessly embarrassed at having "outsiders" (and this would include Rome) to correct a U.S. Catholic document, when in a normal situation an official draft of a Church viewpoint should have been well-nigh perfect. Fellowship member J. Brian Benestad published his major work, *The Pursuit of a Just Social Order*, about the time the economic pastoral was in process. He compared the policy statements of the bishops (1966–1980) with the overall thrust of Catholic social teaching going back at least to Leo XIII and Pius XI. He discovered that the new USCC statements, compared with those prior to 1962, failed to confront issues posed by the country's "liberal" secular establishment. Said Benestad: "The bishops have unwittingly allowed the secular world to set their political agenda." Whereas the NCWC statements were concerned with character formation and unjust personal behavior, the post-Vatican II episcopal statements have been preoccupied with structural changes in society, with no particular emphasis on conversion.

The economic pastoral is a good example of the ideological bias of staff writers and chosen consultants. Since so much of the popes' social criticism has been anticapitalist, Catholics cannot be blind to the evils of the American system. But Catholic writers, in spite of the insistence of the same popes on the rights of property owners, can be overly statist. Thomas M. Macioce, a New York businessman, objected to this latter prejudice among the writers of the 1986 pastoral. Before a St. John's University audience on February 20, 1986, Macioce made the following observation:

> The present moral condition of our economic system is not as bankrupt or as decadent as one would believe from reading the draft of the bishops' Pastoral Letter on the American Economy of November 1984. It was most interesting to me to note a tabulation of the number of people interviewed by the bishops' Committee in prepar-

ing this letter as well as the backgrounds of the interviewees. The Committee prepared a letter on the American Economy and our economic society interviewing approximately 150 people, and my tabulation indicates that 7 American businessmen were interviewed among this group. The Committee involved in addition 15 consultants without any representation from the business community. It would seem to me that if one were preparing a letter dealing with the basic subject of the American economy more than 5 percent of the people interviewed should be those dealing with the subject on a daily basis.

BISHOPS AND THE NCCB

Something must be said at this point about the staff and procedures of the NCCB/USCC complex. Over the years the controlling bishops have ceded extraordinary powers to the General Secretary, the person in charge of daily operations. He is not accountable to the body of bishops for the staff people he chooses. The staff does the research and prepares the position papers for later presentation to committees headed by bishops. Since Vatican II there have been five general secretaries—Joseph Bernardin, James Rausch, Thomas Kelly, Daniel Hoye, and presently Robert Lynch. Bernardin negotiated the unsuccessful conclusion to Charles Curran's attack on *Humanae Vitae* in 1968. Rausch concealed for an entire year (1975–1976) a Roman decree on contraceptive sterilization, as if it were the private affair of the USCC alone. He once told a Midwestern bishop that the latter's choice of an appointee to a USCC committee was unacceptable to staff, even though the bishop in question was only interested in bringing balance to a committee on family life stacked with feminists. Thomas Kelly was unembarrassed by the number of dissenters his agencies consulted. Daniel Hoye rejected an Eastern bishop's effort to balance his committee with the rejoinder, "It's about time you bishops realize you don't run the USCC." When, to correct this situation, Los Angeles Archbishop Roger Mahony proposed an episcopal overview of all such appointments to staff, he was sidetracked.

The USCC procedures are as important as the staff for any understanding of the NCCB/USCC operation. Once upon a time central headquarters, which was relatively small and poorly financed, turned out few statements a year, most of them dealing with strictly religious, moral, or institutional concerns. Today, a large and well-financed bureaucracy turns out dozens of working papers for action by the bishops or by a bishop-headed committee generally on hot political issues affecting any of the populated continents. If the preparations deal with fund raising or archives or construction, the national hierarchy has little reason for concern. But when the ecclesial judgments required deal with controversial political or ecclesiastical issues, the arrival of a set of thick books a mere ten days before an annual or semi-annual bishops' meeting hardly gives the members time to study in depth or consult with their own advisers about the debatable points. Consequently, when bishops finally arrive in Washington, they are afforded opportunity only to ask short questions and to receive short answers in reply. The number of bishops allowed to speak, even in executive sessions, is rarely more than 10 percent of the assembly, as Bishop Austin Vaughan, one of the few theologian bishops in the Conference, has pointed out. How much debate and discussion can go on in any depth prior to settling a host of complicated issues such as AIDS, Central America, doctrinal dissent, divisions in religious life, changes in the liturgy, and the proper allocation of millions of dollars of Catholic people's Sunday offerings?

More important than anything else, therefore, is the openness of the episcopal leadership in power and the correctness of its governing ideology. No one expects bishops from all across the continent to be one in their political judgments or their administrative practices. The U.S. Church grew amazingly well and together in the nineteenth century even though bishops in key sees battled each other over colonization, education, even over relationships with Rome. In this century the rivalry between Cardinal

Spellman and the so-called Midwest Axis (Chicago, Detroit, Cincinnati) delighted many on both sides of the Hudson River. The NCCB has created a mood which suggests unity, but often this is a patina of oneness which belies real divisions, not entirely excluding ideological disagreements over what the Second Vatican Council really taught and over what the Church still teaches as true. Of course, the posture of unity and the pressure to maintain unity help reinforce the control of those already in command of the U.S. Church's direction, as reflected in the daily conduct of the United States Catholic Conference. When the presiding bishop rises at the end of a debate to admit that prepared documents are not perfect, but unity requires that the body of bishops go along with a committee that has worked so hard for five years, the argument has a persuasive ring to it. Many a breakaway bishop has been silenced by the ploy.

The 1986 meeting was something of a watershed, exposing at least two ideological strains at odds with each other within the Conference. This was the year that Seattle's Raymond Hunthausen was disciplined by Rome for various doctrinal and disciplinary aberrations, receiving nonetheless a remarkable amount of underground support from fellow bishops. That November meeting was filled with tension. Only Washington's Archbishop James Hickey, the chief investigator of the Seattle condition, put the Conference back on track with a didactic account of how Hunthausen was judged. The Seattle ordinary had intimated that he was treated unfairly. Hickey made clear to his peers that Hunthausen had been an active participant in the entire process, and that if he had accusers, they were people whom he had approved as witnesses. From the moment of Hickey's intervention, the bubble of Hunthausen support burst. (Subsequently, Rome restored him to full duty.) The actual situation in Seattle was bad and Rome hoped to obtain sufficient reforms without tearing the diocese asunder. Only time will tell whether the decision was a wise one or whether it merely served notice that bishops could flout Roman directives without fear of stern discipline.

Nonetheless, the emotional reaction of some bishops in

145

Hunthausen's favor gave the media an opportunity to play up the unhappiness with Rome within the Conference. Later, the seventy votes in favor of Milwaukee's Archbishop Rembert Weakland for vice president of NCCB was a remarkable statement in itself. Weakland, hardly one of Rome's favorite bishops, had the previous month, in his own diocesan newspaper, no less, challenged the Holy See's preoccupation with orthodox belief. There was no question that he had the Curran and Hunthausen cases in mind. There was no question, too, that the bishops voting for Weakland knew what he stood for and what their vote signified.

By the end of this 1986 meeting, a significant split in the American hierarchy was evident to all, with NCCB leadership clearly on the anti-Roman side. This leadership showed its hand during the vote for vice president. On the second ballot Bernard Cardinal Law, considered the leader of the pro-Roman wing, was in the lead with 106 votes to Cincinnati's Archbishop Pilarczyk's 92. On the third ballot Archbishop Weakland's 70 votes went *en bloc* to Pilarczyk. Law went on to be defeated eight times, the last time by an obscure bishop from the Far West. Granted that Law may have injured his chances earlier by endorsing publicly the Holy See's action on Hunthausen, but even so the NCCB leadership saw to it that he could not be elected even to the lowly role of alternate delegate to the 1987 Synod! It was political power used in the mold of Chicago's Mayor Daley.

The issues that divide the hierarchy, as they divide the rest of the U.S. Church, are not simply expressions of the Roman versus the American experience of the Catholic faith. Americans are not Italians to be sure, and they never practiced their faith in the Italian mode. Historically, the U.S. Church was Irish more than American, the result no doubt of the dominance of Irish-born priests and prelates in the nineteenth century. Andrew Greeley once remarked offhandedly that the trouble with New York Italian-Americans was that they had been "hibernicized" by their priests (i.e., they were trained to attend Mass on Sunday). In any case, the fidelity of the U.S. Church to the Holy See from high

146

prelates to lowly immigrants was by Continental European standards unique.

For the first time perhaps in U.S. Catholic history, doctrinal differences between bishops were beginning to emerge. The Hunthausen case certainly involved more than discipline—the meaning of the Eucharist, the indissolubility of Christian marriage, the Sacrament of Penance, and the Church's sexual ethic. Friends of the Seattle prelate asked why pick on him, since whatever was wrong in his diocese was observable in other bishops' jurisdictions. It was the argument Charles Curran made earlier on his own behalf, claiming for himself the private support of more than forty bishops, something unthinkable prior to Vatican II. Hunthausen's troubles, like Curran's, were sometimes attributed to "extreme right-wingers" in the U.S. or to the authoritarianism of Rome. But, in truth, the situation was much more serious than that. The issues were doctrinal and disciplinary.

The Church was beginning to reap what had been sown from 1965 onward—a preoccupation with humanist causes and the relaxation of traditional Church pieties. Not only this, but the positive assurance that the Church had ready answers to social problems grew to quasi-certainty about the time ecclesiastics were becoming uncertain about Catholic dogmas and the Church's inherited moral code. During this period bishops were very assertive with their social pronouncements and very silent about heaven, hell, and purgatory. Making disciples became a matter more of liberating people from unjust social structures than of getting them to stop sinning. The American agenda, developed out of the thinking of the Catholic elite, including many bishops, made the declericalization and de-Romanization of the Church a major priority. Democratic procedures, lay ministry, feminism, pluralism in doctrine, freedom of conscience (especially in matters of sexual choice), and social action replaced concern about mortal sin, eternal life, fast, abstinence, penance, believing all the truths which the Church teaches, and chastity as the dominant ecclesial values. Force and power were used to bring conformity to this new Church-in-the-making and against any group that wanted to

147

KEEPING THE CHURCH CATHOLIC

talk sin, suffering, sanctity, and discipline. As a result, the *Wanderer* Church grew to confront the *Reporter* Church, leaving the truly faithful Catholics with only the Pope reinforcing their beliefs and the way of life they learned from the Church.

The bishops' machinery began to reflect the theories of social science more than the wisdom of their own tradition. The bureaucrats began their thinking with the human condition and, in their laudable search for human answers, often failed to consider the divine equation. Many of their pronouncements sounded more like Peter Berger than John Henry Newman. And their investigations were often one-sided, skewed by the kind of researchers they chose and the closing off of real internal debate. To prevent further embarrassment long-time *NC News* correspondent Patrick Riley once suggested that at the very beginning of any draft process, adversary scholars be chosen to write different position papers, with ample opportunity for criticism and rebuttal. Riley thought such a procedure would "enable the bishops to decide whether they wish to issue any statement and, if so, what its drift should be." The bishops would know well in advance the pluses and minuses of material presented to them by bureaucrats. At "a pre-decision stage," continued Riley, "they would be better prepared to discuss or challenge the final draft on the floor of the bishops' meeting."[5] As will become evident, the NCCB did not take Riley's advice.

THE SOURCE OF THE DIFFICULTY

It is my judgment that a minority of bishops changed the course of the Church in this country by the control they obtained early in the formation of the NCCB and which they managed to centralize in the years between 1968 and 1988. It is also true that large numbers of bishops permitted this to occur by remaining politically inactive at the national level while supervising as best they could their Catholic islands in a free-floating Catholic sea. There are those, too, who insist that the radical change of purpose and content of the U.S. Church could not have occurred without the active collaboration of high-placed prelates in Rome. A case can be made that Apostolic Delegate Jean Jadot, Rome's bishop-maker in the U.S. between 1973 and 1980, contributed over one hundred bishops to the American scene, some of whom were in sympathy with the new theology and the pluralistic forms the Church was adopting. In any event, the emerging American Church was not the creation of dissenters, no matter how much they prized their own views over those of Magisterium. In the final analysis bishops run the Church, not academics.

The evidence in support of these propositions is uneven. Catholics do face the strong statements of Paul VI, the stronger affirmations of Catholic faith by John Paul II, and the many declarations of Rome's Sacred Congregations, correcting one or the other aberrations of national hierarchies. On the other hand, while the "official" Church says one thing, the day-to-day Church that people experience lives another. John Paul II makes a point to bishops in Los Angeles that status in the Church as "a good Catholic" precludes dissent from the Church's norms of sexual and conjugal morality. The following month (October 1987) the diocesan paper *San Francisco Catholic* has a headline, quoting John Quinn, the Archbishop there: "Dissenters Not Necessarily Bad Catholics."

No one's sincerity on either side of the assent-dissent dichotomy need be doubted when people ask how these two churches grew up side by side. They did not evolve by accident, nor could dissenters by themselves have institutionalized a church within a church. And abstract principles, even of authentic faith, cannot take flesh without people.

What we are inclined to forget is that important bishops came home from Rome with an anti-Roman virus. Detroit's Archbishop John Dearden, who as bishop of Pittsburgh was known as "Iron John" for his strict enforcement of ecclesiastical rules, as a member of the Papal Birth Control Commission voted with the contraceptionists. When elected president of NCCB in 1966, he chose as the first General Secretary for the USCC, the bishops' civil arm, the young Bishop Joseph Bernardin of Atlanta, whose

149

Archbishop happened to be Paul Hallinan, the first major American prelate to demand the retention of Charles Curran at the Catholic University of America. From the moment this Dearden-Bernardin team took over the management of the NCCB, "birth control" became for all practical purposes a dead issue in the authoritative statements of the national hierarchy. During the 1968 debate over *Humanae Vitae,* the U.S. bishops published their own "Human Life in Our Day," with a section on the conditions under which public dissent from Church teaching was legitimate. Twenty years later Washington's Archbishop James Hickey, during the controversy over Curran's dismissal from CUA, would repudiate that section, but in 1968 it had been negotiated into a national pastoral after consultation with Charles Curran, of all people. One of the negotiators was Bernardin, but he was not alone. The NCCB was advised by priests like Austin Vaughan (later a bishop) not to make this "compromise," but the compromise entered the pastoral anyway with little seeming regard for the effect this concession might have on the conjugal life of Catholics, who up to this time were reasonably concerned about Church norms. Thus began a strange era in parochial life. What Richard McCormick happily called "the great silence" on matters of sexual ethics fell from a great episcopal height on local pastors who, it is commonly acknowledged today, do not challenge any more the sexual proclivities of their parishioners.

One only need recall those priests, but mostly those married couples, who because of bishops' clear and firm teaching once looked upon the doctrine contained in *Humanae Vitae* as the Word of God and who carried the worldly crosses because they believed the bishops who so taught them in Christ's name. But the problem goes even deeper.

THE STRAWS THAT BROKE IN 1987

The American preparations for the 1987 Roman Synod on the Laity, the visit to the United States that year of John Paul II, and the November meeting of the bishops saw competing forces within the hierarchy come out of the closet.

The four bishops elected to represent the U.S. hierarchy at the Roman Synod—Cardinal Joseph Bernardin, Archbishop John May, Archbishop Rembert Weakland, and Bishop Stanley Ott— went to Rome with only one thing on their minds—expanding the role of lay people within the Church, especially that of lay women, and they spoke there accordingly. The subject of women's priestly ordination was always in the background of their thinking and, as one participant remarked: "The least we can get this time is altar girls." It had been one of the minimal requirements of Call to Action ten years earlier. This viewpoint did not reflect the world's hierarchy accurately. The Roman Synod gave no one altar girls, nor did it spend a large amount of time on Church structures for the laity. The emphasis instead in Rome was on the lay people's role in sanctifying the world. Whereas the U.S. bishops and their advisers looked within the Church for expanded lay roles, the Third and Fourth World bishops were preoccupied with the "outside world," where Moslems, Buddhists, and Fundamentalist Protestants impeded the Church's own evangelization efforts. This is the world to which those bishops hoped the Synod would direct the laity. It was a chord which harmonized with John Paul II's repeated admonition against any attempt to clericalize the lay people of God.

The 1987 visit of the Pope to the United States also demonstrated the cleavage between John Paul II and the U.S. episcopal leadership. One chosen spokesman on women after the other addressed the human needs of U.S. Catholics exclusively, in defense of their vaunted free spirit, of their unique educational freedom, of their cultural pluralism, as if somehow we might be dispensed from the universal norms of the Church. In each instance the Pope accepted the challenge, reasserting the Word of God, suggesting that the Church does not bend this Word to satisfy the demands of culture, calling upon bishops to refashion culture so that it adapts more closely with the gospel. John Paul was funny at times but never missed the point he wanted to make. To Fr.

Frank McNulty's favorable suggestions about married priests and women priests, the Pope rejoined with a smile on his face citing words of a World War I song: "It's a long way to Tipperary." To Archbishop Weakland's claims about the superior educational level of U.S. Catholics, John Paul wanted to know, if that be the case, where was their influence on American culture in evidence. Obviously, nowhere.

But it was the November 1987 meeting of bishops in Washington, D.C., that exposed once more the role of NCCB leadership in compounding the critical problems of faith, morals, and discipline which are today deeply laced into the fiber of the U.S. Church. Among the many issues separating the American body from its traditional close relationship with Rome, three surfaced at this meeting–dissident theologians and canonists, rebellious religious men and women, and wrong-headed teaching on matters of sexual behavior. The dissident theologians and canonists are found in the Catholic Theological Society of America and the Canon Law Society, the rebellious religious by wide margins dominate the Leadership Conference of Women Religious (LCWR) and the Conference of Major Superiors of Men (CMSM). The wrong-headed moral teaching consists in portraying the Church's sexual norms as a Christian ideal, which in today's real world may in good faith and for good cause be ignored or flouted.

The first proposal to the assembly by the Bishops' Committee on Doctrine sought to establish cooperative procedures between bishops and theologians for dealing with doctrinal disputes. The document failed in its purpose because it suggested a parity between the disputing parties, when in fact there is none between bishops and theologians. It assumed also that the issues in controversy were of such a profound nature that some negotiating procedure was necessary to protect a creative theologian from a bully bishop. The fact is that the average bishop is not dealing with a creative theologian like Henri De Lubac, not even with a contumacious troublemaker like Hans Küng. On a day-to-day basis he deals with complaints that some little-known faculty member teaches that Jesus did not really found a Church or that direct abortion is permissible, and so forth. Rome has established and tested procedures for dealing with the "big guns" of academe, which any hierarchy is free to use. The problem with the 1987 proposals "for promoting cooperation and resolving disputes between bishops and theologians" is that they create formality for what in ordinary circumstances is an informal relationship. If a bishop has to negotiate with every theology teacher who demands personal privilege every time the bishop attempts to correct error, his role as teacher, pastor, and governor of his diocese is compromised. We have ample evidence in contemporary civil affairs of how interminable and undue is the process for dealing with lawbreakers; for any serious Catholic to wish those stalemates on the Church seems incredible. Such a process sacrifices the common good, in the Church's case the common faith, for private privilege or the right to subvert the Catholic commitment.

Since assent to the Faith is the first demand on a Catholic, even a theologian, it is foolhardy in the extreme to wrap anyone's claim of the right of dissent into quasi-legal or collective bargaining procedures. Since contemporary academics write for the public as often as they court respect from their peers, the loser in such negotiations will be the faith of the people and the authority of bishops to protect that Faith.

Here again the ideology of the episcopal machinery came to the fore. The "proposals" to the bishops were drafted by a handful of bishops in concert with CTSA and CSLA, the two societies of theologians and canonists who have been stonewalling Rome for twenty years. No other body of scholars was asked. When Archbishop John Whealon enquired from the floor whether The Fellowship of Catholic Scholars was consulted, he was told it was likely done at an earlier time. The Fellowship was never consulted. The committee report failed to pass because a quorum of bishops was not present for the final vote. It has been remanded to the Committee on Doctrine, where some bishops hoped it would remain buried. Others agitated for its reappearance. It was scheduled for reappearance in November 1988.

More scandalous still was the treatment at this meeting of thousands of religious women who belong to the Consortium Perfectae Caritatis and the Institute on Religious Life, two post-Vatican II creations of nuns who wished to renew religious life in accordance with the requirements of Vatican II and with the norms of the Holy See. The CMSM and the LCWR, pre-Vatican II federations originally created by Pope Pius XII, who died in 1958, have been at odds with the Holy See more often than not since the Council. The Consortium and the Institute members total about thirty-two thousand women who on principle do not intend to join the LCWR. However, to simplify the relationship of the NCCB with the country's religious communities, the bishops' meeting decided to create a Tri-Conference Commission from which both the Consortium and the Institute were excluded. Fifteen members, five each from NCCB, CMSM, and LCWR, will shape the future of religious life in the United States and will also have the dominant voice in distributing the millions of dollars bishops will collect from pastors in the next ten years, moneys allocated to nursing care of old religious. These latter for the most part are nuns who devoted fifteen-hour days for half a century to teaching or to social service as members of communities which no longer are institutionally committed to these Church apostolates. In many communities attached to the LCWR, the "presidents" (no longer wishing to be called "superiors") refuse to accept Roman norms for religious life or wear religious habits, obey bishops or the pope, or commit their orders to hierarchically approved religious works. Their new understanding impels them toward individual lifestyles, secular dress, secular occupations, and usually some form of political action here or abroad.

The LCWR, while comprising communities with a total membership of approximately 100,000, is in fact a declining federation, since half of its constituency is over 60 years of age and their newcomers are few in numbers. (The men superiors are hardly in better condition.) Furthermore, the lifestyle of these communities, because it is secular, is costly. The orders also lack income from young sisters and so are unable to support the ever-increasing medical bills of their own aged. The Bishops' Conference has been dealing regularly with these federations since 1970, even though most of the member communities are locked in a doctrinal struggle with Rome over the meaning of religious life. Their revolution has decimated Catholic schools and the Church's welfare institutions, yet they continue to enjoy privileged status in episcopal circles because once thirty years ago their forebears, then totally devoted to Rome, enjoyed special status and papal sanction.

Consortium and Institute members, including Mother Teresa's burgeoning Missionaries of Charity, only 30 percent of the LCWR's gross statistics (obviously a much larger proportion of today's working nuns), observe all the Roman norms of religious life, wear habits and veils, live in community, obey superiors (even bishops), practice poverty, normally work for diocesan stipends, maintain the Catholic institutions to which their predecessors committed themselves, and command to this day the affection and respect of the Catholic laity. Besides, they are the only communities attracting young women to the service of the Church, the only religious congregations that have a chance of taking care of their own aged nuns. If they have $100,000 to spare, they assign it to the care of their old sisters. In this important sense some of these houses may not need $100,000 of bishops' money. Yet these are the only communities presently excluded from the bishops' Tri-Conference Commission even though the NCCB could have allotted them "at large" representation.

Cardinal John O'Connor asked the right question at the 1987 bishops' meeting: Are these organizations, such as the LCWR, really canonically erected? He was assured by a USCC canonist that they were, on the basis of a thirty-year-old papal decree by a Pope Pius XII who would, if he were alive, not give his approval to such communities. The canonist effortlessly closed out the Cardinal's question because these episcopal meetings are bogged down in a format incapable of dealing with vital questions of ecclesiastical policy in three minutes. In any open-ended congress of bishops, the follow-up questions would have to be posed: Why do we maintain canonical status for religious orders who no longer believe such status is relevant? Why do we freeze out of the episcopal community our only institutional supporters? Why do we reward the disobedient and punish the obedient? These are the critical issues which the Holy See, if not the NCCB, must ultimately face.

THE BISHOPS' CONDOM WAR

Probably the most distressing aspect of the 1987 bishops' meeting was the event that never happened—the failure of a USCC committee to submit a report on AIDS to the body of bishops for approval or rejection. On November 14, two days before the opening of the national assembly, a committee of four bishops, of whom Cardinal Bernardin was the dominant member, approved an AIDS statement for later issuance to the public with no more than a handful of bishops privy to its content. The report included paragraphs which approved the dissemination of factual information to students about condoms as a barrier to the spread of AIDS.

Four days later (November 18), the bishops' body as a whole did discuss and approve its own "Statement on School-Based Clinics," which covered some of the ground any report on AIDS could be expected to cover. The "Clinic" document provided two important guidelines for educators: (1) "Pluralism should not be used as a pretext for giving a diluted message or a double message about moral responsibility to teenagers." (2) "School officials must be wary of proposed 'medical' solutions that may be counter-productive. For example, most parents and teachers would presumably oppose the distribution in the schools of sterile intravenous needles to prevent transmission of AIDS, since this gesture would undermine efforts to teach students to 'say no' to drugs. The distribution of condoms to prevent pregnancy and the sexual transmission of AIDS deserves similar skepticism." These cautions seem clear enough, even in a Church document which missed a more basic teaching opportunity, namely, to explain why contraceptive intercourse of itself is intrinsically immoral. Still, the mind of the U.S. bishops on the limited role of the nation's schools in dealing with the AIDS crisis seemed clear and firm.

Then, out of the blue, three and a half weeks after the NCCB seemed to have closed one door by unanimous vote, the AIDS Committee opened another by issuing its controversial statement, which immediately ran into an ecclesiastical buzz-saw. The statement contained the following paragraph:

> Because we live in a pluralistic society, we acknowledge that some will not agree with our understanding of human sexuality. We recognize that public educational programs addressed to a wide audience will reflect the fact that some people will not act as they can and should, that they will not refrain from the type of sexual or drug abuse behavior which can transmit AIDS. In such situations educational efforts, if grounded in the broader moral vision outlined above, could include accurate information about prophylactic devices or other practices proposed by some medical experts as potential means of preventing AIDS. We are not promoting the use of prophylactics, but merely providing information that is part of a factual picture.

The best goodwill of those bishops who would like to obstruct the spread of AIDS and care for its victims could not prevent the statement from being looked upon—as long as the above-cited paragraph was included—as a new concession by the Church on contraception. Not only would the media, who always search for chinks in the Church's moral armor, tell it that way, but so would many Catholics see it that way. Bishops think that giving up sodomy and drug abuse is the only real way to stop the spread of the AIDS virus, but for them also to endorse telling people the facts "about prophylactic devices or other practices," as a lesser evil than AIDS is a radical departure from Catholic teaching practice. (By way of parenthesis "prophylactic devices" means condoms; "other practices" includes mutual masturbation or sodomy with one steady partner rather than the many in customary homosexual relationships, which are promiscuous.)

Almost immediately upon publication individual bishops reacted negatively. John Cardinal O'Connor said he would not allow instruction about condoms in AIDS education programs in New York. He characterized the 30-page policy paper by the USCC Board as "a grave mistake." Seventeen bishops from New England led by Boston's Bernard Cardinal Law, five bishops from Washington, D.C., led by Archbishop James Hickey, plus others led by Archbishop Theodore McCarrick of Newark, Cardinal Krol and Archbishop Bevilacqua of Philadelphia, Archbishop Roger Mahony of Los Angeles, Archbishop Joseph Ryan of the Military Diocese—about seventy bishops in all—objected to the statement that had been prepared over eighteen months by a committee of four bishops including Covington's William Hughes, Savannah's Raymond Lessard, Greenburgh's Anthony Bosco, and Chicago's Joseph Cardinal Bernardin. Bishop Lessard was chairman of the NCCB's Committee on Doctrine, responsible for the Church's authentic teaching, whose chief staff officer was Fr. Michael Buckley, hardly recognized as a consistent supporter of the Church's doctrinal absolutes. Fr. Michael Place, a Chicago priest who helped draft the AIDS document, is a proportionalist who was comfortable with Catholics who chose not to live according to Church norms.[6]

Although it has been recognized for many years that divisions existed within the U.S. hierarchy and that many bishops disagreed strongly with the leadership of the National Conference, this was the first time since 1966 that the split was so wide and so public. Some called it a "happy fault," a miscalculation by the Bernardin forces which might rouse bishops outside the "inner circle" to stand up and assert their rights over the conduct of the Conference. Too often had many of them been ignored or put down on the floor of their national meeting or felt helpless to counter unsatisfactory prepackaged proposals about which they had little advance information or time for study. The "AIDS Document" looked like the straw that broke long-suffering bishops' limit of patience. Cardinal Bernardin, some thought, had gone too far this time. His big mistake (and that of Archbishop John May, NCCB president) was retaining the AIDS statement within the

158

task force he dominated and not sending it out well ahead of time to the body of bishops where it could be discussed and voted upon during the general meeting, November 17–21, 1987. Most bishops never saw the full text, though a few tried unsuccessfully to obtain advance copies of the draft. Cardinal Bernardin justified the procedure later by explaining that he showed the document to leading archbishops during the assembly and that they had no objection to its content at the time. Still, the covert nature of the operation left many bishops dissatisfied.

What makes the ultimate publication by a committee difficult to comprehend is that throughout the task force meetings doubts raised later in public were discussed quite openly in private. In the September 22–24 meeting, for example, Archbishop Hickey thought the statement was too neutral on Catholic doctrine and on the teaching of Catholic morality. Bishop Anthony Bevilacqua (then in Pittsburgh) thought it would be difficult to get through the body of bishops, and others thought it would open the way to misunderstanding on the Church's teaching of morality. Archbishop Pilarczyk wanted to know how he could explain why the statement on "School Based Clinics" (which treated AIDS education) went to the full body while the task force statement did not. During the November 14, 1987, meeting Bishop Norman McFarland of Orange, California, and Bishop Bevilacqua, both trained scholars, spent a great deal of the task force's time trying to insert language into the document which would save the bishops from being misunderstood or from appearing to compromise the Church's teaching. They both feared that the extant wording would suggest that bishops were willing to water down Catholic teaching simply because they lived in a pluralistic society. Each objected to any hint that they were tolerating condoms. Archbishop Pilarczyk again warned that the task force leaders would need to have a "brief, cogent, and convincing explanation ready when someone asked from the floor why this action was taken in the Administrative Board and not in the general body." Bishop Robert Banks of Boston still was not satisfied that the statement went far enough in condemning the undermining of our nation's moral beliefs. He argued that what goes on in public schools today is not within "the broader moral vision" the bishops were recommending and that the programs there do try to sell contraceptives. At the end of the November 14 meeting Bishop Thomas Connolly of Baker, Oregon, inquired again if the statement could be considered by the full body, only to be told by Archbishop May that it would not be possible prior to June 1989. With that advisory completed, the minutes record: "The Chair called for a vote on the Statement. No voices were raised contrary to the motion and the Statement as amended was approved on a voice vote."

Later, when the U.S. bishops' AIDS statement had aroused international controversy, Roman authorities saw to it that *L'Osservatore Romano*[7] published an unsigned article from a declared "authoritative source" which advised: "The only truly effective measure is prevention, avoiding the cause of contagion, which means in 95 percent of the cases abstaining from sexual activity outside of marriage and from the use of drugs . . . [Further] . . . To seek the solution to the problem of contagion in the promotion of prophylactic means, therefore, promoting a way that is not only untrustworthy from a technical point of view, but also and above all unacceptable from a moral point of view."[8]

The bishops' AIDS Statement had other things wrong with it. William May, member of the Pope's International Theological Commission, in a letter to all the bishops, dated February 2, 1988, raised a few of them: (1) He questioned the task force's use of the "toleration of a lesser evil" in endorsing factual information about condoms, indicating that such education amounts to "cooperation in evil." (2) Since the statement did not reflect a consensus among the bishops, it was a violation of collegiality. (3) Regardless of intention, "The impression was created that the Administrative Board was trying to go over the heads of the bishops and certainly over the policy of individual bishops, particularly if their policy disagreed with that of the Administrative Board." (4) "The publication of the statement divided the bishops on a most important issue of public ecclesial policy. The situation seems to be unprecedented in the history of the bishops' conference and, I am sorry to say, it causes scandal among the faithful." In addition, Professor May suggested that the statement be withdrawn "for the good of the Church and the salvation of souls."

Theologian Fr. Ronald Lawler, O.F.M. Cap., raised other questions. Why were not other bishops' conferences consulted? The Vatican and the Italian bishops rejected a major AIDS program largely because it made provision for teaching children in school about condoms as part of a program against AIDS. Why was the U.S. statement muted about the fact that the primary cause of the AIDS epidemic is homosexual acts and drug abuse? Why did the bishops speak naively about "accurate information about prophylactic devices," when all the world knows that such courses to be effective must teach the young how to use condoms and encourage their use? Why were the bishop authors of the AIDS statement surprised when the media interpreted them to mean: "Since some people are determined not to live in the wise and good ways we commend, perhaps it would be better if they knew about and used condoms?" Do some bishops not know that one may never do the slightest moral evil to avoid any physical evil whatever? Why did not the bishops in question use this opportunity to explain and defend the grave sinfulness of contraception? Why was there such silence on this moral evil, even as "information" about condoms is offered as preventive therapy for AIDS?[9]

Denver's Archbishop J. Francis Stafford gave the strongest rebuttal to the USCC's task force and its "toleration" of "information": "The principle as articulated by Aquinas permits toleration of social evil by civil authority, but not toleration, and still less real or tacit cooperation in its transmission, by bishops and the Church community."[10]

Partisans of the AIDS statement insist that, properly understood, it does not promote the use of condoms. Indeed, it disavows such an intention. Nonetheless, for bishops to tell the young that, whenever they are unlikely to be good, information about condoms may be helpful in keeping them disease-free, is tantamount to removing their sense of guilt about doing wrong. It also suggests that homosexuals and drug addicts are beyond the pale of conversion. The concession implicitly adopts the posture that it is hopeless to talk morality to contemporary youth. The approach suggests that the most important thing in their young lives is to stay healthy, even if that means committing sin. Intentions apart, the suggestion is unacceptable coming from bishops. A moral norm is not an ideal to be compromised given sufficient reason, physical well-being is not a higher value than moral probity, and what the Church holds to be intrinsically evil is always evil.

SEXISM AND BISHOPS

The first draft of what the bishops' committee called *A Pastoral Response to Women's Concerns for Church and Society,* appeared in April 1988 for consideration by the NCCB at its June meeting in Collegeville, Minnesota. While the document has been subject to critical analysis from many quarters, the only sections of interest to this presentation are those which concern Catholic doctrine. A "pastoral" normally is a teaching instrument of hierarchy aimed at reinforcing the mind of the Church on the critical issues of a given time or country. A "response" is a reply, usually to criticism or objections. In many ways "the woman's pastoral" is not a pastoral, certainly not a response to the plethora of objections against Catholic doctrine the bishops allow to stand without comment.

The draft is instead a sociological survey of opinion, mostly negative opinion, whose ultimate effect will be to confirm the view that basic doctrinal positions of the Church are in a state of flux and fair game for continued questioning of a doubting nature. Far from being an instrument to promote unity around Catholic faith and morals, the draft (even if radically altered in its final form) will likely foster additional disunity by encouraging dissidents to think their views are legitimate.

Five Catholic doctrinal positions were brought into play during the bishops' hearings—homosexuality, divorce, abortion, contraception, and the priestly ordination of women, calling for response from the hierarchy.

1. "Lesbian women deserve special understanding and support from the Christian community," the bishops say (No. 176), but nowhere do they provide a solid doctrinal teaching on the evil of homosexual behavior.

2. Divorced and invalidly remarried women wonder aloud why they cannot receive Holy Communion (No. 67), but nowhere in this draft do bishops explain why this is not possible nor, in fact, why valid Christian marriage must always be indissoluble.

3. The draft leaves standing without comment (No. 76) the following complaint: "Some women are also concerned that the dialogue about abortion appears to be closed. They suggest the need for a 'realistic approach to family planning (including discussing the abortion question as a complex issue with diverse options).' "

4. After lengthy citations from women to the effect that the Church's teaching on contraception is wrong or does not square with the American experience (Nos. 73–75), the best the bishops offer in reply is the following: "We especially encourage a spirit of compassion toward those who in good conscience have not lived in accord with the ideals set forth by the Church" (No. 121). Ideals? This is the language of Charles Curran, used in a pastoral in spite of John Paul II's instruction that contraception is not a matter of free discussion, even among theologians, and that such attitudes are indeed obstacles to the reception of the Eucharist and to the designation "good Catholic."

5. Although all participants in the consultation process that preceded the publication of this draft, understood the pressures that were to be brought on hierarchy to soften the climate within the Church against the priestly ordination of women, the bishop-authors merely report the Church's heritage on the subject and cite Rome's 1976 declaration. Not only do they not make their own the constant teaching of the Church, they report without comment the fact that some Catholics find Rome's arguments unpersuasive. Indeed, they call for further study of the question, as if to suggest that the final decision on this matter is still to be made. This is the kind of ambiguity which twenty years ago helped undermine the Catholic consensus on contraception and led to a weakening of the Church's teaching authority on the entire area of sexuality.

The doctrinal shortcomings of the draft apart, philosophical and methodological difficulties run through the draft. The bishops assume they must write more as facilitators or therapists than as authoritative teachers. In one part of the draft they say (No. 109): "We must work to ensure that no one will feel excluded or alienated because of our teaching and pastoral care." This statement flies in the face of day-to-day reality, where truth and right divide, and contradicts New Testament theology, especially Christ's famous dictum: "My mission is to spread not peace but the sword,"[11] a reference to the fact that his teaching separates fathers from sons. The ones entitled to be alienated by the bishops' monitum are those who believe what the Church teaches, not those who do not believe; and those who do not believe what the Church teaches have reason to grow more angry once they are led to believe that the future belongs to them. But in this latter case the fault is not theirs.

THE 1988 MEETINGS

The June 24–27, 1988, meeting of the entire hierarchy (minus 71 absent bishops of the 300 eligible to vote) promised to be a watershed of one kind or another—not necessarily a confrontation as much as a shift away from what one bishop (who preferred not to have his name used) called "the one-party system," which had existed since the NCCB organized in 1966. The published summary of the episcopal discussion indicates that Pittsburgh's Bishop Donald Wuerl (with the AIDS statement obviously in mind) noted why "the need for actual rather than presumed ratification or approval by all bishops of actions taken by a subgroup of the Conference" was necessary to episcopal credibility. Dubuque's Bishop Daniel Kucera wanted to know just how much the present structure helped the leadership role of bishops. Los Angeles Archbishop Roger Mahony objected to the issuing of a major statement without prior approval by the body of bishops. Such dubia about episcopal leadership became the newsworthy aspect of the four-day session. "Catholic Bishops Vote to Retain Controversial Statement on AIDS" wrote the *New York Times.* "Catholic Bishops Vote to Rewrite AIDS Policy," said the *Washington Post.*

The "Bernardin wing" of the National Conference had enjoyed quiet possession of the episcopal machinery for a generation, unchallenged even by what the media called the "conservative bloc," whose leadership, if it existed at all, seemed amorphous or indecisive. It lacks a single bishop or combination of bishops with the political will or talent to steer an agenda more favorable to the Holy See through the committee structure of the NCCB. Chicago's archbishop, on the other hand, possesses the genius for moving his program successfully. Until 1988 his operation went unchallenged by the *corpus ecclesiasticum.* Bishops first came together once a year, then twice, to tackle complicated questions, more often controversial issues pertaining to peace and justice, about which bishops normally would need advance briefing and long discussion before they were ready for qualified judgments. Frequently the complicated documents from the USCC came late (perhaps ten days before a meeting), and the November meetings were so stacked with items sent to the floor with favorable recommendations from small committees that the rubber-stamping of bureaucratic judgments became routine.

In-depth floor discussions were impossible and challenges usually were brushed aside by an appeal to "expert" opinion or by a suave clarification by Archbishop Bernardin, who usually had ready access to a floor microphone. There were no minority reports from committees, even on nondoctrinal issues where minority reports were by circumstance a natural outcome. "Unity" demanded that such divisions not come to public attention, and, since most votes on substantial issues (such as the publication of the AIDS document) were voice votes, strong chairmanship facilitated agreement, when really there was substantial division. Even when a second mid year annual meeting was first proposed (in June, at Collegeville), NCCB leadership saw to it that the most intense discussion took place in small table groups ("buzz groups," they used to be called) on questions preset by leadership, with reports from the floor summarizing the bishops' table discussions made by a facilitator chosen by the national leadership. "Buzz groups," which do facilitate discussion, also prevent bishops from grasping the opinions of the total body. Grumbling might go on at lower levels, but the course of the NCCB was set for the next six months at least. These very procedures led to the ratification of many of the substantive programs which in the long run led the American hierarchy into tension with Rome over such issues as First Communion, lax annulment processes, unsatisfactory sex education guidelines, Charles Curran, etc. Bishop Wuerl was perfectly correct when he observed that the political shift to take place at the 1988 meeting was "minor" (i.e., procedural), but "important."

But "the establishment" does not give away power easily in the Church or elsewhere. Following instructions from the 1985 Extraordinary Synod, Rome sent every national conference a draft document which purported to define the nature and role of such bodies as administrative and juridical units of the Church, while denying them a theological base or a magisterial function. Because each hierarchy was called upon to provide a formal response to the Holy See, St. Louis Archbishop John May, the NCCB president at the time, had the opportunity to affirm what the Vatican draft denied, especially the doctrinal authority of national conferences. Hartford's Archbishop John Whealon was more sympathetic to Roman concerns, reminding his peers of the dangers presented by the NCCB/USCC bureaucracy to the individual bishops, especially when documents are issued without unanimous consent.

Brushing aside such concerns, Archbishop May at the end of his presidential address asserted the prerogatives of office by telling his brother bishops: "I am pleased to announce a committee of the former [NCCB] presidents to coordinate the drafting of the official Conference response." Few could argue against using the experience of the seven past presidents. Archbishops John Dearden, now deceased (1966–71), John Krol (1971–74), Joseph Bernardin (1974–77), John Quinn (1977–81), John Roach (1981–84), James Malone (1984–87), and John May (1988–) certainly represented the foundation years of the National Conference. But, Krol excepted, these were important promoters of policies unacceptable to the Holy See and prelates who coexisted without evident discomfort with those dissenters in the U.S. Church who broke with Church norms, at times obstreperously. At no time during this twenty-two-year period, before or after *Humanae Vitae,* did the national hierarchy confront dissent the way John Paul II does regularly. In spite of those blank spots in recent NCCB history, it seemingly did not occur to a single bishop to take the floor in Collegeville to suggest that some younger bishops, or at least different voices, should be named to help fashion the American response to Rome. John May's prepackaged *fait accompli* was allowed to stand without amendment.

It has long been understood that political advantage belongs to the "ins," and the Dearden-Bernardin party has used the bonus of power with remarkable skills, one of which was always to make sure that the General Secretary chosen to run the day-to-day NCCB/USCC structures was "simpatico" with the objectives of the controlling bishops. Once chosen by an administrative committee and ensconced in office, he had large powers over staff, research, committee assignments, contracts with outsiders, and was independent enough to stonewall bishops who did not like what was going on under his auspices. The Collegeville meeting tilted that power somewhat. Revised statutes as approved give a majority of the bishops' assembly the right to approve or reject by secret ballot all future nominations to this post. The "ins," however, did not lose complete control of their bureaucracy. When

167

Green Bay's Bishop Adam Maida proposed that bishops also have a wider say over the appointment of associate general secretaries, who are usually closer to the particularities, the bishops were advised to vote no and did.

The more interesting exercise of in-power was the retention by the Washington staff of Cardinal Ratzinger's letter on the AIDS issue, keeping it away from bishops-in-the-field until the last minute. The Roman letter, dated May 29, was forwarded to the General Secretary by Archbishop Laghi's office on June 6 and stamped with the arrival date June 10. Yet, it was distributed to bishops as part of a documentary package only as they arrived in Collegeville for the June 24 meeting. Considering the crucial importance of the issue to a divided hierarchy and the level of Ratzinger's authority on moral matters, holding the letter in escrow for two weeks can hardly be considered an enlightened example of open communication between staff and bishops.

The bishops-in-the-field eventually had their day in open court, as it were, when a majority approved a two-year contract with Mother Angelica and her Eternal Word Television Network (EWTN). The vote seemed to shock the establishment, many of whom were anti-Angelica almost from the moment she began operating in 1981. The Catholic Television Network of America (CTNA), founded by bishops about the same time, had consumed millions of episcopal dollars with little production to show for the outlay. EWTN, on the other hand, was a flourishing 24-hour network, with a four-million-dollar annual budget, no debt, and a fixed standard of Catholic identity. Mother Angelica was not in competition with CTNA, although she recognized dissent from Church teaching in some of its discussion programs. Some bishops thought Mother Angelica's programming was "narrow," precisely because she insisted on fixed norms whenever Catholic teaching or interests were presented to the public. In her proposal to the bishops, she claimed the right to reject any program from USCC (i.e., one lacking a bishop), if EWTN's review board ruled it insufficiently Catholic. This demand stuck in the craw of those bishops closely identified with the USCC.

Indeed, a few accused EWTN of "doing a hatchet job" on the bishops' performance at the November 1987 meeting in Washington, D.C. Several of Mother Angelica's priest commentators at that time did express negative comments on three items on the NCCB agenda, one of which concerned the Birmingham nun's TV operation, but these were items about which there was division within the hierarchy itself. It was a strange criticism to come from the floor of a bishops' meeting, where for twenty years those bishops have not criticized priests who disparage the Pope and the teaching which binds all believing Catholics to the Church. The complaint is difficult to measure for another reason. Msgr. Daniel Hoye's letter to Mother Angelica during negotiations asserted that the USCC's own telecommunication system—CTNA, although owned by the bishops, is an "independent entity." Bishops-in-the-field could hardly have been pleased with some of the direction taken by that office. Mother Angelica is much more likely to be cooperative with bishops, even when she raises constant questions about the commitment of USCC staff to John Paul II's vision of what it means to be Catholic.

However, after much huffing and puffing the bishops' body voted not to increase the amount of monies going to CTNA nor allow it to join an ecumenical network. Once Mother Angelica agreed to a five-man episcopal board to arbitrate differences and the bishops realized that her services to them came *gratis*, the majority vote came her way. If Palm Beach's Bishop Thomas Daily emerged as a hero in "selling" her cause to his peers, the valiant daughter of St. Clare turned out to be the meeting's Pearl White. Against bishops who argued that an ecumenical television tie by NCCB would kill Mother Angelica, Greenburgh's Bishop Anthony Bosco responded: "Anyone who knows her knows she cannot be killed." Archbishop John Quinn, usually a friend of women's causes, tipped his mitre to the lady's strength of purpose with the remark that "the bishops' conference might be engulfed by the power of that personality." Still if EWTN is alive and well and for two years at least is the official television outlet of the NCCB, the reasons can be found nearer to New York's Bishop

Austin Vaughan's observation that the bishops needed outreach through television—and there was no reason to keep CTNA alive except for the money already spent on it unfruitfully.

The closed-door session on Cardinal Bernardin's "AIDS Booklet" promised to be exciting, but it turned out to be jejune. Not only did Ratzinger's letter have its effect, but the Apostolic Pro-Nuncio was busily at work in advance on a "gentleman's agreement" between the antagonists in the "condom war." The result was Cardinal Bernardin's proposal of a new statement on AIDS, worked out with the entire bishops' body and with Rome. Cardinal Law was a good choice to second the motion because this partnership made all differences of episcopal opinion moot. It remains to Archbishop May to choose the committee which will work out a new statement.

What will remain of historic interest, of course, will be the attacks on the content of the original AIDS statement by Rome and by important U.S. bishops.

Cardinal Ratzinger's objections were five and curtly stated:

1. He regrets the moral confusion among Catholics caused by the document, and by the appearance of doctrinal disunity among bishops.

2. It is dangerous for episcopal conferences to go off on their own in such matters without advance consultation with the Holy See.

3. It is incorrect to propose a morally unacceptable technical solution to a medical problem.

4. In giving information about condoms, "one would not be dealing simply with a form of passive toleration, but rather the kind of behavior which would result at least in the facilitation of evil."

5. Catholic schools specifically must remain fully faithful to the Church's moral doctrine "without at the same time engaging in compromises which may even give the impression of trying to condone practices which are immoral."

Whenever a high Vatican official accuses a national conference of bishops of aberrations such as the above, this is news. But, at the Collegeville meeting even U.S. bishops indicted the NCCB. A little known bishop from Tulsa, Eusebius J. Beltran, decimated the AIDS statement, ending with a pointed recommendation: "I suggest that the body of bishops should use this unfortunate episode as the occasion to reconsider very carefully the policies, practices and procedures involved in the issuance of documents by the NCCB and the USCC. At times there seems to be an almost frantic urgency in those organizations to issue statements, testimony, policy papers, pastoral letters, and the like." He objected strongly to these becoming known as "statements of the body of bishops." Dubuque's Archbishop Daniel Kucera used the occasion to suggest "a thorough investigation of what we are about as a national conference of bishops." The structure of NCCB/USCC "obstructs rather than fosters full participation of bishops in the process of decision-making." Cardinal Law described the AIDS statement as a "tragic situation." Although Cardinal O'Connor in his oral presentation expressed regret for seeming to cause "trouble" for the conference by his initial opposition to the Bernardin statement, his written intervention recommended "a rewriting of *The Many Faces of AIDS,* omitting the paragraph on condoms which has become a *cause célèbre.*" A number of bishops associated with NCCB leadership defended the Administrative Committee's action, but they were in a small minority and out of harmony with the declared mind of the Holy See.

There was no mood of *noblesse oblige,* however, in the Bernardin camp. An early attempt to retract the original AIDS statement, errors and all, was stonewalled. The irenic motion to write a new statement would likely have died there, had anyone, including Rome, insisted on retraction. Indeed, Chicago's archbishop continued to insist that the rejected Administrative Board document was merely misunderstood and misinterpreted, and had the blessing of Savannah Bishop Raymond Lessard's Doctrine Committee. He also made it clear that he did not intend to have his handiwork repudiated. Indeed, by Collegeville meeting time, he already had the statement printed as Publication No. 195-4 of the Office of Publishing and Promotion Services of the USCC, a booklet thirty pages in length, which will remain on sale in the USCC's bookstore. The maneuver was episcopal sleight of hand at its best by a political master, but not an exercise in authentic ecclesiastical leadership.

The AIDS controversy was brought to an official close at the November 9, 1989, bishops' meeting in Baltimore. By a vote of 219–4, the NCCB approved a new and solidly Catholic statement on the subject under the chairmanship of Los Angeles Archbishop Roger M. Mahony. The new document entitled "Called to Compassion and Responsibility" attacked condoms as one of those "quick fixes" that "actually leads to a greater spread of HIV and AIDS." The pertinent paragraph reads as follows:

> Not only is the use of prophylactics in an attempt to halt the spread of HIV technically unreliable; promoting this approach means, in effect, promoting behavior which is morally unacceptable. Campaigns advocating safe/safer sex rest on false assumptions about sexuality and intercourse. Plainly, they do nothing to correct the mistaken notion that non-marital sexual intercourse has the same value and validity as sexual intercourse within marriage. We fault these programs for another reason as well. Recognizing that casual sex is a risk to health, they consistently advise the use of condoms in order to eliminate the risk. This is poor and inadequate advice.

At a later press conference Mahony called the suggestion "dangerous" which would consider such prophylactics preventative of AIDS. Pressed more than once by the media representatives, he (like Archbishop May) denied that the 1987 defective booklet was being repudiated or withdrawn. The reporters seemed unconvinced by these assertions. Nonetheless, "The Many Faces of AIDS" will continue to be available at USCC headquarters until the present edition runs out. The NCCB leadership insists that the new document is merely a more forceful and more authoritative presentation of the Catholic view and that "The Many Faces of AIDS" remains a Committee Document of the USCC, even though it was criticized by seventy bishops, by Cardinal Ratzinger, and eventually rewritten.

What made the 1988 meetings more interesting than most is that the full scope of episcopal thinking came to the fore, even when there was general agreement. The proposal to criticize President Reagan's Strategic Defense Initiative (SDI) was upheld, although the committee phrase "morally deficient" was deleted at the request of bishops, who feared the words might be interpreted as condemning SDI as immoral. Archbishop Joseph Ryan of the Archdiocese for Military Services objected strongly to the "whole section" on the Strategic Defense Initiative as "seriously flawed." "It rests upon factual data that is highly controverted, supported by an obviously politicized scientific report and blatantly designed to undermine the declared intention of the [U.S.] government." Archbishop Philip Hannan of New Orleans thought Cardinal Bernardin's presentation manifested little sensitivity either to Archbishop Ryan or to the intentions of the President of the United States, unlike John Paul II who, he said, shows appreciation for the efforts of the U.S. government to reduce the dangers of nuclear deterrence.

The same latitude of expression characterized the discussion of General Absolution. The new *Code* (Cn. 961) permits bishops to allow it in danger of death and in cases of special necessity, for example, when there are too many people and not enough confessors, so that the penitents would be deprived of grace or the Eucharist "for a long time." Such special necessity occurs at times in rural parishes and in scattered dioceses. Rome wanted to know, however, how long "for a long time" is for penitents in the United States. Prodded by Arlington Bishop John Keating's Canonical Affairs Committee, the bishops voted to set a thirty-day limit. In other words, bishops are not to give blanket permissions for General Absolution—only in cases of "special necessity," with the understanding that private penance is available within a month. In some dioceses General Absolution was being administered repeatedly without any demand that penitents in the state of mortal sin must go to private confession. Some bishops at Collegeville still insisted on no limit or argued for a longer limit. Retired bishop William McManus of Fort Wayne defended the notion that General Absolution actually brought people back to confession, although the empty confession lines belied that claim. Milwaukee's Archbishop Rembert Weakland, responding to an earlier assertion that some Catholics think there is "magic" in General Absolution, said his priests would be offended to hear this charge: "That description would better fit the thirty-second confession with no chance of conversion." St. Paul's Archbishop John Roach thought it was wrong to concentrate on such a small matter and advised further study.

It was Bishop Vaughan who spoke for most bishops when he called for some standard to be set. He granted that the breakdown of the penitential discipline was a broader question—children not educated to go to confession, bad examples set by adults, seminarians who do not go, disbelief in sin or hell among Catholics, priests who give different advice on birth control, etc. Retired bishop Jerome Hastrich of Gallup saw part of the larger problem in priests who do not show up at scheduled times for confession. Archbishop Whealon cited the theological opinion that many current General Absolutions are invalid because people do not bother to go to private confession afterward.

The relevant aspect of this discussion was Bishop Keating's reminder that the Pope has been asking for clear norms on General Absolution as far back as 1978, and that the Canonical Affairs Committee itself had been studying the subject from 1986 onwards. The bishops voted with Keating. The larger issues, especially the one raised about the unworthy reception of the Eucharist currently going on, was left to another day. The Canonical Affairs Committee also forestalled Bishop Lessard's Doctrine Committee from enlarging the preaching role of the laity during the liturgy. Lay persons are already permitted to preach in churches (Cn. 766), but not during that part of the liturgy reserved for a priest or deacon, namely, at homily time when the mysteries of the Faith and the norms of Christian living are to be expounded (Cn. 767, No. 1).

While the formula for distributing monies to retired religious evoked no significant controversy, the two hottest political potatoes—the draft statements on women and on the doctrinal responsibilities of bishops vis-à-vis theologians—were deferred to the November 1988 meeting, with only minor discussion of the former, none at all of the latter. The draft of the "women's pastoral" had been in the public forum since March 23, greeted lukewarmly by feminist partisans and favorably by liberationists generally, lambasted by almost anyone who expects Church teaching, not popular or unpopular sentiment, to frame the character of a Church pastoral letter.

The difficulty in which bishops find themselves today over letters such as these goes back at least to *Call to Action* (1976), when someone sold the Dearden-Bernardin leadership the policy of conducting Church business more as American politicians than as bishops. Going out to the hustings to discover what is politically viable before they propose a bill or enact a law is what Congressmen do. Only the naive, or the politicians, consider these so-called "input" or "feedback" sessions to be genuine town meetings. Activists and veto groups usually dominate such hearings, leaving the eternally silent majority more unheard than ever. "Listening sessions" on behalf of the "women's pastoral" may prove more dangerous for bishops than those held for the peace and economic pastorals, because the issues involved here are intimately personal and radically familial, and also because the feminist bloc, now so experienced at harassing bishops, annoys other Catholic women who are uncomfortable with bitter politicking within the Church, which some of them are seeing for the first time in their Catholic lives. Joliet's Bishop Joseph Imesch, for example, dismisses Helen Hitchcock's Women for Faith and Family as a "minority" force in its opposition to his draft as written. But Imesch is caught in the trap of his own methodology. If a poll-taker stood in front of most churches on a

175

given Sunday morning, he would find that most churchgoers have not the foggiest notion of who Bishop Imesch is or what he has been doing for the past five years.

Indeed, after a series of open pastorals alleged to be openly arrived at, it is said, the Church in the United States seems more disunited than ever on the basics of what it means to be a man, a woman, or the roles of the sexes within marriage as distinguished from their civic roles. Questions have been raised before about how openly arrived at these pastorals are, how open are the intentions of those who write the original drafts. Some people also wonder what other public institution permits a "committee of few" to publish an imperfect document, which at times questions the priorities and policies of the institution it serves, without the consent of the ruling officers of that body. Philip Lawler, editor of Cardinal Law's *Boston Pilot,* raised similar questions a few years ago (1986) in a booklet he entitled *How Bishops Decide: An American Case Study.* Lawler reminds readers that the first draft of any bishops' letter is not a pastoral at all, but the statement of five bishops and whoever they choose to prepare the material. Yet, it is this first draft, often seriously defective, even biased, which receives the most media attention, even from the Catholic press. Nothing that bishops do to improve the final statement offsets the impressions of the first draft. What people come to think bishops said often ends up better remembered than what they finally do say. And, because three to five years may pass before the Church receives the magisterial pronouncement, the initial committee, though insignificant of itself, may be an instrument of Catholic opinion-molding in ways the full episcopal body did not anticipate.

Consider the first draft of the "women's pastoral." Immediately, and not surprisingly, the media seized and spread abroad the notion that the Church now considers sexism to be a sin. Who among the public knows that at Collegeville Helena's Bishop Elden Curtis asked for clarification of this notion? Certain forms of discrimination and different treatment of men and women are necessary, he said. The media also wondered aloud whether the

176

bishops' pastoral was edging toward a favorable view of women's priestly ordination. Bishop Daily immediately asked why the committee's draft spoke of the position of the Congregation for the Doctrine of the Faith on that issue, and not the teaching of the Church. These novel forms of episcopal speech did not enter the draft by accident.

Partners in the Mystery of Redemption is in difficulty largely because of the methodology that shaped its character and slanted its research. It is almost inconceivable, for example, that a pastoral on the subject of women would not take into account Stephen B. Clark's *Man and Woman in Christ,* (1980), a scholarly study of the roles of women in the light of scripture and the social sciences. This masterpiece deserves mention, if only to be rejected, but instead the bishops or their consultants chose to ignore it. In a letter to me dated June 18, 1988, Mr. Clark made the following observations on the bishops' draft:

> Scripture is not heavily used in the text. Most sections make no references to scripture at all. Where scripture is used, it seems often employed more as a Christian embellishment to the text than the actual source of the statements.

He concludes the letter with this observation:

> To be sure, the feminist approach to exegesis is not obtrusive in the document, because the use of scripture is not. My recommendation is that less scripture, in fact, be used. A more fruitful and exegetically solid use of scripture would require a re-casting of the whole document in a way that is alien to its current intention.

A thirty-three-year-old Jesuit at Harvard provided an even more critical analysis of the draft. The following are his most substantial points:

1. It permits the reading that abortion should become part of a "dialogue" on family planning.

2. It imperils the authority of *all* Church teaching by stating without specification that Catholic doctrines have been and are tainted with sexism.

KEEPING THE CHURCH CATHOLIC

3. It states that New Testament teachings were influenced by cultural bias, thereby weakening their authority.

4. It adopts as its own in several places language that has specific origins in anti-Catholic polemic.

5. It seriously misrepresents the breadth of the concerns of Catholic women by the suggestion that "alienation" from the Church is felt only by women who see it as too traditional.

6. It studiously and even ostentatiously avoids any reference to God the Father, which permits the reading that the American bishops are prepared to dispense with this confession as a sexist interpolation.

In the judgment of more people than Fr. Mankowski, the proposed letter on women contains what can be called deliberately placed time bombs, buried deep in long paragraphs, fused to explode in the new listening sessions as they take place. Not only is Church order at stake, but the authority too of Scripture and the teaching office of the Church itself.

Perhaps more serious to the future of the Church is the contemplated episcopal letter on the doctrinal responsibilities of bishops and theologians. Tabled by the bishops at their November 1987 meeting with the recommendation that a wider group of scholars be consulted, it has taken new form without wider input. The appointment two years ago of Jesuit Michael Buckley as executive director of the Doctrine Committee takes on enlarged significance.

By the time of the Collegeville meeting the "theological letter" was still shrouded in secrecy, a bad omen of itself, not unlike the case of the Catholic Theological Society's book *Human Sexuality*, whose content was closely guarded until it was published by the Paulist Press in 1976. Although the volume was later criticized by American bishops and the Holy See, the long-range damage that it inflicted on Catholic moral fiber is incalculable. Much has been said since Vatican II on the responsibility of bishops to guard the Faith and on the right of Catholics to the Church's authentic teaching, on the duties of theologians to Magisterium, and on the difference between legitimate and illegitimate pluralism, the Doctrine Committee at present is wedded to a document surfeited with sociotheological jargon difficult to reconcile with Catholic tradition which, therefore, will be difficult to interpret in favor of Magisterium's superior rights.

The November 14–17, 1988, meeting in Washington, D.C., as far as the substantive issues relating to faith and morals are concerned, was a repeat performance. The U.S. leadership was on one side (followed after some infighting by the rank and file episcopacy) and Rome on the other. The professions of loyalty to the Holy Father were profuse, but the alienation of leading bishops from the Roman perspective, though attributed by some to the press or to Catholic reactionaries, was clear enough. This estrangement is not of recent vintage, to be sure. Neither does it simply involve matters of procedure or of Roman versus American experience. There was visible annoyance when Joseph Cardinal Ratzinger's office, for the second time in a year, intervened immediately prior to the November meeting. Through his episcopal secretary, he expressed grave concern over the NCCB's plan to approve a document entitled *Doctrinal Responsibilities,* (thus killing it, at least for the time being). This paper, fifty pages in length, in the works for eight years and passed over the previous June in Collegeville, was expected to be approved this time, even though seriously flawed.

The pique was attributed to the alleged last-minute timing of the intervention, although it is clear from the record that Ratzinger's office received the final draft only a few weeks earlier. Perhaps the previous scuttling of the AIDS document because of Ratzinger, and John Paul II's apostolic letter *On the Dignity of Women* (August 15, 1988), which effectively placed on ice the NCCB's proposed pastoral on women, were contributing factors to the annoyance. Whatever irritation Archbishop Alberto Bovone, the secretary to Ratzinger, felt, if any, would be due not to faulty procedures, but to the failure in this case of the U.S. machinery to safeguard doctrine or doctrinal authority. Archbishop Bovone concluded his five pages of observations with the following paragraph:

The impression one gets from the quotations cited and from the entire document is that it tends to formulate the problem of the relationship between bishop and theologian principally as a question that concerns the subjective level and, thus, as a problem of the defense of the rights of the persons involved. At the same time the question of the objective level of the content remains on a secondary level. It is on this level of the content that the bishop (especially when one treats of subjects already dealt with by the magisterium) has, for the good of the faithful, an ultimate and specific responsibility.

It was this "ultimate and specific responsibility" which Denver's Archbishop J. Francis Stafford rose to defend against this document at the 1987 meeting. Even so, other things were wrong with *Doctrinal Responsibilities.* Leveling of bishops and theologians to the same plane, so that they would negotiate their differences as equals, so that theologians' right to teach freely would not easily be negated by hierarchy, so that the faithful's dependence on hierarchy for Catholic truth and guidance would be compromised by the co-existence of a rival theological establishment with something different to teach in the name of Christianity, were not small matters for the Holy See.

The average bishop on a day-to-day basis deals hardly at all with academics. There are many, however, who talk or write freely about the "People of God Church," as if it were independent of hierarchy, about a second magisterium, about exceptions to Christ's moral absolutes; who profess a virulent distaste for *Humanae Vitae,* while justifying contradictory norms that would allow believers to sin without guilt, who no longer consider mortal sin an obstacle to a graceful relationship with God, and who fault Magisterium's insistence on indissoluble marriage, private confession, and personal absolution by a priest in cases of mortal sin, and so forth. Doctrinal Responsibilities, as Archbishop Bovone rightly observed, makes a large point of such academics' subjective rights to pursue their agenda among the faithful, but leaves diocesan bishops relatively helpless against such dissenters. Does anyone remember an outpouring of support from this theological establishment for Magisterium's judgment on Charles Curran, Richard McBrien, Anthony Wilhelm, Philip Keane, Matthew Fox, to name only a few Americans who have come under the Vatican's censure?

Yet, the chief consultants of the NCCB who prepared the draft on doctrinal responsibilities were of the same academic mindset as those who have supported one or the other of the opinions listed above, all of which have been rejected by Rome, not once but repeatedly. Their names, all well known to the Washington, D.C., theological complex, would have remained hidden from view had not Bishop James Malone been pressed by Cardinal Bernard Law to name them. The bishops' drafting committee earlier had demanded that the Roman Congregation reveal its sources. Regardless of how one rates on a magisterial scale the individual theologians singled out by Malone as consultants, the fact is that not one of those named has an unblemished record of defending the teachings of the Church as those teachings have been articulated by the last four popes or the nine synods of bishops. A few days before Malone made that announcement, an International Congress on Moral Theology was held in Rome under the patronage of John Paul II which featured the following American scholars—William May, Ralph McInerney, Germain Grisez, Lorenzo Albacette, Carl Anderson, Benedict Ashley, Ronald Lawler, David Liptak, Thomas O'Donnell, William Smith—all but one of whom were excluded from the normal consultation process of the National Conference of Catholic Bishops under its present leadership. And this in spite of the fact that bishops on the floor a year before had requested wider consultation for writing the paper on doctrinal responsibilities!

These inclusionary and exclusionary tactics for dealing with matters of doctrine and ecclesiastical policy have been characteristic of the U.S. episcopal machinery for two decades. Rome, on occasion, has intervened in U.S. Church affairs to correct a theologian, to withdraw an imprimatur, or to demand changes in the constitutions of rebellious religious communities, without any follow-up in similar cases by the U.S. hierarchy. In these quarters there does not seem to be sufficient awareness that the "modern man" bishops today are called upon to respect is really the creature of street "theologians," not the Christian character formed traditionally by the magisterium of hierarchy. These "theologians," whom bishops seem to accept as allies, are experts more at doubt and search than at unqualified affirmations of revealed faith. Rome and many U.S. bishops recognize the critical significance of a statement by a particular hierarchy on doctrine. Catholics differ on many things because there are so many uncertainties in life. The bishops cannot afford to leave uncertain whether Jesus is God's Son who rose from the dead and founded a Church, whether there is a heaven or hell, whether mortal sin estranges people from God, whether sacramental consummated marriages are indissoluble, whether the Mass is an important sacrifice and men its only celebrants, and whether pope and bishops can bind in conscience.

Confusion about Catholic priorities probably explains why the more newsworthy, but less significant, decision of the November 1988 meeting was rejection by a vote of 205 to 59 of the Vatican document on episcopal conferences. The byplay among bishops over this issue had its moments of drama, and the inner state of the U.S. hierarchy was exposed without settling the theological fate of episcopal conferences. Do national bodies of bishops have real teaching authority? Obviously yes. But without Rome? The draft document from the Holy See would limit the autonomy of national conferences; the U.S. bishops (like many others) tend toward the view that their quasi-independence should be institutionalized. Hardly more than a century old, the rationale for the existence or function of national conferences was insufficiently developed, with the Pope inclined to stress unity in a universal Church and bishops favoring flexibility and diversity. Church history provided no clear or settling evidence on the question, except to say that the Pope is the final decider.

What displeased some bishops was that other bishops, especially the committee of ex-presidents, used insensitive and at times somewhat patronizing language in rejecting the Roman

draft. The suggestions that Rome should follow more open procedures, reveal sources, be objective, and acknowledge that its conclusions sometimes are prudential, not necessary, were considered
disrespectful language. Ex-presidents Joseph Bernardin and John
Quinn recognized the need for softening the language, and they
made an effort to do so before the meeting began. Other bishops
still were not satisfied even then. The most dramatic moment
came in the vote on Detroit Cardinal Edmund Szoka's amendment
to strike the section which contained the unseemly language. Cardinal Bernardin rose five times to defend the tone as necessary to
make the Holy See realize the true meaning of the American
response. The final vote defeating the Szoka amendment was
127–127, a measure of pro- and anti-Roman sentiment, if there
ever was one. A *National Catholic Reporter* correspondent ended
his summary of the vote with the line: "Perhaps reflecting the
differences within the conference, an observer muttered as those
opposing Szoka stood: 'The Jadot regime.' "

Softened language was later adopted, but not before New
York's Auxiliary Bishop Austin Vaughan, former president of the
CTSA, startled his peers with blunt speech of his own. While he
himself was critical of the Vatican draft, neither was he impressed
with the ecclesiological competence of the ex-presidents responsible for the American response. He compared the committee's role
to the guarding of a hen-house in the hands of foxes, "friendly
foxes, but foxes" nonetheless. This was a reference to the role
played by NCCB bishops in raising Rome's anxiety quotient over
national conferences. The Dutch hierarchy's position on clerical
celibacy, the European episcopal disagreement with the U.S. pastoral on war and peace, and lately the American document on
AIDS were part of Rome's ongoing nervousness about local bodies of bishops. Vaughan went further, criticizing the NCCB leadership for its lack of collegiality in dealing with its own bishops in
the field, among other things hiding Roman documents from
them.

Most of the people-in-the-pews were hardly aware that these
proceedings were taking place, let alone touched by the issues

raised in Washington about doctrinal authority. The elite, however, were not so detached from the goings-on. The *National Catholic Reporter* capsulated their expectations in a headline: "U.S. Bishops' Conference, In Lopsided Vote, Rejects Vatican Bid to Curb Collegial Church." This edition featured priestless parishes, with one local community expressing favor for a weekly communion service run by laity, rather than a Mass celebrated by an "outside" priest. As the bishops' meeting was drawing to a close, a Jesuit professor of the Berkeley School of Theology, which itself already enjoyed representation within NCCB, told an ecumenical gathering in New York that the real disease-bearing Catholics in the contemporary Church were fundamentalists, who intimidate bishops and progressive theologians by their hostility toward women's rights, gay Catholics, and Third World liberation theology, and who hide behind the popular John Paul II. The parties engaged in what the Jesuit called a "fratricidal war" are clearly visible, found in every diocese whenever two pastors living side by side tell parishioners contradictory things on what it means to be a Catholic. Apostolic Pro-Nuncio Pio Laghi touched lightly on these senseless divisions when he spoke to the U.S. bishops on their Hispanic ministry. In view of the fact that Hispanics are now the largest Catholic minority in the United States (twenty million), Laghi called on bishops to "provide the supportive ecclesial environment that nurtured the faith of earlier generations of (immigrant) Catholics" and to emphasize for Hispanics "three pillars of our Catholic faith": "deep devotion to the Holy Sacrifice of the Mass and the Blessed Sacrament; veneration of the Blessed Virgin Mary, the angels and the saints; and respect and love for the Holy Father as Vicar of Christ on Earth." These demands are not exactly what the *National Catholic Reporter* or the Berkeley Jesuit had in mind.

Several years ago, sitting around the apartment of a denizen of the Roman curial scene, two Americans became fascinated at how often the word "schism" cropped up in the conversation. (A schism is like a lesion, enough blood-letting to indicate a wound, but not enough to kill—yet). Would there be a schism in the

United States? The Americans did not think so. Too many committed bishops, too many believing Catholics whose faith is that of Paul VI and John Paul II. Everyone seemed to agree that the Dutch Church was in virtual schism—six bishops bull-dozed by academics, and Catholic religious observance, once about the highest in Europe, now infinitesimal, with animosity to Rome at a high pitch. As if out of nowhere a curial cardinal present interjected himself into the conversation with the observation: "Brazil is a more likely place for schism—many more bishops fighting Rome and an undercatechized population." The usual symptoms of potential schism are present—many bishops turning over the national Catholic machinery to a few, the few permitted without oversight to develop a bloated bureaucracy headed by "nationalists" who favor de-Romanization and decentralization of the Church, the conference taking positions unanimously or almost unanimously, with individual bishops hardly having time to grasp the long-range significance of many votes, documents circulated through the mass media which do not represent well the Church's best understandings, runaway pastoral programs, runaway seminaries, runaway base communities, illicit, sometimes invalid, Masses, bad imprimaturs from cooperative bishops, and so forth. The pattern was very familiar to the Americans present. They all knew the problems, but at the moment they were not prepared to deal with them in any systematic way.

THE 1989 MEETING IN SETON HALL

At the June 16, 1989, Bishops' Meeting at Seton Hall University, the National Conference gave overwhelming approval (only nine negative votes) to its long-prepared statement on "Doctrinal Responsibilities," the one to which Cardinal Ratzinger had objected in November 1988. Archbishop Oscar Lipscomb, now the chairman of the Committee on Doctrine, cited a March 11 letter from Ratzinger, (following a personal meeting in Rome) in which the German Cardinal expressed satisfaction "with the way in which the Bishops' Conference had chosen to deal with this matter." Lipscomb's committee subsequently made linguistic changes in its draft to accommodate Ratzinger. For example, whereas the draft spoke of bishops' teaching authority "exercised in the name of the Church," the final reading said that this authority "is exercised in the name of Christ." This change, and others of its nature, was made to tighten the language, especially as it related to protecting the authority of bishops.

While it is correct to say that Ratzinger, after the March meeting in Rome, moved out of the way and was no longer an obstacle to the NCCB in its desire to publish this document, it is not fair to say he approved of it. Very little discussion at Seton Hall met the substantive Ratzinger challenge head-on. Accompanying the Cardinal's letter to Lipscomb was a four-page critique of the NCCB draft, which in some ways is stronger than the remarks sent earlier to the Bishops' Conference by his secretary, Archbishop Bavone. Ratzinger's major questions remained the following:

1. What good can come from "unduly juridicizing" the dialogue between bishops and theologians?

2. Is there not danger in giving the impression that bishops and theologians are on an equal footing and that their interests in dialogue are similar?

3. In speaking of the "authority" of the theologian, does not the NCCB run the risk of legitimating within the Church a second teaching authority, when in truth the only authority Catholic theologians have is from their canonical mission granted them by hierarchy?—and when the primary concern of the bishop is the authenticity of the doctrine taught, not the theologies explaining it?

4. Will not the proposed "committee to screen complaints" insulate theologians from criticism and "hinder the faithful from bringing to the bishop their legitimate concerns regarding particular teachings"?

5. Does the procedure not make the bishop's task of guarding the faith more difficult, making him "the villain" if his dialogue is considered unsatisfactory, and does it not provide dissenting theologians with a respectable platform for promoting their views more widely?

6. Does not the bishop alone, especially on subjects already dealt with by Magisterium, have the unique and ultimate responsibility for making judgments in doctrinal conflicts, a responsibility (says Ratzinger) "which must be clearly acknowledged not only theoretically but also practically and procedurally?"

Unquestionably, the Lipscomb committee, in response to these questions, fine-tuned the language to limit the potential misinterpretations or the improper use of the document. But, when all is said and done, the "Doctrinal Responsibilities" statement still juridicizes the relations of unequals and, by the very nature of the procedure, institutionalizes parity between bishops and theologians. This document has the built-in defects of a formalized marriage contract, tilting the relationship away from its fundamental givens and from the typical free play of matrimony toward ambiguity of roles and legalistic determinations likely to be made to suit a popular mood rather than the well-being of the organic relationship itself. At this moment in Church history, the academic establishment favors theologians over bishops and a variety of theological opinions, too, over cohesive religious truth. As the Ordinary of one of the country's most prestigious sees said to me prior to the June 16th meeting: "I think any type of statement such as this would be dangerous to the relationship between the bishops and theologians. My fundamental objection is that I fear that the juridicization of the relationship between the bishops and theologians will prove detrimental to the status of bishops." The bishop becomes a facilitator in his diocese, not the legislator or judge of matters Catholic.

Obviously, Archbishop Lipscomb and most bishops think otherwise. Certainly the June 16 vote represents a victory for the Joseph Cardinal Bernardin–Archbishop John May leadership of the NCCB. It presumes that dialogue will sift out the clear meaning of particular Church teaching, that the rights of inquiry are more important at this time than doctrinal precision, and that more peaceful relations between bishops and theologians will be the natural result. Other assumptions also underlie what is clearly the present institutional policy of the Catholic Church in the United States: that all is well between the hierarchy and theologians, that the state of the Church itself is quite good, that whatever tensions exist are created by so-called conservative Catholics, and that the governing authority of bishops is not to be used against dissenters in a coercive manner, although it may properly be so used against conservatives.

One aspect of the problem is illustrated by the solid bishop who praised the document profusely on TV, calling it a means of cementing good relations with theologians. The lights were no sooner off and the camera stopped running than he turned to a reporter on the sidelines to say: "This document is going to cause a lot of problems."

Bishop Austin Vaughan was a lonely figure again. This time at the June 1989 meeting, when he asked for clarity about the line in the "Doctrinal Responsibilities" document which suggested that bishops' theological consultants "be selected from as many segments as possible on the spectrum of acceptable theological opinion." Would a theologian be acceptable, he asked, if he did not believe in Mary's virginity or in the moral doctrine embodied in *Humanae Vitae*, or favored women's ordination and selective direct abortions? At a later press conference one prelate responded to a similar question by saying that those opinions would today be contrary to the teaching of the Church. However, is such a theologian acceptable to bishops today? Many present-day episcopal consultants do hold similar views. Does "today" for a Catholic bishop mean that the above-mentioned teachings will change? Many theological consultants to the NCCB really think so.

During the Seton Hall meeting several bishops stressed the congenial bishop-theologian relationship as the reason for institutionalizing ongoing juridical dialogue. Archbishop Lipscomb went so far as to say: "I would like to think that the Curran affair

188

might have had a different outcome if such a process had been in place very early on." One wonders how close these views are to reality, considering the recent reactions of theologians in the Western World to the new oath of fidelity demanded of future appointees to theology posts. What bishop reading the annual proceedings of CTSA could come away with the impression that all is well in the American theological community? Notre Dame's Ralph McInerney says the theologians he knows could not take the fidelity oath without lying. What makes anyone think that structured dialogue will soothe the savage breasts of their disciples? When Richard McBrien feels free to question Avery Dulles in a left-handed manner for the latter's call for submission by theologians to Rome's oath of fidelity, the theological household cannot be so pacific, after all, as Archbishop May would have us believe. One would also think that Rome's withdrawal of important imprimaturs would be red flag enough to bishops.

But more important than the state of American theology is the question: What happens when a bishop runs into doctrinal dissent within his own household, in the public forum, and before his very face? Not long ago (April 5, 1989) *Education Weekly,* a Washington-based publication, reported how a woman professor of theology at Chicago's Mundelein Seminary told the 1989 convention of the National Catholic Education Association that serious dissent from Church teaching is often necessary "for the sake of the gospel." And because the Church's rationale for its teaching "does not reflect Jesus Christ and is unjust and untruthful, we are bound to examine," she said, "both what the Church teaches and what nags at us that we cannot accept." In defending her feminist cause, she received loud applause when she said: "Jesus proclaimed God's love. He did not appoint a pope or ordain anyone." The weekly concluded its report as follows: "Cardinal Bernardin responded at the session that the Church would be unable to deal with Ms. Graff's criticisms until it resolved changes in the mission and function of the Church that have been discussed in the wake of the Second Vatican Council." Is this the proper episcopal response? And how would structured dialogue change the patently antimagisterial views of the seminary professor in question?

Finally, there was an interesting byplay at Seton Hall which says something about the U.S.-Rome relationship. While Cardinal Ratzinger declared "no contest" over the "Doctrinal Responsibilities" position of the U.S. bishops, even though he thought the document denigrated the episcopal office, the Americans were not so apathetic about the Holy See's gestures toward converted Lefebvrites. Rome's norms for returning members of the excommunicated sects are more lenient than U.S. bishops would prefer, sometimes giving permission for the Tridentine Mass directly over the head of a reluctant local bishop. Anti-Roman feelings among bishops over the bypass, and the general ambiguity of the norms themselves, spilled over at closed meetings, even though Lefebvrites, converted or no, are hardly a major threat to the U.S. Church.

THE REMARKABLE ADDRESS OF ARCHBISHOP MAY

Ten days before the Seton Hall meeting (June 7, 1989) the president of the NCCB addressed the annual convention of the Catholic Theological Society of America in his own St. Louis Archdiocese. He quickly focused on the complaint made that the archbishops in the Roman meeting did not defend their theologians. Archbishop May explained: "The reason that no one pursued this issue in defense of the theologians in the United States is that the soundness of our relationship with you seemed so obvious, so taken for granted, so unquestionable among us." He praised those theologians who assisted in the drafting of the peace and economic pastorals and assured his audience that "you have the strong and grateful support of your bishops." Apparently oblivious of the American theologians that Rome has censured (to single only a major source of criticism), he attacked critics of modern theologians as quasi-McCarthyites, who make sweeping and generalized accusations without appropriate evidence. His substantive judgment was expressed as follows: "Very bluntly, I think the Church in the United States suffers from too many anxious, warning voices that would divide bishops against theologians."[12]

This address was delivered to a convention which before it completed its deliberations "overwhelmingly" supported Charles Curran in his contest with bishops, called for the CTSA Board to address the issues raised against Magisterium by Bernard Haring and 162 other German-speaking dissenters, and whose president publicly expressed the Society's anxiety over Rome's prescribed "oath of fidelity" for theologians.[13]

This is the Society whose one-time president declared (1974) the institutional Church "out of phase with the demands of the times," and also asserted (1976) that Vatican II implicitly taught the legitimacy of dissent, which in 1977 published *Human Sexuality*, a book censured by the Holy See and the U.S. bishops' conference, which denied (1978) that there was any valid reason why women should not be ordained priests. Its leading members have consistently opposed Rome's disciplining of dissenting theologians (even Hans Küng) and have contributed numerous articles, books, reviews, and lectures to general audiences in support of dissent. The CTSA has also conferred its highest annual award on a variety of virulent critics of Church teaching and the Magisterium which proposes it as true.

What is doubly ironic about Archbishop May's presentation is that it was made to an audience that for twenty years has declared itself out from under episcopal supervision, also that it directed fire at scholars who have consistently claimed membership in the Catholic academic community because they acknowledge their subordination to bishops' authority. Now, apparently, the "outs" are "in." Even more strangely, in one of May's footnotes to the original manuscript distributed at the CTSA meeting, the Archbishop named three scholars that he would consider irresponsible and who have created "a cloud of fear that would poison the air in which we do our work." They were philosopher Ralph McInerney of Notre Dame, political scientist Fr. James Schall, S.J., of

Georgetown, and historian James Hitchcock of St. Louis University, all critics of dissent surely, but all recognized scholars, too, and indefatigable supporters of the teaching Church. The footnote did not appear in the *Origins* reprint, indicating that May belatedly reconsidered its significance.

THE 1989 MEETING WITH THE POPE

On March 8–11, 1989, the active cardinals and more than thirty other American archbishops met with John Paul II and leading members of the Roman Curia to discuss the ongoing problems of the U.S. Church. First requested by the NCCB president in 1986, then insisted upon by the Pope, the high level visitation was intended by the Americans to help John Paul II understand the U.S. Church better and to offset the picture painted (so the leaders said) by "conservatives" of a sagging, divided, and frequently rebellious Catholic body. The NCCB leaders tried to back away from the meeting after John Paul II's 1987 visit with them in Los Angeles, lest a special trip to Rome might look like a confrontation or a chastisement. The Dutch Synod of 1980 was an example of the one, and the 1986 meeting of John Paul II with Brazilian bishops, though more friendly, was an effort to rein in bishops overly smitten with the excesses of liberation theology. The U.S. leadership simply wanted to chat with the Pope, but when they suggested that NCCB elect the participants, the Pope said archbishops only, and when they proposed that "evangelization within the American context" be the subject matter, the Pope added "with special stress on the bishop's role as teacher of the faith." Although an unfriendly Jesuit critic suggested that sitting archbishops were an easier audience for the Pope (he chose half of them), the more relevant fact is that under Church law (Cn. 436) archbishops are responsible for overseeing the faith and ecclesiastical discipline of dioceses within their province and are obligated to inform the Pope of any abuses and to visit a neighboring see in their province should it be neglected by the local bishop.

The Roman summit meeting seems to have been in fact what the participants called it—a success. The words used to describe the discussions which followed ten archepiscopal presentations were "candor," "conviction," "kindness," and "cordiality." The announced euphoria resulted partially from the low expectations of both the American and Roman sides. Joseph Cardinal Bernardin, comoderator for the visitors, made it clear that the conference was not designed to be action-oriented but was merely a friendly discussion of the Catholic situation in the United States from two differing perspectives. He anticipated a better Roman understanding of the difficulties faced by U.S. bishops and a modicum of patience with their strategy for dealing with them. The calculated irenicism did not entirely mute the different perceptions attendees had of the benefits to derive from the sessions. One West Coast archbishop said tensions with Rome still existed, an Eastern prelate told an audience that there were no real differences between the Pope and the U.S. hierarchy, while a Midwesterner thought that he and his peers were vindicated. If one Roman informant can be trusted, even John Paul II was relieved that no fireworks occurred to scandalize the faithful further. The Pope's confidence in the future apparently rests on his ability to choose the right bishops. As one wag on St. Peter's square summarized the meeting vis-à-vis the Americans: "If they're happy, fine, but wait till they see the next ten bishops."

Sideline observers of the Roman conference found most interesting the manner in which the U.S. bishops spoke of their local churches. No one did this more enthusiastically than John Cardinal O'Connor, whose summary of American impediments to episcopal teaching was lucid and scholarly. O'Connor was forthright in pointing out the failure of the Church (here he could only mean the hierarchy) to prepare the faithful for the meaning and sense of Vatican II, the four years of waiting for *Humanae Vitae*, liturgical experiments run wild, and the rise of paratroopers for a new Church in the persons of Xavier Rynne, theological confounders, radical feminists, publishers of ambiguous catechetical texts, and distorters of Catholic college teaching. The controlling pragmatism of the secular culture, especially of the media, was not helpful either, the New York Archbishop said, and as if that hindrance were not enough, a bishop had reason to worry whether his particularized battles on behalf of authoritative teaching would enjoy the support of Rome or of the NCCB machinery. On this latter point Cardinal O'Connor did not provide specifics. Neither did he allude to differences some bishops have had worldwide with policies and definitions of the Holy See.

However, specifics were provided by Joseph Cardinal Bernardin in his summary published in *Origins* of the results of the summit meeting. Without proposing any concrete solution of the differences, he listed a number of what he called "issues"—the nature and conduct of religious life, First Confession of children, inclusive liturgical language, altar girls, General Absolution, fallen away Catholics, annulments, Catholic higher education, seminaries, clerical celibacy, and so forth. These "issues" surely have divided bishops from bishops, bishops from Rome, at times evoking strong feelings because some of the controversies have involved doctrine or universal policies of the Church that reinforce doctrinal demands. Bishops who would, for example, overturn Rome's policies on First Confession, General Absolution, dispensations from the priesthood or annulments (and there are bishops who make it clear in one way or another that they disagree with Rome on these matters) help create or perpetuate uncertainty about which demands of Catholic life really bind.

Cardinal Bernardin proposed as a response to these ongoing issues more dialogue, better arguments, further study, leaving "the issues" unresolved or open to suspected future relaxation for those inclined to think so. The Church will survive altar girls (whatever their presence does to the pool of altar boys), but it is not going to be credible in the long run to believing Catholics if the Church looks like it is really dissolving sacramental marriages under the guise of updating annulment procedures.

One interesting paragraph of the Bernardin summary concerned traditionalists:

> Concern was expressed as to the rationale for placating a small but vocal number of people who side step the local bishop's authority and, at times, seek to undermine that authority. They would appear to present a distorted image of liturgical life in the U.S. and absorb a disproportional amount of time that could be better given to other more urgent matters. In regard to the Tridentine Mass, it was made clear that the hesitation to permit its more frequent use is not with the Mass per se, which was the center of the Church's liturgical life for so many centuries. Rather, it is the attitude of some of those who request the Mass toward the local ecclesial authority, as well as toward many of the developments introduced by the Second Vatican Council.

No one who has ever run a parish or a diocesan agency or a catechetical center or a theology department would disagree with Cardinal Bernardin's view of traditionalists, particularly of Tridentines. Whether converted Lefebvrites or no, they are often self-righteous, hardnosed, and bitter, and in pursuing their narrow religious interests they are frequently a nuisance. Why they think that Mass in an old Latin form with the priest facing the back wall of a Church is worth their anger or their pestiferous behavior is difficult to understand. Still, traditionalism, even of the Tridentine variety, is not a major problem for the U.S. Church, or for bishops either. One is reminded of an old Depression adage among farmers, which went something like this: When wolves are ravaging your crops and wounding your children, it's no time to be worrying about flies. Furthermore, the Tridentine Mass has been restored by the Holy See as a favor and under normal Church rules is to be permitted to those to whom it applies. Yet, in American dioceses (at least initially) the "favor" was granted only under the strictest constraints, at times ungenerously by bishops who themselves have played loosely with strict norms set by Rome for the First Confession of children, General Absolution, annulments, and so forth.

Bernard Cardinal Gantin, comoderator of the summit meeting, gave no synthesis of "the issues" for the Roman side. Had Gantin, the Prefect of the Congregation for Bishops, responsible for nominating all the bishops appointed by the Pope throughout the world, chosen to do so, his summation would perforce have included many observations of Vatican officials relative to the reason John Paul II had the Americans come to Rome.

1. Cardinal Ratzinger made the major point that bishops have to a large extent acquiesced in the reduction of their office to that of moderator of theological differences, becoming dispensers of pious advice rather than witnesses to binding truth. Catechesis, he observed, has largely been turned over to professionals. The price of exalting the competence of theologians over that of bishops has—in his words—"begun perhaps to erode the faith itself." Ratzinger called upon bishops to be on guard and to be martyrs to the truth, if this is what is required.

2. Antonio Cardinal Innocenti, the Pope's chief catechist, asked bishops to guarantee that priests, especially teachers and seminary professors, present Church doctrines "without distortions or erroneous subjective interpretations."

3. Jerome Cardinal Hamer, who currently deals with religious institutes, following his stint with Ratzinger's Congregation, reminded the U.S. archbishops that religious orders are not autonomous of their bishop connection.

4. Eduardo Cardinal Gagnon, president of the Pope's Council on the Family, proved to be as directive as Ratzinger. He warned bishops about allowing programs of Natural Family Planning to be interfaced with methods of artificial contraception, about their sex education guidelines which the Holy See wants revised, about judges on their marriage tribunals who do not believe in the indissolubility of marriage, about marriage preparation courses that do not reflect *Familiaris Consortio*, about the ordination of married deacons who have been sterilized, about ministries to the divorced that have degenerated into dating services for Catholics who are not free to marry, and about people on bishops' staffs who reject *Humanae Vitae* and are prochoice on abortion.

5. Martinez Cardinal Somalo, who oversees divine worship and the sacraments for the universal Church, reminded the prelates that they are the principal protectors of liturgical norms, issued precisely and in writing by Rome, and that "bishops who do not exercise their authority in a timely way" create difficulties —over the use of "exclusive language" (which "touches on biblical and theological questions"), the use of altar girls, modification of approved liturgical prayers that express the faith, the proper order of First Confession and First Communion for children, and so forth.

6. Whether Catholic colleges are really Catholic, whether training of future priests is always wholesome, whether professional accreditation of seminaries has not actually lowered theological standards, whether a generalized concept of ministry has replaced a specific concept of the ordained ministry, whether in dealing with priestly formation celibacy is treated as a problem— these are matters of concern that emerged when formation of future U.S. priests was analyzed by William Cardinal Baum, the Pope's man for Catholic education.

7. Achille Cardinal Silvestrini, the chief justice of the Church's supreme court, objected to the 37,538 annulments granted by the U.S. tribunals in 1985, 80 percent of the world's total nullities. Of the American cases accepted, only 3 percent of the decisions were negative. Silvestrini complained: "Various tribunals in the United States have introduced their own method (of adjudication) not fully in conformity with the Code of Canon Law." Here the reference was to nullities improperly based on "psychic incapacity" (Cn. 1095). The Italian Cardinal made three particular charges: American judges were translating what modern psychologists call "immaturity" into the Church's "canonical immaturity," an entirely different concept; they were also confusing marital difficulty with incapacity for marriage; and equating the unhappy marriage with the invalid marriage.

197

One of Silvestrini's indictments received little press comment: "grave violations of the right of defense." Historically, under canon law procedures the "Defender of the Bond" was an important officer of the tribunal. His job was to defend the indissolubility of what appeared to be an indissoluble sacramental marriage. Because Christ's clear words "what God has joined together let no man put asunder"[14] represented a seemingly infalliable and irreversible judgment, the Church has always placed the burden of proof against indissolubility on the plaintiff, with the "Defender of the Bond" named in Catholic law as the official adversary. The New Code of Canon Law (No. 1432), for example, says he is "bound by office to propose and clarify everything which can be reasonably adduced against nullity or dissolution." Complaints have reached the Church's Court of Appeals in Rome (the Rota), often from spouses who object to attempts to declare their long-established Catholic marriages null and void, that the system which once stood for indissolubility now stands for annulment, the burden of proof of indissolubility now being placed on defendants, not on Church authority. Furthermore, while bishops subsidize at great expense their diocesan tribunals (and so the annulment process), spouses who choose to fight the dissolution of their marriage are often greeted with hostility by tribunal personnel (especially if they appeal to Rome), are denied access to appropriate documents, are forced to expend large amounts of their own money to defend what once they thought the Church defended freely. Cardinal Silvestrini reminded his audience that "bishops, even more than the officials who make up the tribunals, are responsible for the administration of justice," and so he counselled them to be "vigilant."

The U.S. bishops defended their tribunals, pointing to the bad American family situation and their own caution in accepting cases for nullity assessment. After the Roman meeting Cardinal Bernardin invited Cardinal Silvestrini to visit the United States for an examination of the American church's tribunal procedures. The critical issue, however, is not the procedures as such, but the substance of the Church's doctrine and law concerning consummated sacramental Catholic marriages.

What was not discussed in the Bernardin summation of "the issues" is doctrinal dissent or the extent of its influence on Catholic formation programs, including those under the direct control of bishops or within the family of bishops, itself. Cardinal O'Connor made several references to it, but Cardinal Bernardin did not, in his summary, list dissent as an "issue." He chose instead to call for clarification of the differences between faith and theological expressions, of the authority of some Church teachings as against others, of the limits of compromise with real life situations, and of the mechanics of conscience formation whenever Church teaching is involved. These were questions easily answered by pre-Vatican II theologians who readily agreed that faith propositions were true, even if they were not defined solemnly or with an added note of infallibility, but they become impossible to answer when academics doubt that any religious proposition can be called true, let alone be proposed infallibly. Even though Rome directed bishops to "placate" Lefebvrites and apologized for the excesses in liturgical and doctrinal matters which provided them with an excuse for schism, it has not manifested toleration of the pick-and-choose Catholicism, dear to the dissenters in Catholic higher education, in religious orders, and in some diocesan offices. Yet, these are the dissenting groups which enjoy the favor of the bishops' national machinery and of individual bishops, not the traditionalists or the outspoken defenders of Magisterium. Virulent dissent was not raised by Bernardin as an "issue" worthy of the serious attention of the U.S. hierarchy.

Year by year pick-and-choose Catholicism continues to be embedded still further in the subculture of the contemporary Church, helped along by assertions (as in Rome) that American Catholics are a freedom-loving people, used to pluralism and "compromise" (to borrow Archbishop Roach's word), and likely to look upon the divine right of bishops as being (in the phrasing of Archbishop May) "as outmoded as the divine right of kings." U.S. Catholics were already in 1962 full-blooded Americans when they were overwhelmingly believing and practicing Catholics. Their bishops then expected no less of them. The recent Council did not dispense Americans from Church norms. What the archbishops did not discuss in any depth was the seedy side of contemporary American culture—the violence, terrorism, moral relativism, sex obsessiveness, crass materialism—features that have overtaken the Catholic subculture, including the lives of many clergy and religious. Also commonplace in our society is a certain intellectual dishonesty which attempts to pass off radical rejection of important norms and denials of religious truths as mere revisionism or updating. While Americans were described as a religious people, little reference was made to the fact that this country's religion is usually defined by poll-takers as generic, civil, philanthropic, neighborly, and earthbound. Few leaders dare any more either to call this a Christian nation or to say that it is any less sympathetic than it used to be to the Catholic Church with its emphasis on dogma, moral absolutes, sacrifice in worship and mode of living, personal holiness, and eternal life. Nor does the "conservative" upsurge among American youth, often of a law-and-order political variety, give promise of offsetting the pick-and-choose Catholicism which within one generation has been inculcated in their lives by many Catholic infrastructures.

What does this dissent say about the purity of the Church's ministry on behalf of holiness and salvation? Bishops cannot control people's response to faith, certainly not their behavior. But is there not institutionalized scandal in teaching which leads to doubts about faith and in instruction which justifies the choice of sinful ways? Bishops cannot remove all of the impediments to evangelization but they can eliminate many of those within their jurisdiction. And by molding a strong Catholic identity, they create defense mechanisms for their people who live amid the temptations instigated by world, flesh, and devil.

Granted that "Catholicity" and "state of grace" are not measurable, the otherworldly side of the Church makes it possible for revisionist commentators or reactionaries to exaggerate or denigrate the effects of good and bad teaching on human lives. Yet, few are bold enough any more to doubt that Vatican II occasioned a revolution within the Church. Some scholars wish it to go further because they believe that faith and morality are human creations anyway and that the time has come for the Catholic Church to assimilate the Protestant Reformation. Some American Catholics who helped energize the original rebellions here can be heard today bemoaning the results of the Council on U.S. Catholicism. "They've gone too far," seems to be their belated cry. But European scholars—Henri de Lubac, Hans Urs von Balthasar, Hubert Jedin, now Walter Kasper—recognized much earlier the excesses that were being fashioned by their academic peers. These latter understood from the very first the nature and extent of the Catholic crisis and along the way compared the passivity of the episcopate in the face of the post-Vatican II onslaught to the failure of bishops before and after the rise of Martin Luther. The use of Catholic institutions and leadership to turn sixteenth-century Catholics into Lutherans was not dissimilar to the effect of the new catechesis and secularized lifestyles on millions of today's sincere believers, who by no stretch of imagination can be dismissed as reactionaries or conservatives.

What few people speak about any more is how dissent, whole or partial, now after twenty-five years, goes beyond the words spoken in classrooms. When Charles Curran says, "Why pick on me?" he speaks out of the assurance that little Currans are everywhere in the Church machinery. The pressure on bishops (and on everyone else) to go along with the dominant trend within their administrative or academic households has become a powerful force. Cardinal O'Connor in his presentation before John Paul II spoke in passing about uncertain support for episcopal defenders of the faith from the NCCB, or even from Rome. Prior to the Council the pressure favored conformity to Church teaching. In 1961, even Richard McCormick and Charles Curran endorsed Church teaching on birth control. On the other hand, the Paulist Press published a book in 1988 by these two authors, called *Dissent*, which not only approves of contraceptive sterilization, but suggests (p. 534) that one hundred bishops favored their position over Rome's.

Years ago (1972 and thereafter) the Holy See established "pontifical" catechetical institutes as an alternative to the dubious catechesis going on in many places. Most American bishops were unfriendly to such institutes and in 1987 Rome withdrew permission for the use of the name "pontifical" by such institutes—as a result of American pressure. Bishops who have problems with the present annulment practice of their tribunals find it difficult to tighten local procedures, since complaints to Rome during several pontificates have not resulted in corrective action. Some bishops at odds with NCCB policies have no interest in participating in the work of episcopal committees or come to realize they are not welcome on important episcopal committees. Other bishops are reluctant to conform to Roman norms (on *Humanae Vitae*, altar girls, General Absolution, religious life, Catholic higher education, etc.) because such implementation will certainly spark negative reactions from their presbyterates, many of whose members were trained under Catholic auspices to consider disagreements with Rome or their bishop as legitimate options. Conversely, dissenting academics and religious, some of whom write regularly for diocesan newspapers and well-known Catholic magazines, pursue their independent course without fear of correction or expressed displeasure from bishops. Catechetical and theological texts are published lacking appropriate imprimaturs without any noticeable challenge to their authenticity from bishops, who know they would have a fight on their hands if they attempted to enforce the requirements of canon law. When in February 1989 Rome issued a declaration requiring an oath of fidelity to Church teaching by all new teachers of faith and morals at the college level and above, the reaction of leading academics was one of indignation and announced rebellion.

John Paul II, and millions of his flock, go beyond those who merely wish to stem the current revolution at its present level. The fundamental issue for the Pope is the truth of revealed doctrine. As the U.S. archbishops were preparing to return home from the March meeting, the Pope, quoting one of their own, said that bishops may not be successful, but they must be faithful. Continued John Paul: "We are the guardians of something given and given to the Church universal; something which is not the result of reflection, however competent, on cultural and social questions of the day, and is not merely the best path among many, but the one and only path to salvation."

We live in a society saturated with personal and social values based on unverified or dubious conclusions of experimental psychology and sociology. The deductions of these social sciences about human nature, about moral norms, about institutions and the function of the common good, about marriage and sex, about religion itself, even about mankind's reason for living are often diametrically opposed to the teachings of any religion which is centered in God or derives from a revelation attributed to Jesus Christ. Modern society, largely influenced by social science theories, rejects such notions as personal responsibility, self-denial, directive authority, chastity in or out of marriage, obedience, sin, guilt or punishment, dogma, immortality, "the other world," etc., rendering the teachings of any respectable church, especially one with a Catholic sense, jejune if not seemingly incredible or ridiculous.

In such secular circumstances, John Paul II's "givens," which he holds to be true because they come from Christ, enjoy little credence today, and even less do they have social support. If for no other reason than the contemporary social situation, the Church must reestablish its own defense mechanisms and institutionalize in the lives of its adherents its own world and otherworld view. Since Vatican II, however, the Church and its American leadership have been awash in social science theories which strip catechesis of any Catholic meaning, which debase the hierarchical priesthood of status, role, and commitment, and which thereby make the Church more an instrument of human aspirations than of Christ's Kingdom of the Father.

One would think that after a quarter of a century bishops would be happy to take their problems to their Holy Father and to seek his help in restoring authentic teaching and good order to the Church. Merely to visit Rome seeking understanding of our deficiencies and to leave without a program of active remedy reminds one of the faulty wisdom of another day and another society—"Prosperity is just around the corner." Only the most irresponsible critics expect hierarchy to wash the Church's dirty linen in public, or to satisfy media lust for ecclesiastical fisticuffs. John Paul II told the archbishops he came to listen and he did, to ponder in the aftermath where he goes from there.

Is there a plan to reform the Church in accordance with the real intent of Vatican II? Are bishops prepared to unite with John Paul II in the effort? Are they prepared to reclaim and to exercise properly the authority which belongs to them alone, and to follow the lead of the Pope in restoring obedience as well as faith in the churches they govern? The faithful need not know the details, but they could use assurance from Christ's vicars that appropriate reforms are in the making. The credibility of the Church for those who sacrifice their lives to its gospel requires no less.

NOTES

1. Romans 3:8.
2. *NC News*, February 19, 1982.
3. Matthew Murphy, Betraying Bishops, published by Ethics and Public Policy Center, 1987, p. 76.
4. *Theological Studies*, March 1974.
5. *Homiletic and Pastoral Review*, April 1982.
6. See Fr. Michael Place's booklet on *"Human Conscience,"* published by the *Cana Conference of Chicago* with Cardinal Bernardin's permission (no date, but circulated in 1988).
7. *L'Osservatore Romano*, March 10, 1988, p. 1 (translated by *NC News*).
8. *Origins*, March 24, 1988, p. 708.
9. See the full comments of Dr. May and Fr. Lawler in the June 1988 issue of the *Newsletter of the Fellowship of Catholic Scholars*.
10. In a December 17, 1987, letter to the people of his archdiocese, reprinted in the *International Review of Natural Family Planning*, Winter 1987 (pp. 310–17).

11. Matthew 10:34.
12. *Origins,* June 22, 1989, pp. 88–89.
13. *St. Louis Review,* June 17, 1989, p. 1.
14. Matthew 19:6.

PART FIVE

The Resurrection
of the Vatican II Church

PROLOGUE
The Miracle of Peter

THERE IS A STORY told about St. Peter which bears on our contemporary ecclesial dilemma. It is an apocryphal tale by all reckoning, passed around in the second century about how the Big Fisherman ran away from Nero's lions, even as other Christians were dying for the Faith. According to the account, Peter, already the pastor of the Church community at Rome, was scurrying down the Appian Way when he ran into Jesus. Caught by surprise but still direct of speech, the Apostle is alleged to have asked, "Quo vadis, Domine?" (Where are you going, Lord?) To which Jesus replied, "I am going to Rome to be crucified." "But you've already been crucified," said Peter. "Yes, I know," was the answer, "but now I go to Rome to be crucified again."

The story ends on a positive note. Coming to his senses as if from a dream, the first of Rome's chief shepherds heard the message. He turned around and headed back for Rome, where he was crucified, his blood and that of other martyrs becoming the seed of Christianity's world-wide expansion. It would not be the first time, even if the story were true, that this pastor or that, headed in the wrong direction, was turned around by the Spirit of God moving through the Church.

In the present crisis within the affluent Churches of the West, it is a good assumption that the Holy Spirit is with the popes of this century, all of whom have demonstrated a touch of greatness, all of whom have been men of intense piety. There is, too, a remarkable continuity in those recent pontificates, in their common teaching. Paul VI and John Paul II differ only in style, in tone of voice, and perhaps in the latter's readiness publicly to instruct and rebuke dissenters and their supporters. And, although John XXIII is alleged to have grandfathered a belated protestantization of the Church, his successors never cease to remind audiences that the Jolly Pope's classic lines at the opening of the Second Vatican Council (October 11, 1962) were: "The greatest concern of the Ecumenical Council is this—that the sacred deposit of Christian doctrine should be effectively guarded and taught." Clearly, therefore, if Christians are to think with Christ and His Church, a sensible process by which this can be accomplished must begin and Church authority must take the lead, not excluding those pastors who are headed in the wrong direction.

SIX

Toward Good Government in the Church as Required by Catholic Tradition and the Second Vatican Council

GOOD GOVERNMENT AND THE ORDER OF THE DAY

WHERE, THEN, is Mother Church going?

Wherever Church government, good or bad, takes her.

Ordinary folk know when government is good or bad. They know when they feel safe in their homes, when they have food on their tables, when their children can grow up to be decent people. They take for granted a certain amount of frailty in leadership, even a little corruption, but they know venality, vice, lawlessness when they see them, when they have to barricade themselves in their own homes for safety's sake or move away to find peace or livelihood.

When a government is good it is the result not only of a decent constitution and legal system, but of good governors who make the system work for the purposes for which the society was created in the first place. Labor is not management, the Church is not the State, and Christianity is not Islam. Yet they share a

211

common feature, namely, a government capable of coordinating special interests or of keeping them in line when they threaten everyone else's general interests. A certain amount of force or threat of force was necessary even in New Testament times to make sure evil did not triumph completely over the good. The young Avery Dulles entered the Church in part because in his circles he wearied of hearing that Christ was a "mild, gentle, even tolerant moralist."

However, good governance involves more than restraining the ambitions and the excesses of those who think with the *National Catholic Reporter*. It involves taking care of the faithful, sustaining them, providing shelter, encouraging initiative, development, and outreach, yet protecting those things which make the faithful one family distinct from all others. A well-run household is a warm place to live, even for the rugged individualist and the "black sheep." Here one usually finds orderliness, moral standards, and obedience, but also more real charity and tolerance, more mercy and forgiveness than is normally found among strangers.

Good governance of the Church is a lived experience, the result of hard work by leaders who have truly Catholic things to say, assisted by efficient and dedicated coworkers with good evangelizing abilities, leaders who can unify their constituencies as the U.S. bishops did successfully between 1840 and 1940. When all is said and done, Catholic purpose and bonding grows out of a common belief in "the message" and from ingrained reliance on obedience to bishops in union with the Pope. Without a clearly identifiable faith and a disciplined body of parishioners there cannot be a vital and growing Catholic Church. Without obedience there can be no religious community, no hierarchy, no vows, and especially no authentic faith. As the Gospel says: "The disciples went off and did as Jesus had commanded."[1]

The Church, called the "mother" of Christ's household by the recent Council, may be a little more difficult to govern today with the presence of a TV camera peering into ecclesial closets under the guiding hands of media czars whose religious sense is far from

Catholic. The Church surely suffers, and bishops too, from networks which roll out as part of their entertainment programs a stream of Catholic iconoclasts, complainers, and dissidents who have little in common with Sunday churchgoers, i.e., those who find purpose and warmth within the Church. Eventually, if only in self-defense, ecclesiastics will find ways to counteract the media masters. But a good TV image is the least of the Church's contemporary difficulties. Catholic infrastructures going their own way contrary to Vatican II's documents and its implementing decrees, bishops who side with breakaway theologians and their institutional confreres, the put-down of "the faithful" in many ecclesiastical circles, these are the well-documented evidence of misdirected governance.

The push by Catholic dissidents for a Church less influenced by the Bishop of Rome and his curial congregations has attracted important segments of Church leadership. It is a theme that plays well in media because academics from Hans Küng to Bernard Cooke to Bernard Haring to Richard McBrien and their many collaborators have poured out reams of propaganda since 1965 belittling papal origins and papal teachings. If U.S. bishops dawdle too long over the temptations placed before our faithful by the dissidents, they will help undermine the credibility of any Church claiming the name Catholic and their own episcopal status as well. The conceptualized new "American Church" under the rubric "privacy" or "freedom of conscience" or "academic freedom" canonizes a popular disrespect for unpopular Church directives, gives special privilege to "veto groups" (academics, religious superiors, etc.) to act outside of prevailing law, and favors restraints or penalties for law-abiding Catholics exercising the freedoms and fulfilling the duties prescribed under canon law when these activities threaten the privileged position of power achieved within the Church by those who claim, however improperly, to represent "the spirit of Vatican II."

The Catholic faithful, especially those blessed with a U.S. baptismal record, also know a good church from a bad one. They know scandal when they see scandal, even if they are part of it. They take for granted the sense of the Church's midday prayer:

> Do good, Lord, to those who are good,
> To the upright of heart,
> But the crooked and those who do evil,
> Drive them away.[2]

Indeed, the Church would be a well-nigh ideal system if it translated the way it prays in its daily eucharistic celebration and hourly liturgy into the way it lives. The U.S. Church has been well served in this regard. Other national Catholic populations have not always been so blessed because their episcopal leadership was tested (sometimes papal leadership) and found wanting.

So where is the present Conference of Catholic Bishops likely to lead Mother Church?

I would like to think where Christ intends her to go, if not today, then tomorrow—making disciples of all nations in God's appointed time and eventually "one fold and one shepherd."

"In God's appointed time" is an important qualification. We Christians must take into account God's providence, neither substituting our judgment for His, nor forgetting that suffering, even of the Church, is a critical element in salvation history. The daily cross of the Church, like that of Christ, is vital to our redemption, even if it is a cross of our own making.

Still, however much God will continue to insist on the things that belong to Him, we as a people must obey the commands that have been imposed by Christ—that we become His disciples by living according to His teaching[3] and that we enter life by keeping His commandments.[4] It is the role of the Church's bishops to make that possible for all who are disposed. People may make the Church look messy, and Christ surely suffered at the hands of His sinful contemporaries. But He did not send His apostles into the ministry to demonstrate their incompetence or their wickedness, although He suffered both. If those apostles and their successors were responsible for His teaching, they were also accountable for

214

the discipline that makes it possible to live the kind of life that the teaching demands.

It makes no sense, therefore, that the Body of Christ should be known for its unsound teaching or its scandalous behavior. It is the function of governance to create the climate which supports believing parishioners in their struggle to live the kind of life Christ prescribes for followers. Ruling is an art, not an exact science, but one of its essentials, beyond reinforcement of norms, is setting limits on tolerable dissonance and misbehavior. That is what legitimate authority is all about in civilized societies, including the right to enforce public law and command obedience. Imperfect churches have existed within the Christian community from the beginning, but at no time in the United States, at least up to now, has false worship of God or denials of Church teaching on matters pertaining to Christian life or eternal salvation been tolerated or held in respect as proper and normal for the believing Church. At no time was it ever conceded that doctrinal "mess" and the immoral lives that result from heterodox teaching are to be the order of the Catholic day.

BLAME THE FALSE PROPHETS, NOT VATICAN II

Permit me to say what I have said many times before, that there was nothing wrong with the Second Vatican Council. It said, and commanded, all the right things. But it did have unexpected dysfunctions because its deliberations were distorted and its documents misused by false prophets (not unknown in Church history) in an effort to refashion the Catholic Church into something it was never intended to be. While the Council quite properly turned the Church in new directions, changemakers seized the opportunity to deny the Church its birthright. But they could not have loosened, in some cases broken, the close ties of several generations to the Church without help from bishops—some during and after the Council siding with the false prophets, others misreading the trouble-makers' intentions, while most sat on the sidelines hoping that the Pope would have the clout to keep the dissidents reasonably in line. Rome tried first by making complaints but without discipline, then promulgated mild censures too late, and afterwards used papal *ad limina* and local lectures to motivate bishops on every continent to the responsibilities of their office—without much help from national episcopal conferences. By 1970 many of these were cuddling with the false prophets.

It is the thesis of this book that the extent of the Catholic disorder has been concealed at the highest levels of the U.S. Church—one documented not only by the research of scholars like Germain Grisez, William May, Ralph McInerney, Fr. Ronald Lawler, O.F.M. Cap., James Schall, S.J., Msgr. William Smith, Joseph Fassio, S.J., Donald Keefe, S.J., James Hitchcock, and many others in the United States (to overlook for the moment the recent anxieties about the Catholic revolution by John Tracy Ellis and Avery Dulles) but also by the fifty documents of the Holy See issued since 1967, including papal encyclicals and exhortations, synodal decrees, and judgments on a variety of doctrinal issues by the Congregation of the Doctrine of the Faith.

The critical issue for the Church of the twenty-first century is not false prophecy per se, which is deep enough, but the present day cover-up of the difficulties by the bishops' national machinery and by more than a few offending bishops.

The majority of the still-going-to-Mass parishioners have been taken for granted, perhaps recklessly. I am speaking of practicing Catholics, generally in or near middle age and beyond, our brothers and sisters perhaps, who believe all that the Church teaches and do the best they can to shape their lives and those of their children accordingly. The shenanigans in the Church following the Council scandalized them. And still do. Far back in my mind are the traditionalists, the privileged upper class Catholics, the political reactionaries, the racists, the ethnocentrics, and all those used as scapegoats for society's and the Church's ills.

I am presently of sufficient age to attend all kinds of gatherings of parishioners, old and new. I now baptize the grandchildren of people I married. It is a good way for a priest to stay young. Do you know what we talk about? More frequently than I care to admit, about what this or that priest, religious, or teacher has done to cool the piety of someone's twenty- to forty-year old off-spring. As I scrutinize the aging faces of people I love, remembering their large families, their daily morning Masses during Lent and their nights spent at parish devotions or apostolic enterprises, the sacrifices they made to give of their little substance toward the cost of a complete Catholic education for their children, I feel helpless to console them. Here are parents and young grandparents who know nothing about secularization or about the psycho-social dislocations that allegedly accompany radical cultural upheaval. They do not even know that ecumenical councils are supposed to have dysfunctional aspects. And, unlike politicized academics, they would have difficulty defining a "liberal" Catholic as against a "conservative" Catholic. They only know what they saw happen to their children within what they thought was a Catholic-protected enclave. They watch Church ties with their young attenuated, the kind of bonds earlier generations of priests and religous had knotted so tightly for their parents and for them.

A SERIOUS MATTER

Why is this leakage a matter of grave concern? Because, for one thing, it represents a lost generation of pious Catholic life to which our American parishes had become accustomed. More importantly perhaps, we face a Church whose relations are presently cold with an age group—the once-hopeful *crème de la crème*—on which so much devotion in the home and in the parish was expended. Without their involvement how can we expect to evangelize successfully the hordes of new immigrants, to say nothing of the extant fallen-aways, who fill up the territories of what used to be called Catholic neighborhoods? Have we really learned anything from the experience of those old-time pastors who were once called "sweet incense to the republic"? They would not have evangelized the earlier newcomers in their rat-infested slums, nor those "hidden" Catholics who always seemed to live on the fringe of the parish, somewhat afraid to be noticed, without hosts of enthusiastic and informed lay people who became the priest's eyes, ears, often his legs and his hands. What would those older aliens and alienated have thought if the Catholic laity they first met were at odds with their pastor, or if they learned that their pastor disagreed with the Pope, or that the religious women were more interested in political causes than in their faith or morals? Those pastors did not go out into the corners of their parishes merely to show human interest or as social workers. They went in to Christianize or reconcile people on the Church's terms. And without the right kind of trained laity in support—the laity that are now dying off—they could not have done that.

Let us face another fact of present-day Catholic life, that which disturbs the faithful whom I love and those whom we must pursue for Christ's sake with love. They no longer see one Church unified around their pastor, their bishop, not even around their pope— Catholic leaders who in their earlier experience were one with each other in faith, worship, and discipline. Their children no longer have a sense of the "true" Church, once the dear possession of their parents. These youngsters, now far from teenage, have lived under Catholic infrastructures which have sowed doubts about matters which Paul VI and John Paul II consider the true Word of God. In the pew, or away, the average Catholic is likely to face any one of four Churches—in addition to the one headquartered in Rome.

There is (1) the "freedom of conscience Church" (sometimes called "the democratic Church") led by partisans of the Hans Küngs and/or the Marcel Lefebvres, which assures the would-be believer that the faith, the morals, and the laws he will obey are his to decide. Then, you have (2) the "human problem solving Church" which insists that Vatican II wanted human problems lifted off the backs of the world's peoples, rather than a repetition of those worn-out abstractions about salvation. Humanity is now the sacred arena, and its Church speaks primarily about the struggle of people for freedom "with little reference to divine mysteries to which the struggle points."[5] One other unexpected post-Vatican II development involves (3) the "There's no going back on the revolution Church." The argument advanced in its favor considers the Council to have been the work of "the Spirit," and that it is this spirit of Vatican II which broke the stranglehold of the hierarchy on the personal lives of Catholics. "Officials" may continue to declare the Catholic line but to no avail. Recently matured Catholics today have the sense to choose their theologians, as once their parents chose their confessors.

Probably the most serious rival to the pope, however, is (4) the "antidogma Church," typified by books like *The Case Against Dogma*, written by a Jesuit in Rome, a church without a constitution from Christ, whose people must be enlightened to accept that "a lot that a bishop has received has not been received from the Lord," that the average Catholic must become aware, painfully if need be, that much of what the bishop teaches is not authentic Christianity.[6]

Many good Catholics, even those still going to Sunday Mass regularly, have fitted one or the other of these "Churches" into their new "Catholic" identity. Had these substantive disagreements been widespread on the first Pentecost Sunday, Peter and Paul would never have made it into the New Testament, let alone into the history books. And we would never have had the catacombs.

The task ahead, therefore, calls for a restoration of Catholic unity, something which is not possible until Church leadership reestablishes its ability to defend Catholic teaching against schismatical or heretical tendencies, and to delimit the scandalous conduct of those who minister to the faithful in the Church's name. The scandalmongers pooh-pooh the old Church system in the United States (which was highly successful), only to impose their own system on the Church body, one which in a few years has manifested a ruthlessness rarely found in the homes of bishops. The power struggle, which the bishops at the moment are losing, is no small matter of Catholic concern, and at this moment unresolved in favor of Magisterium.

THE BUCK STOPS WITH BISHOPS

Bishops must reassess their lack of authority over the impact of these defections or their part in their proliferation. If Catholic structures are not administered in full accord with the basic thrust of magisterium, including its defining role, they have no right to function in the Church's name.

I do not maintain that "runaway" academics, or bishops for that matter, fully explain our present troubles. Nor do I think that heavy doses of episcopal authority, after years of nonuse for defense purposes, will solve the Church's problems in the short run. But the only promise of reasonably restored unity and respectable Catholic performance is the proper exercise of episcopal authority based on solid Catholic principles, and exercised in close harmony with the Pope. Catholic doctrine cannot institutionalize itself, and the best the Pope can do is to supervise the American effort. He cannot govern every local church. He has authority to appoint bishops who will do their job well and to weed out bishops who have no intention of following the universal laws of the Church.

All this is easier said than done, of course, and anyone who has ever taken over a dying parish, or a dead one, knows quite well the amount of effort and pain that goes into its revitalization. A divided or a delinquent diocese is a much headier challenge, and no local pastor has arrayed against him the powerful enemies a bishop faces today; sometimes within his own chancery office.

GOVERNANCE OF THE CHURCH BY UNFORMED GOVERNED CAN EQUAL LAWLESSNESS

While bishops are being terrorized by hostile thrusts from behind convent walls and ivied halls of learning, pugnacious bishops are hardly the appropriate episcopal response. Satisfactory

220

instead would be bishops whom everyone knows to be in tune with Rome (and who cannot therefore be played off against the Pope) and bishops who know how to bishop. (Bishop dissenters are the Pope's special problem.) With all due respect to Archbishop May, the U.S. hierarchy has a revolution on its hands, partly of its own making. Denial of the crisis does them little good and additional dialogue with dissidents, after twenty years of trying, has only left the Church antagonists convinced that their way of mastery works. If U.S. presidents with their high-priced negotiators and military might have done little to free hostages or Cuba, or Nicaragua either, their counterparts in the hierarchy should know by now that virulent recalcitrants are not likely by persuasion alone to restore their Catholic institutions to the Church, of which bishops are the visible heads.

I am not too sure how many of the bishops have really insisted with authority that this be done. Colleges have declared themselves nondenominational with hardly a by-your-leave to the local bishop, whose predecessors helped them get their start and promoted their development. The ones who have suffered the consequences of these alienations have been ordinary believers. Yet only bishops, not the faithful, could have prevented the breakaway. Had Cardinal Spellman stayed alive and well, Woodstock College would never have come into New York, only to cause scandal and die. Almost overnight bishops decided that Charles Curran did not belong at a Catholic university but then surrendered to pressure from the news media and a campus strike. Twenty years later under pressure from the Holy See, they did what they should have done in 1967. This defeat, duplicated everywhere in subsequent years, spawned alienated college presidents, even rebellious pastors. Today, the only victims of episcopal sanctions are likely to be traditionalists, who often deserve what they get but who, because of their small numbers, are incapable of inflicting the deep pain on the U.S. Church presently caused by the boldness of the false prophets.

The arrogance of dissenters is manifest whenever John Paul II is called an Ayatollah or Cardinal Ratzinger a Torquemada, while bishops continue to greet cheerfully those who sponsor these commentators or give them space in their diocesan newspapers. In May 1989 a major religious community, with the "strong recommendation" of its archbishop, wrote to a Vatican cardinal describing the Pope's earlier letter on religious life in the U.S. as "pre-Vatican II." The superior made very clear, as her predecessors have for twenty years, that her community does not intend to follow the lead of any authority, save its own. This is the leadership which is bringing a prominent order toward extinction, their once lush institutions too. Notre Dame's Richard McBrien, a former president of the Catholic Theological Society, only two years ago expressed public pique at the appointment during the 1980's of "ideological" bishops who stress Church authority. Drawing on his experience as a prominent Church divider, he avers that such bishops drive a wedge between hierarchy and the people, especially among Catholics who are "less than willing to see themselves as simple faithful and sheep." McBrien thinks that the Church of the twenty-first century would be better served if the appointments to major American sees were drawn from a list "with names like Esther, Judith, and Ruth." Actually the Church might be better served if bishops quarantined the Richard McBriens, those prime antiauthority figures who use Catholic institutions (like diocesan newspapers) to denigrate John Paul II's administration of the Church.[7]

OLD TIME SENSE OF GOVERNANCE SEEMS TO BE LOST

When one old-timer decided not to discipline a priest for his misuse of a Catholic institution to the embarrassment of his archbishop, he instead sent his vicar to carry a warning to the priest with the following advisory: "In my position I expect from time to time to have my throat cut, but I'm not going to pay for the razor." Some contemporary bishops are doing precisely that.

BISHOPS PRIMARILY TEACHERS WITH AUTHORITY

Bishops are not simply disciplinarians. If that becomes the dominant impression they create, they will not be effective. First and most importantly, they are, like Christ, teachers with authority. They do not speak to hear themselves talk. And when they teach they are not giving their private opinion. They expect to be heard with respect and obeyed if that is what the teaching or the correction of error calls for. In the two cases mentioned above the archbishops in question would have been better advised to chide that religious community instead of endorsing their impertinence, while the bishops who pay McBrien for his divisive columns should have published an open letter of objection, unless they decided to drop his weekly column completely. If bishops have become accustomed to remaining silent in the presence of querulous or disruptive academicians, university presidents, or religious superiors, then they cannot blame faithful Catholics for choosing sides against them. If, on the other hand, bishops' teaching is clear and repeatedly so, and if they are willing to initiate corrective actions to the extent they consider necessary or appropriate, then those same Catholics will come to know the legitimate range of Catholic membership and make informed judgments accordingly. Whenever bishops fail to uphold or defend their own authority, or that of the pope (and silence in the face of dissent is failure), then they undermine the authority of the pastors of their parishes.

Part of the contemporary episcopal difficulty is that bishops have allowed pop social science to redefine their role. And many of them have play-acted to a script which eviscerated the episcopacy of its God-given meaning. They may not have been taken in by the "call me Jack/Jane syndrome," as many priests and religious have been, but a large number fall over backward to avoid being called triumphal, i.e., appearing unusually formal or acting authoritatively. They prefer somehow to appear as hail-fellow-well-met "nice guys," as "democratic" types (whatever that means), especially among those whom they perceive to be potential troublemakers. They have been persuaded that they are more effective when they act as facilitator, as a debating friend, therapist, or chairman of the board, rather than as the legislators, the judges, and the heads of the Church they really are. They tend to let fall into desuetude the social distance that exists between them and the people they govern in Christ's name. Christ was a friend but not a "pal" to his disciples.

As a result, the scale of balance of reverence, respect, and obedience has been tipped against their exercise of independent and final authority. In an era of imperial presidents (even of universities), the bishop is often looked upon as just another wheeler-dealer by those who think they can get him to bargain away the content of Catholic faith and discipline. The ones prone to submit to his authority without a fight are those predisposed by training and conviction to do as the bishop directs.

I recently stood in the midst of a dozen or more priests waiting for a parish celebration to begin, time spent with seniors in the group reminiscing about the crazy aspects of our relationships with prelates like Cardinals Francis Spellman and J. Francis A. McIntyre, archbishops like John Maguire and Thomas Donnellan. Some of the related experiences turned out to be funny indeed. Suddenly one of the younger priests interjected this comment: "You guys still talk respectfully of them, even though you didn't like many of the things they did. Today when we go into the chancery we respect no one, not even the bishop."

In my better days more than a few of us were friendly with many bishops, all kinds of personalities, from cold to gregarious, even on a first name basis. But when we sat with any one of them as our bishop, suddenly we knew at that moment he was no longer just our friend. He was boss and he made us know it even when he was rewarding or complimenting us. The internal enemies of the Church lack respect for the authority of bishops (even cardinals) as the following conclusion to a letter from the major superior mentioned above to the Roman Cardinal makes clear:

"Not only is the letter's pre-Vatican II stance [this referring to John Paul on U.S. religious life] not helpful to us, but it is detrimental to the perception of our Church by the larger public in this country." As long as that state of mind prevails uncontested in important Church centers, the bishops will be the losers.

BISHOPS ARE HUMAN

There is a story told by a one-time university president which describes the bishop who never failed to announce once a year at graduation time that he was the chief teacher in the diocese. "He said it in such a way that you got the idea that he considered himself the only teacher in the diocese," the storyteller related. Then, the bishop went to the Second Vatican Council, where he became so intimidated by the intellectuals he encountered that never again did he assert his supreme teaching role at home.

Most of the bishops I have known or with whom I have lived were good men and first-rate priests, who did their best always to accommodate their role and the use of their office to the human needs of parishioners or diocesans they served. If Vatican II changed their lives it was not the result of any new doctrine about their status—*Lumen Gentium* on the Church devotes more space to the hierarchy than to the "people of God"—but because the climate of revolution during the 1960's upset the Church system as it did civil order. Many bishops had been chosen in more peaceful times for their administrative experience or their close ties to senior bishops, not for their ability to deal with controversy and conflict. And the U.S. Church was seemingly developing so well that governing was relatively easy. The bishop's life then might have been busy, but the controversies were manageable. When antiestablishmentarianism invaded the Church it made its way quickly into the Cathedral precincts. Many of them never had to do serious battles with their own, certainly not about the faith. They gained esteem then for defending the Church against outsiders and anguish later if they tried to maintain public order in the

225

Church. Soon after the Council, almost as if it was mandated, they adopted the policy of avoiding confrontation with those who could do the Church a great deal of harm. It was a human first reaction to the uncertainty over how to promote legitimate change without compromising the unchangeable. One bishop, well known nationally as a prelate with the courage of his convictions, made three tries after the Council to rein in an errant theologian at a local college. After the last effort, he sighed plaintively to a friend, "What more can I do?" The following week he publicly threatened to suspend a pastor who insisted on keeping his Sunday Masses in Latin. And the pastor in question mended his ways.

Later, bishops avoided the semblance of correction or confrontation, at least with virulent dissenters and public sinners. They began to sound as if they had been programmed to accept ongoing dialogue as the ultimate substitute for anything that looked like a hardhearted decision, even in defense of the Faith. They failed to see that recalcitrants use talks to play for time, not to come to terms with Magisterium. They became part of Philip Rieff's "therapeutic generation," accepting the explanation of moral and social aberrations as more the result of mental quirks than of evil choices. The maintenance of discipline, especially by interdiction, came to be considered uncivilized behavior. Such mindsets are evident in the address in 1987 by a bishop warning religious educators about the dangers of "corporate severity" in the Church or by a neighboring archbishop whose archdiocesans were instructed in a weekly column that "fanaticism and small-mindedness" were the result of orthodoxy. While few sensible Christians would oppose tenderness or mercy toward anyone in sin and error, these are hardly the dominant, or exclusive, bases of governance, not unless balanced by considerations of justice, the common good, and the maintenance of that juridical order necessary for civilized or faithful living. It is surprising, too, that at the moment when public educators and government officials were searching for ways out of the permissiveness that had corrupted American society, ecclesiastics were advocating blind humanism

226

in a Church whose convictions about mankind's original sin were based as much on empirical evidence as on faith.

Younger bishops became caught up in another unexpected development—the existence of dissent from binding Church teachings or norms within the episcopal body itself. On the twentieth anniversary of the *National Catholic Reporter* (October 26, 1984), whose Catholicity was once rejected by its founding bishop, nineteen U.S. bishops sent words of public endorsement. During Charles Curran's doctrinal fight with Rome (1986), the dissenter claimed support from more than forty bishops. In his 1988 book *Dissent in the Church,* Richard McCormick, whose contrary views on the morality of contraceptive sterilization are well known, cited a bishop friend claiming that a hundred of his peers agreed with him, not with the Holy See.

If Abraham Lincoln found it impossible to govern a nation half slave, half free when it was conceived and dedicated to the proposition that all men are created equal, then John Paul II cannot preside over a Church half Catholic, half not Catholic; half moral, half immoral; when it was created to establish the reign of God on earth. What Catholic people do in the privacy of their lives is not within the scope of the Pope's authority. But what goes on in Catholic institutions and in the lives of bishops he appoints to supervise local Catholic communities is his major responsibility. In his travels around the world the present Pope goes out of his way to deal with the human condition of his local Churches and their hierarchy. It is his governing role, also, to see to it that the Code of Canon Law is implemented.

NOTES

1. Matthew 21:6.
2. Psalm 125.
3. Luke 10:16.
4. John 8:31–32.

5. Henri Nouwen, *Gracias: A Latin American Journal* (Harper and Row, 1987), p. 170.

6. *National Catholic Reporter,* November 23, 1979.

7. See Richard McBrien in an NC News release published in the *Long Island Catholic,* September 29, 1988, p. 6.

SEVEN

Restoring Christian Living Through Observance of Church Law

CITIZENS of every society who are mindful of the law expect it to be enforced to the benefit of their lives. Indeed, good governance of State or Church is a boon to the well-being of all. Law-abiding citizens have enough sense to realize that a cop on the beat helps them resist betraying their informed conscience. Within the Church, too, the faithful accept pope and bishops as their spiritual fathers. Whatever patterns of order and disorder typify secular society, Catholics normally look upon the House of Faith as also a House of Obedience, in imitation of Him whose life was one of self-abandonment. Catholic elites, even the clergy, are no more exempt from obedience than the "little ones," who were singled out by Christ as models of fidelity.

It is the function of Church law to direct Christian conduct towards heavenly purposes and to frustrate, if need be, those who would lead the people of God astray. Law, even its enforcement, does not guarantee peaceful community life, but its very existence does support the efforts of those who wish to live according to

229

norm, and its proper implementation keeps disturbers of the peace in places where they can do the least harm to souls.

The authentic message of Christianity has always begotten a variety of reactions from those who bear a saint's name—too many demands for some, too little for others, too otherworldly or too mundane, too irrational or too philosophical, too stern or too compassionate, too sacristy-bound or too political, too encouraging toward lust or interfering toward passion, and so forth. In every age complaints are often heard from those who wish to belong to the Church without committing themselves to every aspect of the Church's message. Although their dissatisfactions lead to a certain tepidity or selectivity in the practice of the Faith, they may also indicate that Catholics generally know what the Church expects of its members. More disruptive types in the Catholic community are likely to be those who do not care about government at all—compulsive lawbreakers, malcontents, revolutionaries, those who think they are outside the law or have been trained to think they are a law unto themselves.

We must not underestimate the influence of canon law on the formation of Catholic character. If that law is inoperative in the lives of those responsible for seeing that believers "observe all things that I have commanded you," the Church is badly served. Why did John XXIII convoke the Vatican Council? His first stated reason was to give the Church a new and better law. Twenty years later, John Paul II promulgated the New Code (January 25, 1983),[1] stating its dominant purpose to be the restoration of Christian living. The prescribed "rules and norms of action," he said, were intended to institutionalize important doctrines of Vatican II, and he asked that these canonical laws "be observed by their very nature," with the prayer that "what is commanded by the head may be obeyed by the body." Thus far the wishes of the last four popes have not been realized.

If law is instructive, it is also demanding. A Church which believes in original sin and the propensity of the best of her flock to do wrong knows how to teach effectively and how to use sanctions correctly. After all, heaven, hell, and purgatory are sanctions, and these are what Cardinal Ratzinger says are the forgotten message of the contemporary Church. The threat of canonical penalties is often a restraining influence on public wrongdoers. One is reminded here of Abbé Louis Duchesne, a nineteenth-century Church historian par excellence, who indoctrinated a young Alfred Loisy with his own anti-Romanism. When Loisy was excommunicated in 1907 by St. Pius X, he was asked how Duchesne managed to escape a similar excommunication. He shrewdly answered: "[Duchesne] was an excellent sailor; he took in his sails when the storm grew wilder." This is what good governance accomplishes through laws, decrees, and statutes.

The only trouble is that Catholics in the pews, those who pay the bills, have no idea of the content of their new Church law, which was finally enacted after dissenters made their points with both Paul VI and John Paul II over two decades. Few of them have any idea that the new Code (in Canons 796–821) specifies that no school can claim the name "Catholic" without the consent of competent ecclesiastical authority; that those who teach Catholic theology at the college level or above need a mandate from the same authority; that bishops have the obligation to take care that the principles of Catholic doctrine are faithfully observed in those institutions. They also would be more than mildly surprised that one of the Code's longest sections legislates on religious life. These Canons, 158 in all (573–730) demand that there be a community life (including contemplation) for the membership; that religious understand the ecclesial nature of the corporate commitment; that a religious habit is important as a witness to the religious consecration; that vows of chastity, poverty, and obedience are to be understood traditionally; and that oversight of how the religious fulfill their responsibilities belongs to bishops and Pope.

As far as the faithful themselves are concerned, they are expected to follow in obedience the teachings and rulings of bishops (Cn. 212), and doctrine is to be taught to them according to the mind of the Church (Cn. 226). The New Code also requires compliance with the Magisterium of the Church (Cn. 218) and defense of Catholic teaching (Cn. 229), "avoiding innovations based on worldly novelty and false knowledge" (Cn. 279) with the Pope's decrees and sentences considered to be the last word (Cns. 331 ff.).

A few years ago Cardinal Ratzinger told two hundred American bishops that the fundamental role of the pastor is to nourish his flock with good teaching. And the New Code, in a variety of canons, goes out of its way to specify that the faithful ought to receive good teaching. Catholics are told to shun doctrines contrary to Magisterium (Cn. 750) and to avoid whatever does not accord with the authentic teaching of Magisterium (Cn. 752). Catholic education is to be based on the principles of Catholic doctrine (Cn. 803). Even though the faithful have the right and duty to make their views known, they are "bound to show Christian obedience to what the sacred Pastors, who represent Christ, declare as teachers of the faith and prescribe as rulers of the Church" (Cn. 212).

What about those pastors? The New Code commands that priests are to be trained to show filial charity toward pope and bishop (Cn. 245), to be formed theologically under the guidance of the Magisterium (Cn. 252), and to avoid associations which cannot be reconciled with their office (Cn. 278). Appointed pastors are to be "outstanding in sound doctrine" (Cn. 521) and are charged to make sure they "safeguard the integrity of faith and morals" by exercising judgment, even condemnatory judgment, over writings of the faithful which harm true faith and good morals (Cn. 823). Religious who wish to publish on matters of religion or morals must gain the permission of their major superior (Cn. 832).

But, then, much depends on how those major superiors and bishops exercise their high office. The New Code has a great deal to say about their role in shepherding the faithful properly with good teaching. First of all, all Catholic associations are placed under the supervision of ecclesiastical authority (Cn. 305). The bishop must "defend the unity of the universal Church," "foster the discipline which is common to the whole Church," "press for the observation of all ecclesiastical laws," and "ensure that abuses do not creep into ecclesiastical discipline" (Cn. 392). Even the apostolic works of religious communities come under the supervision of diocesan bishops. Bishops must insist that religious be faithful to the discipline of their institute (Cn. 678) and must deal with abuses in those religious institutes, if that becomes necessary (Cn. 683).

Furthermore, bishops are to see that religion teachers are outstanding in true doctrine (Cn. 805) and that the principles of Catholic doctrine are faithfully observed in universities (Cn. 810). The same ecclesiastical authority has the right to impose penalties on those who teach a doctrine condemned by the Pope or who obstinately reject the authentic teaching of Magisterium (Cn. 1371) or who provoke Catholics to disobedience against ecclesiastical authority (Cn. 1373) or who join an association which plots against the Church (Cn. 1374).

How well or poorly the New Code works depends on its implementation and enforcement, and here the Church relies on particular determinations by all those who work (under John Paul II) in positions of responsibility. The Church cannot solve ecclesial problems by throwing papal documents at them anymore than civil society can cure social ills by throwing money around. There must be a consistent and graced performance by those entrusted with the care of Christ's Mystical Body. We must learn once again to approach this body—that Church—with the reverence due to its sacred character. The Church is not the House of Savoy or Tammany Hall. Pastors must not allow her to be treated as such. Canon 1373 of the New Code reads: "A person who publicly incites his or her subjects to hatred or animosity against the Apostolic See or the Ordinary because of some act of ecclesiastical authority, or who provokes the subjects to disobedience against them, is to be punished by interdict or other just penalties." Canon 1374 calls for similar punishment of persons who belong to an association which plots against the Church.

If false teaching and bad example by priests and religious are the critical pastoral problems of our time, they must be confronted. The Catholic flock does not adequately represent Christ if everyone wanders over the countryside of the Church on his own. Cardinal Ratzinger wondered aloud recently why a dissenting teacher would want to teach in the name of the Church or even give that impression. There is an additional question: Why would anyone in authority allow such a person to teach in the name of the Church?

NOTE

1. *Origins,* February 10, 1983, pp. 555–57.

EIGHT

The Apostolic Church —
Always One, Always Holy,
Always Catholic

JAMES GORDON BENNETT was a prominent name in Catholic circles about the time the Church of New York was coming into its own. The founding publisher of what became the well-known *New York Herald,* and a member of the social elite, often used the bully pulpit of his editorial office to expound at great length on matters Catholic. On one occasion in 1837 he sallied forth to do battle with his pen, boasting: "I am a Catholic. I believe in our Church. I venerate her absurdities—but I do all this in my own way." And then as if to make sure everyone understood what his way was, he added: "We never would and never will submit our mind's free thoughts to the shackles of any man or set of men under heaven, calling themselves priests or prelates. . . . There is no species of Christianity that could more easily link itself with the higher order of civilization than Catholicity, independent of the old fools and blockheads of the Vatican."[1]

Mr. Bennett was not much of a believer. Although an ex-seminarian in Scotland, where he was born, a churchgoer he did not

235

remain. Married by a priest, he hated religious authority nonetheless, blaming churchmen for his personal and religious problems. New York's first notable bishop, John Hughes, was not long in his cathedral chair when the *Herald*'s editor consigned him to a social level only one notch above Irish churchgoers, whom he looked upon as members of the pig family. Still, Bennett never cut his ties with the Church, preferring to be considered a Catholic, not a Protestant. He mellowed somewhat in later life, grudgingly conceding that the deceased Archbishop Hughes (d. 1864) was "the best friend of the Catholic Church in America." John Cardinal McCloskey, Hughes' successor, soothed Bennett's savage breast sufficiently to return the old curmudgeon to the sacraments on his deathbed (1867).

I recount this tale because it has relevance to the Church of our day. James Gordon Bennett was a common enough Catholic type, who stayed in the Church but was never considered by himself or anyone else to be an exemplary Catholic. He and Hughes understood the limits of their respective roles in the Church. The one sensed how far he could go with bishop-bashing, the other the boundaries on his authority to excommunicate. In any confrontation the odds favored the bishop, since as the father of the Catholic family, he was the one responsible for the well-being of all. It would never have occurred to Bennett, for example, that he had the right to incite Hughes' "pigs" against their bishop or to redefine the faith against the mind of Gregory XVI. Nor would such a crusade have been tolerated by "Dagger John." The Hughes-McCloskey era may have represented the infant U.S. Church struggling to find its way in an unfriendly world, but it also drew clear lines around the truth it was teaching, defended the faithful, as well as their faith, and manifested enough solicitude for the errant to keep querulous publishers from dissolving or cutting their baptismal ties with the Church. The heterodox mind and prodigal behavior might not have occupied honored seats in respectable Catholic chairs in those days, but pastors were quite good at keeping them in view and praying for miracles of grace, if only on a deathbed.

A century later this system, which worked so well to the amazement of Protestants, began to break down. Today a scholar's half-belief and antipathy to Magisterium, even a publisher's, are no longer disqualifications for acceptable status in the teaching Church. Disciplined restraint is expected only of bishops. For moderns, Bennett's chief offense would be his public contempt for the underprivileged Irish, not the private state of his sinful soul before God. Arthur Jones, one-time editor of the *National Catholic Reporter,* stated the new case as well as anyone: "American Catholics in new generations are formulating their faith practices without regard to heritage." They are independent of bishops, he says, and Jesus-related, not structure-related, who would make Martin Luther comfortable in today's Church. The Jones agenda goes still further. While he does not expect Catholics any longer to rally behind Roman battles on behalf of orthodoxy and conformity, the ground swell of "base communities" at the parish level will eventually force the Pope (and hierarchy) to become more sensitive to people's needs in matters like in vitro fertilization and homosexual activity. The pope has no monopoly, he avers, on what it takes to be a Catholic or to be saved.[2]

Neither Bennett's lifestyle nor Jones's agenda represent the Catholic norm, much less the Catholic ideal. Yet James Gordon Bennett would be shocked at the latter's post-Vatican II agenda. Jones seems certain that the Church is going his way. More than that, he attributes the present Catholic drift to the dominating influence on Church constituents of American independence and American Protestantism. But does his design accord with that of the bishops' national machinery, where the governing authority over the Church really lies? Run-of-the-mill Catholics have reason to hope not, since for reasons of faith they presume that the government of the Church today will conform with the Catholic understanding of its nature and purpose. Based on the evidence offered by Rome and found in this and other books, they also have reason to worry. Such Catholics are not disposed to brawl with bishops, as virulent dissenters do. They expect bishops to defend what other bishops taught them to be true. Yet it is clear that the complaints of these Catholics are frequently ignored, if not resented, by the bishops' bureaucracy, even as one concession after another continues to be made to the dissenting apparatus, without any discernible Catholic good deriving therefrom.

When all is said and done, therefore, the Church's structure and organization must have a truly Catholic direction to maintain their institutional integrity. The most serious failings of the post–Vatican II Church, certainly in the United States, have been the confused signals to come out of its aftermath about what it means to be a good Catholic. This has happened before in ecclesial history, but elsewhere. Most people are "born" into their religion and likely most remain attached to, or are affected by, a family or an ethnic religious tradition, even if in later life they do not take its rituals or its content seriously. Catholics, however, have a special problem. The Church does not simply say: "We are a tradition." It says: "We are from Jesus Christ and He is from God." The Church does not simply say: "We are a religious people." It says: "Here is what God has to say to you and what we say to you is true because it is God's word." So, of its nature, the Catholic religion is cerebral. Its claims and its content must make sense, not necessarily to the pagan nationalist, but to those who accept the authority of Jesus Christ and that of the Apostles with their successors. If those "successors of the Apostles" leave the impression that the Church is confused about its *nature, function,* and *priorities,* they must expect strong negative reactions from those who have given the Church their intellectual commitment and allowed it to shape their lives.

No matter how well governed it can become, and regardless of the secular social purposes it continues to serve, the Catholic Church is in trouble with its own if its nature, purpose, and priorities are unclear.

I would like to single out four sources of confusion which must be removed by bishops if Catholic sanity is to be restored:

1. Whether the Church anymore considers itself or is to be considered the Church of Christ.

2. Whether working for personal salvation and eternal life is the ultimate Christian priority.

3. Whether there are any moral norms that bind Catholics absolutely, whose observance is important to salvation and the worthy reception of the sacraments.

4. Whether bishops can bind the consciences of Catholics and to what extent.

Many other things rattle Catholics these days—the lifestyle of priests and religious, the quality of Catholic education, poor liturgies, the impersonality of parish life are just a few. But answers to the four questions I ask are central to the credibility of the Church. There is little reason for Catholics to maintain their commitment to an uncertain or confused Church, except perhaps as an exercise in nostalgia. Certainly there would be little motive for men or women to devote their lives to celibacy in such a doubtful enterprise.

I would like to make brief comments on each of the four sources of present Catholic disarray. There are many ways to say what I am about to say. The Second Vatican Council called for outreach to other Christians, to Jews and Moslems, even to atheists. Further, it called for a greater concern by the Church for the human difficulties of people during their pilgrimage on earth. Finally, it directed members of the Church to use their freedom creatively and productively in those matters in which as Christians they are free, obligated to no higher law than good sense, prudence, and concern for the freedom of others. I am not gainsaying any of these challenging directives. In some respects they are long overdue. Among other things they demand that we be careful of our language and that we show greater respect for those who do not share our common faith. Still, it would be a serious mistake to think (1) that one can interpret these directives to include a denial of binding Catholic teaching or (2) that differences of opinion on these matters can be considered merely the result of different personalities (order-loving versus freedom-loving) or of the use of different theological methods, or that they simply represent legitimate disagreements among scholars. Quite to the contrary, we touch here on vital Catholic truths and priorities about which Magisterium has spoken authoritatively but which some scholars nevertheless reject or at least attempt to change.

With these cautions in mind let us proceed.

1. There is only one Church of Christ and this Church is found concretely in the Catholic Church.

This is a basic Catholic given. If this proposition is not true, then the Catholic Church is simply one of many Christian communities, some of which also claim to be Christ's Church. Others would assert that all Christian bodies, considered collectively, and more or less equally, form the one Church of Christ.

However, Vatican II reaffirmed something different[3], and Paul VI in his 1968 Credo of the People of God professed the Church's faith in its uniqueness and its establishment by Jesus Christ.[4]

As declared by the Church this conviction remains a serious bone of contention in ecumenical circles, where the prevailing view is that a multiplicity of churches should seek to reestablish bonds of communion with one another on some other basis than Catholic teaching. The Catholic Church cannot endorse such a view and, following Vatican II, has specifically disallowed it in teaching statements issued from the highest level of the Church's teaching office.[5]

Catholic teaching, of course, affirms and does not deny that elements, sometimes very many elements, of the one Church of Christ exist in other Christian church communities. One thinks here immediately of the Orthodox Churches, which the Catholic Church has always (since their eleventh-century break with Rome) viewed as Churches and which, ironically, profess the Catholic conviction even more restrictively than popes. They assert that their communion is the one and only Church of Christ.

The doctrine about the fullness of Christ's Church being concretely realized in the Catholic Church alone—although it is the foundation of Catholic identity—is being nuanced, muddled, or denied out of existence for Catholic audiences, especially at the college level, and even in some diocesan catechetical centers.

Consider the views of Richard McBrien, chairman of Notre Dame's Department of Theology. He would demote the Church to the status of one among many Christian bodies, having the Catholic Church subsist in the larger Church of Christ, rather than the other way around. He argues that the contrary position consistently maintained by the Congregation for the Doctrine of the Faith (issued March 20, 1987) "tones down" the Vatican Council. He tries to use Johannes Cardinal Willebrands, president of the Vatican's Secretariat for Promoting Christian Unity, to refute Joseph Cardinal Ratzinger. Willebrands insists, as a matter of fact, that although elements of the Church, including sacraments, are found among non-Catholic Christians, "the one and genuine Church of God is found in the Catholic Church."[6]

These efforts, sometimes subtle, occasionally bold, have as a direct result spread uncertainty among the young as to whether the Catholic Church is concretely the Church of Christ or whether Christ has any Church today He can call His own, or even that He intended one at all.

Consider how these "nuances" work their way down to the grass roots of the Church.

About a year ago a young lady from a distant but important diocese visited St. John's University to explore a course of study there and by chance visited my office. In the course of conversation she explained how she was a new parochial school teacher at home and, as part of her initiation into the system, was required to attend orientation classes. When she finished her story, I asked whether she was willing to put her experience in writing for the attention of her bishop. She was willing, and this is what she wrote:

> Sister informed the class that children should be made aware of the fact that the Catholic religion is just another Christian religion, no better, no worse than any other religion—Christian and non-Christian alike. She stated that the Catholic Church no longer believes

itself to be the one, true Church, nor does it teach any greater truth than any other religion. Sister said that this is the valid, post-Vatican II teaching regarding the truth to be found in the Catholic Church.

The Catholic Church is the linchpin of Christianity. It cannot permit its true identity to be denied, even as the result of a hand of friendship extended in Vatican II to other Christian and non-Christian bodies. Whatever we know of Christ today or believe about Him as true is so held because there is a Church which calls herself *His* Church, one which verifies, for those who can never in this life know Christ personally, the truth of what He said. The Catholic Church makes this claim.

However, more than a claim is involved here. We are dealing with a doctrine of faith—"the sole Church of Christ," as Vatican II calls her—and a fact of Christian history. Even those inclined to doubt the miracles of Christ acknowledge the miraculous continuity of the Catholic Church from Christ.

When, therefore, one allows the impression to gain credence within the household that there is no one true Church of Christ, one no longer speaks of the Church to which the Manichean Augustine returned to become one of its greatest bishops; not the Church of the younger Henry VIII of 1521, when Leo X conferred on him the title "Defender of the Faith"; not even the Church which Martin Luther four years earlier only wanted to purge of her impurities; certainly not the Church to which Anglican John Henry Newman made submission at the feet of Father Domenico Barbieri.

As early as the fifth century the priest St. Vincent of Lérins gave witness to the issue that plagues the post-Vatican II Church: "In ancient times our ancestors sowed the good seed in the harvest field of the Church. It would be very wrong and unfitting if we, their descendants, were to reap, not the genuine wheat of truth but the intrusive growth of error."

Affirming that there is only one Church of Christ and that this Church is found concretely in the Catholic Church in no way diminishes the propriety of ecumenical dialogue and intercredal cooperation, including appropriate common worship. The declaration only makes the dialogue and the cooperation realistic, while reasserting for Catholics what the Church believes to be true.

2. The Church's primary reason for being is to lead humankind to a life of holiness here and salvation eternally hereafter.

This is another Catholic "given" about which little of substance is said anymore in Catholic circles, save on the occasion of a funeral. The belief does not underestimate or undervalue the importance of human life on this earth: it merely gives it final purpose, and specifies the role of the Church in contrast to the role of the state.

Some years ago a bishop made this enlightened statement to a meeting of liturgists: "For me the most important thing to come out of Vatican II was learning that as a priest my most important obligation is not to save souls but rather to build a Christian community on earth."[7] No one in the audience thought to ask the bishop what purpose did he think his newly defined Christian Community was supposed to serve.

The bishop must be very uncomfortable today with the final canon of the Code of Canon Law for the Latin Church (No. 1752) which reads: "The salvation of souls always remains the supreme law of the Church."

In his 1987 visit to the United States, John Paul II called the Church "the sacrament of salvation for the whole human race." Specifying that "the ultimate goal of all Catholic education is salvation," "the goal of all apostolic service is communion with the Most Holy Trinity," the end result of faith being "salvation and eternal life."[8]

Who hears stirring sermons today on the four last things— death, judgment, heaven and hell. These are not often spoken of in polite Catholic circles. Nor do we with any regularity indict Christians today for their sinful choices or speak of God's indignation over sin, unless it be the wrongdoing the secular society already holds in disfavor. We find sin more easily in social struc-

243

tures, and if we happen upon outrageous conduct, we are more likely to call the offenders "weak" or "sick," than to say they are sinners. The words of the Act of Contrition have become a dead letter: "I detest all my sins because I dread the loss of heaven and the pains of hell. But most of all because I have offended Thee, My God." The few who go to confession today are treated to God's full mercy, and some priests treat the requirement that habitual sinful lifestyles be corrected almost as a relic of another Church. Hell is never mentioned because all modern Catholics are allowed to assume they are irrevocably saved, making conformity to disagreeable Church norms no longer necessary.

New Testament piety made conversion from sin a Christian obligation. The New Testament states the Christian priority as follows: "There is no eternal city for us in this life but we look for one in the life to come,"9 and, again: "I strain ahead for what is still to come. I am racing for the finish, for the prize to which God calls us upwards to receive in Christ Jesus."10 Seeking first the kingdom of God and "His way of holiness,"11 specifies the Church's nature and function, its priorities, its reason for discipline, and its formation procedure. Eternal salvation is, indeed, the *raison d'être* of the Church.

But if all this is so, why are so many contemporary Catholics absenting themselves from Sunday Mass? From the confession of sins? Why are they receiving Holy Communion in a state of serious sin? Leaving the Church to join fundamentalist sects? Or, staying in the Church with little faith in its teaching? Why are the sexual attitudes of Catholics, and their practices relative to illicit premarital and extramarital behavior, including abortion, closer to the prevailing American mores than to the norms of the Church? Why has there been a virtual wipeout parish by parish of so many "private devotions," created by the Church in earlier centuries to reinforce personal piety and love of God? Why are these acquired deficiencies not a matter of the highest priority, since they reflect badly on the effectiveness of the Church's apostolate?

Today we have conferences on "the recovery of the sacred," i.e., the sense of God's presence in our lives. But how did we lose that sense, this Church of ours with its ancient penitential discipline and its notable ascetic streak. The saints, living and dead, are visible witnesses to the holiness demanded by Catholic formation procedures. And popes, even when they direct the attention of their flock to the reform of social institutions, still insist that reform of people's morals is the higher priority. Reformed institutions managed by immoral people are in the papal view hardly likely to represent the public progress contemplated by the social encyclicals.

Following the Council two alien philosophies began to dominate the thinking of those responsible for the renewal of the Church's pastoral life—Freudian psychoanalytical theories and Marxist political ideology. Catholics no longer were to be burdened with undue anxiety about punishment for sin and thoughts of eternal damnation. Inducing guilt trips was out in Catholic catechesis, even though Karl Menninger's popular post-Vatican II book, *Whatever Became of Sin?*, argues that remorse following wrongdoing is a necessary internal control of antisocial behavior. The Marxist accusation that Christians justify the injustices of this world with promises of consolation in the next took deep root among Catholic teachers. Concepts like "judgment" and "eternal damnation" are obnoxious to unbelieving social scientists. Instead of "blood and thunder" parish missions, we are likely to be offered exercises which make us feel good about ourselves and the world or to encourage good works on behalf of our neighbor or our environment.

Can successors of the Apostles remain comfortable with this present state of affairs in view of the Church's Sunday night prayer? "Lord Jesus, when tempted by the Devil, You remained loyal to your Father, Whose angels watched over you at His command. Guard your Church and keep us safe from the plague of sin so that we remain loyal to the day we enjoy your salvation and your glory."

3. There are moral absolutes that bind Catholics absolutely, whose observance is important to salvation and the worthy reception of the sacraments.

I have always had confidence in the Catholic *sensus fidei,* even among those who do not make Mass every Sunday.

It is not possible to know, of course, what goes through the mind of every parishioner that crosses our path but, generally speaking, people who called themselves Catholic used to know the difference between right and wrong. They might not have been able to recite the Ten Commandments as Moses promulgated them to the Hebrews, but they realized that murder was wrong, so was adultery and stealing someone else's husband, too. Somehow those who could not spell "blasphemy" understood they were not supposed to curse God or to go into court and lie under oath. Believers may not always have obeyed these commandments, which Christ Himself reaffirmed to be God's very word, but they learned to distinguish the good from the bad if only by osmosis within the Catholic community.

I find out now that others disagree with this reading of Catholic opinion.

THE SENSUS FIDEI

In a lecture last year I illustrated this "sense of faith" with the case of a couple, who over twenty years of living together without benefit of a Catholic marriage (the union was later validated) never once attempted to approach the altar rail for the Eucharist, although by reason of family connections they were sorely tempted on many occasions. At this point in the lecture a director of catechetical formation in her religious community raised her hand to say that my observations no longer applied. By and large, she claimed today's young do not have such a *sensus fidei.* They are not convinced about the details of their Catholic commitment and are inclined to think that if there are moral choices at all, the options rest with them. A Jesuit schoolmaster from a Catholic prep school on the East Coast joined the discussion to agree with the nun.

About the same time of the year a moralist friend of mine asked a nearby parish priest how he dealt with sins against the sixth commandment. The young man who had been saying Mass long enough, one would think, to have a grasp of the priest's role in the Church, answered the question as follows: "I don't talk about those sins at all. They're not the most important things in the Catholic catalogue. What counts for me is that most of the people are in good faith on these matters."

If Catholics are becoming unclear about what the Catholic way of life entails, and if the shepherds of the flock are losing the sense of their mission to motivate and support parishioners to do the right thing, then the Church is in trouble with the Lord. Granted that adultery is not blasphemy, both are mortal sins. As far back as the days of St. Paul, Christians knew of their obligation to receive the Eucharist worthily. And it was Christ Himself who spoke of the "second death" for those who by sinning permanently and impenitently separated themselves from God.

In the authentic Catholic lexicon, therefore, the Ten Commandments are not simply nice things to know about. They are expressions of God's grand design for human happiness. Not only are these directives meant to enrich the quality of our personal life, but they are intended to guarantee a reasonably peaceful society to live in. The God who ran planets around the sun in orderly procession did not send the "lords" of his creative enterprise—those made in his image and likeness—into an unplanned and senseless world. We who live in urban America today should realize, better than most, how well-off the country would be if the citizenry lived by God's moral laws.

Those "absolutes," as the Church calls them, are not only serious demands made on us by God for our benefit, but they are foundations of holiness. They are so important to our well-being that we may not violate them, not even to save our lives. Nor to save the Church. Another absolute taught by the Church says that we may never do evil, even if some good might come of it.

The believer looks to God for clear and certain guidance on matters of right and wrong, and to Christ who spoke for His Father. To be Christian is to be in fellowship with the holiness of Christ. And in the concrete order of our daily lives, the Church speaks for Christ. Not only about perennial issues like fornication and homosexual behavior, but about the application of fundamental moral norms to new situations: the natural right of workers to form unions and to bargain collectively; the evil of nuclear war or the obliteration bombing of noncombatants during wartime; the evil, too, of experimenting on live human fetuses. Complicated moral choices are not always easy to make. Is this strike (or this war, or this operation) morally justified? The Church does not have all the answers to complicated questions, like the fair distribution of wealth, but it does know when a particular moral demand binds everyone absolutely. The bans on all-out nuclear war or first-degree murder are good examples. If the Church was not certain on these matters, it would be a poor Church for Christ to have established.

The priest has the special responsibility of speaking authoritatively for the Church on these moral issues, using the common teaching of the episcopal Magisterium and the opinions of theologians which harmonize with the Catholic tradition whenever fine points of application are to be considered. Are the present wage scales of bus drivers just? May nonunion workers take the jobs of strikers? What is the morality of providing military aid to Nicaraguan freedom fighters? On occasion the priest may leave a questioner or a penitent in good faith about his actual or potential wrongdoing, for example, when the facts are not fully known or when serious illness is involved. Normally priests are obligated to help form the consciences of their people correctly, to help them do good rather than evil. If they lead their people into error or sin, even by silence, they commit the sin. Members of the Church are obligated to form their consciences in accord with Catholic norms received from apostolic times. If they are not sure what they should do, they must ask a competent moralist. The parish priest or confessor is normally their first recourse.

Catholics face special difficulty today with priests who do not speak the mind of the Church, yet are permitted to continue as the Church's official voice; sometimes they are rattled as a result of defective moralizing by prominent Catholic politicians. Governor Mario Cuomo's public declaration that a woman's personal conscience is the ultimate determinant of a proabortion choice may be a fact of life with which the Church must live, but it is hardly a morally sound judgment for the Catholic woman to accept or for the Catholic officeholder to endorse.

THE CHURCH AS A MORAL FORCE

The Church is sometimes excoriated for not standing up and being counted when some great moral outrage occurs—as the excesses of Hitler before and during World War II, the bombing of Hiroshima and Nagasaki by the United States during the same period, or in the period when Catholic kings carried on the slave trade. Granted that popes always do more and better than Church-haters like to admit, it is also true that they sometimes compromise their moral leadership by being too cagey or by playing it too safe. They concede too much to the public mood of kings or commoners, or they seem unwilling to play the martyr's role. They often delay decisions until their judgments are of little account. As a consequence history passes them by.

Every nation and every historical period has favorite sins it wants the Church or the government to extirpate. In the nineteenth century America's ethos demanded that we get rid of alcohol and dirty sex. So a crusade was organized to pass laws against both. In the twentieth century we still want something done about liquor and drugs, but political savants advise us to leave sexual activity completely up to personal choice. Sex is no one's public business, they say, not even if it leads to killing the unborn in their mother's womb, or to a breakdown of public morals. Even the Church finds itself caught up in these trendy movements, pulled hither and yon by accommodating theologians who think that Catholics who insist on confessing their sins to a priest should more appropriately ask forgiveness for working on the Exxon tanker that spilled oil over the Alaskan shoreline rather than for their use of contraceptives.

One of the particular problems of the contemporary Church is the relative silence of pastors on matters of sexual behavior. If youngsters believe today that sexual fun is okay as long as they do not hurt anyone else, it is the fault of their spiritual leaders, as much as that of funloving youth. The responses of several national hierarchies to *Humanae Vitae* muted the moral force of the encyclical, putatively out of concern about the burdens on modern couples. Unwillingness on the part of the hierarchies to oppose the sensuality of the culture was the more likely reason.

Perhaps this is as good a place as any to speak of compassion. God knows, every parish priest should be filled with compassion for those who can benefit from its expression. If a priest is good at what he is supposed to do, he shares the burdens of his people and sits with them in their darkest hours. He suffers with them even if their wounds are self-inflicted. If a priest, or anyone else, can alleviate or remove pain, or carry other people's crosses on his own shoulders, he performs a necessary Christian service. Some life-situations are extremely painful and beyond belief in this world. These are the times, too, when the best the priest can do is to provide companionship as a friend, and to pray for God's intervention one way or another. But as John Paul II had occasion to remind bishops on September 5, 1983, compassion is not indulgence. Beyond the support it already supplies, the virtue of compassion also calls for encouraging people to face reality, for speaking the truth, for setting out proper guidelines to live by, for raising people's sights to what is true and right, with a helping hand always nearby. Under the guise of compassion, indulgence often sneaks into a relationship. This is harmful, and perhaps sinful, if it compromises Catholic truth or misleads people about the need for virtue or if it *de facto* supports them in a life of sin.

Pastoring does not include going down in a quagmire with the flock to wallow in shared error or errant behavior. Christ rejoiced in the prodigal son because he was found after being lost, because he came home after abandoning his wasteful life. He did not rejoice because the suffering son remained prodigal.

To return, then, to Christian formation in the proper use of one's sexual powers—this is vitally important because powerful psychophysical tendencies are involved which, allowed to run riot, can destroy the human happiness of otherwise decent people and cause a large amount of social distress. In a quick-fix era like our own, when the technologists, and often the politicians, see the need for controlling everything but the human being, Christian absolutes on sexual behavior, which are intended to fashion a self-controlled sexual being, are counted as ridiculous and irrelevant.

Who spoke more authoritatively than Christ of "two in one flesh," the two being, of course, a man and a woman (i.e., monogamous marriage)? When Jesus spoke of indissolubility of the marriage bond, of the adultery involved in marrying another man's wife, of lusting as adultery of the heart, of the sinfulness of evil thoughts,[12] was he not teaching moral absolutes? Where did St. Paul obtain the idea but from Christ that sexual immorality is antithetical to the demands of Christ's kingdom, whether it take the form of fornication, adultery, or homosexual activities? Why did the early Church (long before the Roman Curia came along) demand public penance lasting a lifetime for adultery and abortion, if these were not understood to be grave offenses against Christ's own norms for Christian behavior? In those first centuries masturbation, contraception, sterilization, pederasty, and copulation with animals came under a similar censure.

When we speak, therefore, of the historic Christian sexual ethic, we refer not to human traditions originating with unenlightened or ignorant people (a description that hardly fits the New Testament authors), but to what God from the beginning deigned to join in such a way that no man who believes in Christ may deny or sunder in good conscience. Christ did not proclaim these

251

absolutes to kill the joy of human creativity, but to guarantee for the commonality of mankind "the greatest measure of earthly happiness in this vale of tears." Particular individuals may not think so, but the society of humankind is never so well-off as when sexual faculties are used within marriage by men and women who are committed to each other for life and who realize the value of fidelity, of God's grace in matrimony, and of their children.

If Catholic young people today are uncertain about any of these truths, it is because the Catholic community has in large measure lost sight of the human benefits of eternal promises.

THE ROOTS OF MORALITY

Let us place these issues where they belong, or should belong, for those who profess the Catholic faith. John Paul II stated in 1984 that the roots of the Church's moral system, including its sexual ethic, are not only written in nature but in the deposit of faith itself. Some years earlier (1979) he told an ecumenical group in Washington, D.C., that the quality of our faith determines the quality of our morals. Even the doctrine on artificial contraception, so often scoffed at today by revisionist theologians, is, the Pope says, part of "the moral order revealed by God."[13] Three years after that 1984 statement the Pope continued to insist that the Church's teaching on contraception was not a matter of free discussion among theologians. He scored their "leading the moral conscience of spouses into error."[14]

THE CHURCH'S SUPPORT SYSTEMS

St. Augustine was quite right in his affirmation that "no one can be ready for the next life unless he trains for it now." But few of us remain in virtue long if everyone around us impresses on us a different lifestyle while our own value system remains unenforced. So, whenever the Church preaches to the world, it is important that its own house be in good order. The Catholic community is never perfect, of course, given the sinful nature of humankind, but it has had at times remarkable success in bringing its people up to standards of belief and behavior first set by Christ Himself. People were able to do this because those demands were reinforced by the Church through single-minded preaching, the penitential discipline, liturgical rituals, pious customs, parish missions, and canonical sanctions—all administered by a clergy that believed in the truth of the Church's message.

4. The bishops of the Church, and the Pope, have the authority to bind the consciences of Catholics on matters of faith and morals and on those things which are necessary to safeguard what belongs to the deposit of faith and the well-being of the Catholic community. Bishops may not bind consciences when the question at issue is a prudential judgment about a particular course of action.*

Peter and the Apostles exercised this "power of the keys" from the beginning,[15] so that, as the New Testament says, "the community of believers were of one heart and one mind,"[16] and the Apostles themselves were held "in great esteem."[17] Paul not only exercised extraordinary authority over his various communities, but he indicted their depravities when the occasion warranted such reproof.[18]

Ever since apostolic times, and with differing governing styles from century to century, the Church has exercised the power of binding and loosing to preserve the unity of its membership and the integrity of its teaching and way of life.

The Council of Trent, for example, specified many doctrines of the faith (and morals) concerning the nature of the Church, the priesthood, the Eucharist, etc., by anathemas. In 1563 it declared: "If anyone says that in the Catholic Church there is not instituted a hierarchy by divine ordinance, which consists of bish-

---

* This latter exception does not extend, of course, to those religious who have a vowed relationship of obedience to bishops and/or the pope.

ops, priests, and ministers, let him be anathema." Closer to our time Pius XII (1948) forbade Italian Catholics under the pain of mortal sin to vote for Communists in their upcoming national election. The Cold War was well underway at that time and Soviet expansion was a threat not only to the West, but to the survival of the Church in Italy. Shortly afterward, at the diocesan level, Francis Cardinal Spellman decried the growing tendency of Hollywood to produce and distribute offensive movies. In 1956 he condemned *Baby Doll* with this advisory: "In the performance of my duty as Archbishop of New York, in solicitude for the welfare of souls entrusted to my care and the welfare of my country, I exhort Catholic people to refrain from patronizing this film under the pain of sin."

Contemporary bishops, and the Holy See, use different language today, but they still emphasize the binding power on Catholics of universal moral principles and authentic Church teaching. The 1983 pastoral letter on peace stressed the obligatory force of the episcopal judgment that "under no circumstances may nuclear weapons or other instruments of mass slaughter be used for the purpose of destroying population centers." They also asserted the nonbinding character of "their prudential judgments based on specific circumstances which can change or which can be interpreted differently by people of good will." They were less certain of their views on limited nuclear war and policies of nuclear deterrence. Others would place in the category of "prudential judgments" bishops' views on unemployment insurance, housing subsidies, national health insurance, affirmative action, specific proposals to ban abortion, capital punishment, etc. The Holy See's action in ordering that imprimaturs be withdrawn from books considered injurious to faith or morals and its censures of Hans Küng and Charles Curran are also examples of exercising "the power of the keys."

The Church, and this includes her hierarchy, makes many judgments in the course of its daily life, many of which are prudential judgments about what at the moment best serves the cause of evangelization, as in papal concordats with nations and actions taken on diocesan Catholic school systems and parish councils. But these decisions are of a different order than faith declarations.

Because God cannot fail, neither can the Church fail in those areas of religion that have to do with the content of the faith of her people. Whatever the Church has received, holds, and hands on to the faithful as the Word of God is believed and taught infallibly. If that is not so, then we have no sure access to God's Word and have been deceived if, under those circumstances, we think we have such access. And, when we use the word "infallibly" here we simply mean the Church cannot be wrong once bishops in union with the Pope, and with each other, teach doctrines and moral norms as coming from God, and as obligatory for all Catholics everywhere to believe or to observe. Whether the Magisterium does this in a solemn or ordinary way is of little account. The truth of the Church is the same whether it be announced in an ordinary way, "Thou shalt not commit adultery," or proclaimed solemnly from St. Peter's Basilica, "Mary was conceived free of original sin." A solemn definition does not make infallibly true what was once considered fallibly doubtful. Dissenters argue that only solemn declarations of the Church are infallibly true. But that position is false. The Second Vatican Council made this very clear in *Lumen Gentium* (No. 25). In that same Council it is not possible to find the word "dissent" used even once. Assent is what the Council fathers expected from the faithful. Bishops can make mistakes in judgment but not when teaching collectively the creeds or the Church's universal moral norms.

Something else must also be made clear. The Church does not want people in good faith to act against their own upright conscience, however mistaken it may be. There are people who believe in the Church but consider it wrong on a given teaching. One troubled Catholic solves the dilemma by conforming his life to the teaching nonetheless. Another Catholic simply cannot give assent for a variety of reasons that seem good to him, even after proper consultation with Church authorities. The Church expects

255

this latter person to follow his own upright conscience and leaves the judgment of that soul to God, even when the person is merely conforming to norms set by his unbelieving surroundings. A different problem may develop later, if the nonassenting Catholic becomes a public dissenter who wars against the received teaching. But then the issue becomes a matter of public order in the Church, not the freedom and duty of an individual to follow his upright conscience.

I was making these distinctions for an audience recently, when a laywoman of some experience asked this question: "All that you have said is very fine. But do you think anyone is listening to bishops, except a few of us old-timers?" When I probed to find out why she felt this way, part of her response was the following: "You referred to Pius XII and Cardinal Spellman. But they spoke with authority. John Paul II speaks with the same authority. Those kinds of bishops expect to be heard and obeyed by the words they choose and by the tone they use. My bishop almost says 'please' whenever he speaks on tough subjects. You'd almost think the choices are all ours."

It is certainly true that the fashionable ruling style in secular life is that of facilitator, not ruler, not governor, not even father. The benign "chairman of the board type" has done little to promote public order or to maintain civil peace. Unfortunately, Church leaders have imitated the worst features of modern society, even though they know that Jesus Himself held the crowds on the Mount of the Beatitudes "spellbound" precisely because he taught as "a man of authority."[19] Andrew Greeley once explained how one becomes a selective Catholic and gets away with it: Be a dissenter and make the bishop dialogue with you, because you have as much of a hand on God as the Magisterium.[20]

There are other things beside loud dissent and the ruling style of bishops which prevent Catholics from hearing the Church's clear voice and heeding its call. Those contribute to confusion who, as working members of chancery offices, do not believe in the demands of Magisterium and say so to audiences and to the press, or who distort or dilute episcopal teaching—and still remain spokesmen for their dioceses or the national office of bishops. Matthew Murphy wrote a book (having a forward by Cardinal O'Connor) with the title *Betraying Bishops.* This is the story of how the 1983 peace pastoral was mangled at local levels, even by USCC officers, through the introduction of "teachings" as official (e.g., on pacifism as an appropriate national posture) which the bishops actually had rejected.

These defects are only part of a larger episcopal problem. Walter Kasper, the German theologian, now a bishop himself, is only one of many churchmen to warn hierarchies against overextending their teaching authority.[21] The more they address in great detail secular issues that do not involve important moral principles or other specific Church interests, the more they jeopardize their role as teachers of God's Word. They also irritate informed lay leadership who have been taught by the highest officers of the Church that the world is their sanctuary.

This is a serious problem for four reasons. First, because intricate social policy statements call for a plethora of prudential judgments which the laity are free to reject. Secondly, it involves them in matters which Church authorities have said many times are beyond the expertise of clerics. Thirdly, it plays into the hands of doctrinal dissenters. Once bishops commit themselves to the nitty-gritty of social programs perceived to be politically partisan, they find themselves as bishops in the middle of controversy with their own people and with each other. Dissent, which is proper in that situation, becomes commonplace. Intra-Church fighting over Mary's virginity or contraception then takes on the flavor of the controversies over the Panama Canal or the MX missile. Fourthly, it creates the impression that one can be a good Catholic if one commits oneself to the social mission of the Church without even being fully probed about his faith in the Church's creeds and moral absolutes. Uplifting the poor to middle class status, to cite only an example, becomes an end in itself without anyone asking whether the poor have been evangelized in the process. This imbalance also explains why a number of newer Catholic social movements speak little of the Church of Christ as Catholic or of the state of grace. In some Catholic circles these have almost become nonissues.

The Church is at its best when it forms the intellectual, moral, and prayerful character of its faithful, training them in the kind of faith and in the virtues necessary for Christian life, and by supporting their witness in the public forum. In the past the Church has often compromised itself rather badly, by relying on secular "princes" to protect its own religious interests and to relieve human miseries. In spite of a tradition as old as Christianity that the sanctification of the world is the special apostolate of the laity, the Church has a spotty record of having developed in any sustained way a lay apostolate that effectively Christianized the culture under which citizens of the world are forced to live. "Apostles" are of little use as representatives of the Church to the world unless they are fully committed Catholics and their spiritual life is in order. That formation is the special responsibility of bishops and priests.

If clerics insist on transforming the laity into "little priests" around the altar, yet fail to form the minds and souls of their flock for their more important and tougher lay role as the leaven of a pagan world, they subvert an important aspect of evangelization. If clerics insist on a veto power over or otherwise discourage dominantly Catholic lay organizations from exercising their independent political judgment, they tend to overextend their authority. This has occurred at times when controversial lay activity has made certain prominent Catholics, and even bishops, nervous, or perhaps contravenes what is considered the prevailing Catholic wisdom. (I speak here, of course, about matters political not doctrinal.) Clerical interference in the U.S. weakened the influence of the once vital *Association of Catholic Trade Unionists*, and more recently the political power of *Right-to-Life* movements. In 1957, the Australian bishops, when they no longer could withstand media heat, literally quashed "the Catholic Movement"—an effort encouraged by their predecessors to have Catholic trade unionists help rid the Labor Party there and affiliated unions of Communist influence. In 1989, the new Italian lay movement *Communione e*

Liberazione was criticized by a Vatican-controlled newspaper merely because it directed attention to the low rates of Mass attendance in that country. Clerics have a difficult time heeding the advice that Pius XII gave them almost forty years ago: Form the laity as Christian leaders and let them go.

There is a no-man's-land here, to be sure. Occupation of the secular domain by the Church's lay forces is to be looked upon as normal. Yet clerics are responsible for the institutional interests of the Church. If laics are not always sensitive to ecclesial matters, clerics forget that most of them are poor politicians, and historically many of their numbers have sold the Church out to the world's trendy forces. The greatest danger in our time is that by so doing they diminish their religious impact in those areas where Christ intended their influence to be felt most.

NOTES

1. Richard Shaw, *Dagger John* (Paulist Press, 1977), p. 126.

2. *National Catholic Reporter*, July 17, 1989, p. 24.

3. *Lumen Gentium, No. 8*. See also Gerard Philips, *L'Eglise et son mystère au IIe Concile du Vatican* (Tournai, Belgium: Desclée, 1967), Vol. I, pp. 118–119; James T. O'Connor in Paul Williams, ed., *Faith and the Sources of Faith*, 1985, pp. 41–58).

4. *Vatican II Post Conciliar Documents*, Vol. II, Austin Flannery, O.P., ed., p. 391.

5. Cf. Declaration of the Sacred Congregation for the Doctrine of the Faith *Mysterium Ecclesiae* (June 24, 1973) in Flannery, Vol. II, p. 429; the Notification of the Congregation for the Doctrine of the Faith concerning Franciscan Father Leonardo Boff's book *Church: Charism and Power* (March 11, 1985), in *Origins*, Vol. 14 (April 4, 1985), pp. 1ff. Johannes Cardinal Willebrands seeks to present an authentic explication of the doctrine in two major essay/addresses: (1) "The Ecumenical Movement: Its Problems and Driving Force," *One in Christ*, Vol. 11 (1975), pp. 210–23; and (2) "Vatican II's Ecclesiology of Communion," in *Origins*, Vol. 17 (May 28, 1987), pp. 27–33.

6. See above, note 5. See also Richard McBrien in the *Brooklyn Tablet*, June 4, 1987.

7. An NC News item in Rhode Island's *Catholic Messenger*, September 16, 1976.

8. *John Paul II in America*, pp. 49, 65, 79, 224.
9. Hebrews 13:14.
10. Philippians 3:13–14.
11. Matthew 6:33.
12. Matthew 5.
13. John Paul II, *Reflections on Humanae Vitae*, pp. 9–10.
14. English *L'Osservatore Romano*, June 6, 1987, p. 12.
15. Matthew 16:17–19; Matthew 18:15–18.
16. Acts 4:32.
17. Acts 5:13.
18. Romans 1.
19. Matthew 7:28–29.
20. *America*, April 30, 1983, pp. 333–36.
21. *The Month*, July 1987, pp. 263–65.

APPENDIX

Summary and Recommendations

In a few concluding words I would like to offer what seem to me to be the most important elements to consider for the U.S. Church in the twenty-first century. Most important, because we priests deal with what may be the best-educated Catholic population in the worldwide Church and also a flood of new poor, whose Catholicity is undeveloped and marginal, even if traditional. The matter is critical, too, because we must speak of the Church as Christ would have it, not as a given populace would wish it.

The Church in the United States has been inspiring as the Body of Christ, as the historical record demonstrates, and its contribution to human betterment cannot be denied. What other voluntary institution over the entire span of this nation's history has motivated so many men and women to devote their entire lives, not only as witnesses to God's word, but as servants of our citizenry? What body of Americans can be found in every nook and cranny of the country raising people's sights about what it means to be truly human and helping them to be the children of

God they were meant to be? Even if the light of the Gospel does not shine brightly in some parts of the world, and if post-Christians no longer show any interest in holiness or eternal salvation, the Church's social and educational services are appreciated everywhere, especially in the United States, where they are so massive.

It must never be forgotten that what made other Americans take notice of the Church as a valuable national asset and as a force within the Church universal, was the conformity of U.S. Catholics, not to the social mores of their country, but to the Gospel requirements of their faith as these were proclaimed by U.S. bishops in union with the Pope.

It would be a tragedy, therefore, if pick-and-choose Catholicism, so commonplace in the weakened Catholic communities of Europe, became the future U.S. Catholic norm, not only for that majority of families whose tradition of pious religious observance has been substantial, but for the new immigrants, who as they rise out of poverty may lose even their Catholic connection or fail to grow into informed and practicing Catholics. Furthermore, during the present drift the alleged "Catholic moment" in U.S. history is likely to pass. The Second Vatican Council was convoked to expand the Church's evangelical possibilities in the modern world. There are not wanting Protestant opinion-molders today who look to the Catholic Church to save Western civilization, in spite of their distaste for certain aspects of its triumphal past. However, if as a result of the problems created for all Christian Churches by the German and French Enlightenments Catholic leaders mute the identity of their own Church and secularize its God-given meaning, then the force of the Church's influence on the lives of Catholics will become minimal, certainly by comparison with the fidelity manifested only a generation ago.

And so we turn to pope and bishops, as we must whenever questions of Church governance are raised. Not only must they teach together as one voice on all matters of faith and morals, but in harmony they must see to it that this teaching is reflected in all the Catholic institutions under their authority, especially in the lives of their priests and their religious. Their most difficult task in the present climate is to offset the powers within the Church which would pressure or intimidate them to accept a watered-down Catholicity as the planned by-product of Vatican II. This is not a new Catholic problem. It was also the major problem of the second and third centuries of Christianity. In his famous disquisition *The Unity of the Catholic Church,* that is, of the one founded on Peter, St. Cyprian, the bishop of North Africa, complained in A.D. 251 as follows: "Certain people, backed by hot-headed associates, seize authority for themselves without any divine sanction, making themselves into prelates regardless of the rules of appointment and, having no one to confer the episcopate on them, assume the title of bishop on their own authority." At the time Cyprian was fighting fellow bishops, as well as pretenders, and interceding with several popes to stand up, to use the authority of Peter properly, in support of Catholic wisdom. Cyprian, the author of the famous aphorism, "You cannot have God for your father if you have not the Church for your mother," died seven years later a martyr for the faith.

So, on the basis of the material in this book, and keeping in mind the scores of official Church documents that apply to the present crisis, and with all due respect to the office of the Supreme Pontiff and the bishops, I would like to propose some steps which are necessary if the renewal of the Church contemplated by the Second Vatican Council is to be realized:

1. Full unity between the See of Peter and the U.S. hierarchy must be restored.

While most U.S. bishops make their profession of faith and take their oath of fidelity to the Apostolic See with the utmost sincerity, and while modern pontiffs have exercised their "supreme, full, immediate and universal ordinary power in the Church" (Cn. 331) with remarkable effectiveness, disagreements between national hierarchies and the Holy See over the administration of the Church are not uncommon, even in our time. Vatican Councils tend to accentuate differences, as I and II surely did

263

for a number of bishops returning home (in 1870 or 1965) resentful of Rome's dominance, and occasionally of its teaching. The reaction to Roman supervision by the vast majority of bishops was and is positive, although complaints of one kind or another did emerge both times. In those situations bishops tend to blame the Pope's Curia, never the Pope. The special problem for us today is the nature of the times, with its compulsive stress on "autonomy" and "pluralism," and a corresponding distaste for "overcentralization" and "papal tyranny." Some bishops ride effortlessly on this anti-Church rollercoaster in spite of complaints from many of their Churchgoers. So does Rome. Consider the way Curial officials have been dealing with post-Vatican II doctrinal dissent.

We have had dissent going on in Rome for years. Since 1965 two voices have been heard from its Seven Hills. That of Paul VI and John Paul II, and a number of their Cardinals, preaching Catholic doctrine clearly and eloquently, who censure bad U.S. theology books and catechisms, as well as the authors, who express anger in various private and official ways against religious superiors, college presidents, and theological establishments which break ties with Peter's See. The city of abbeys, basilicas, and catacombs has also been a place where dissent has flourished, and still flourishes, in pontifical universities, in episcopal colleges, and among a few curialists I have known. U.S. priests have learned rebellion and unseemly lifestyles there, and acquiescence to the vagaries of national bishops' machinery is commonplace. It is difficult to fathom whether Pius IX, Pius X, Pius XI or Pius XII could have lived at peace with themselves in the present atmosphere.

How under normal circumstances of the modern Church (1989) could Charles Curran's mentor, Redemptorist Bernard Haring, of Rome's Redemptorist College, so easily resurrect himself to withstand John Paul II or to rekindle anew the sexual revolution he helped organize as early as 1962 against Paul VI? Not too many years ago bishops I knew, and an occasional cardinal, would complain: "I cannot insist, if Rome does not insist, especially if the

Pope's congregations speak with different tongues." Recently, Roman authorities have acknowledged mistakes they made in dealing with the early complaints of Archbishop Marcel Lefebvre. Why, then, do they now go over the heads of local bishops unilaterally, to grant reconciled schismatics special privileges, instead of demanding compliance by national conferences with the universal norms. If Paul VI, speaking of bishops, could once ask: "Where are our faithful sons?," who down the line of the Church would have been able to provide the appropriate answer? If John Paul II assembled the entire U.S. archepiscopacy because he perceived a high-level crisis to exist in our Church and if the prevailing words to result were "all is well," "things are better than ever," what can the faithful at Sunday Mass think or say that would be meaningful?

The tales of the U.S. bishops' activities recounted in these pages record events which really happened and which are well known in general outline, if not in all their detail, within the Catholic community. They are known to people in the pews, to academics who enjoy the tug-of-war going on between bishops and Rome, and to the National Conference of Catholic Bishops; and they have been known to all recent popes, including John XXIII during the early days of the Catholic Revolution.

The faithful in the pews are asking a simple question: What are the Pope and the U.S. bishops doing to protect the Church's unity and their faith? Why are believers floating by themselves in a sea of what St. Cyprian called "disloyal troublemakers"? Among these "troublemakers" I would situate the "radical traditionalists," although their influence in our country is miniscule. What are bishops in union with the Pope prepared to do about the "radical dissenters" whose influence is more powerful over Catholic opinion and practice? The "gates of hell" will not prevail against the Church, as we believe, but many of the faithful are not too sure. The Catholic hierarchy alone has the final say about what is Catholic and what is not, what is to be institutionalized and what is not, who controls the infrastructures and who does not. I do not know of a pope in my lifetime, and I have known of

265

only a few bishops, who approve of doctrinal dissent or of antiestablishmentarianism, either of which would make anti-Catholic views a new orthodoxy.

The Catholic manuals, to say nothing of Church documents, make much of the phrase "bishops in union with the Pope." The Pope is the one who confirms bishops as authentic shepherds of their local flocks, and unity with him is the basis of their claim to teach infallibly. Historically, strong popes have removed bishops who were embarrassments, sometimes after weak popes have permitted them to continue their scandalous ways over many years. In making such judgments a certain amount of sound political judgment is required. But these are the kinds of decisions we expect responsible officials to make.

In the immediate post-Vatican II period, Paul VI, and later John Paul II, prodded U.S. bishops to conform the U.S. Church to Roman directives—particularly as they related to the theological, catechetical, and liturgical enterprises and to the administration of Catholic institutions, especially religious orders. Roman complaints have slowed down the innovations and made change-makers more cautious, including some bishops. But has anything significant changed? The Pope has not been successful in turning the Jesuits back to the Ignatian norms of "thinking with the Church," and the U.S. bishops (with Rome appearing less influential on them today) have all but legitimated the dissent being carried on within the sanctuaries of religious communities, Catholic colleges, and the reigning theological establishment. Bishops and popes of the twenty-first century are left to face the consequences. One of the anomalies of the contemporary Church is the ready acceptance of the appointment by Rome of an American cardinal as an ambassador to those communities of religious women who have observed all the Roman rules for religious life. The suggestion seems to be that *they* make peace with the Leadership Conference of Women Religious, who have repeatedly made it clear that they intend to accept no supervision from men, even if they be successors of the Apostles. Archbishop May's endorsement in 1989 of the Catholic Theological Society could not have been made if the views of the Congregation of the Doctrine of the Faith were controlling. And, as of this writing, the leaders of the American Association of Catholic Colleges and Universities, with support from powerful U.S. prelates, are providing public indication that Rome will back away from demanding episcopal oversight of the lifestyle of U.S. Catholic higher education, even if this means turning certain canons of the New Code into dead letters. However much these signs of the times reflect the *de facto* Catholic reality, they represent ecclesiastic politics at its worst, surely not the most salvific interpretation of the rubric "bishops in union with the pope."

Some commentators think that John Paul II has decided for the moment not to crowd the U.S. Church any further, hoping that his appointments to the episcopacy will heal the wounds and in due course set the Church on a proper course. In his first address to our hierarchy on American soil (October 5, 1979), he said: "Our leadership will be effective only to the extent that our own discipline is genuine." Nothing in this book makes any sense, if that prayer is not translated into reality without delay.

2. Newly appointed bishops—ordinaries of dioceses and auxiliary bishops as well—must have demonstrated prior to nomination an ability to govern the Catholic community according to the universal norms of the Church and under the supervision of the Pope.

Given the nature of the times, the selection process for bishops must involve more than meeting the minimum requirements of canon law (e.g., thirty-five years of age) or simply fulfilling the Holy See's "Norms for the Selection of Bishops in the Latin Church." Future bishops must only be priests who have a well-defined and a public record of fidelity to the Church's authentic teaching and discipline and an acknowledged talent for providing authentic direction to the Church they are to rule, for dealing firmly, however skillfully, with the need for appropriate correction of error and misbehavior within their household.

The choice of auxiliary bishops has acquired new significance because many of these later rise to become heads of dioceses and because under the New Code they are to be given special responsibilities within a diocese, usually as vicars, general or episcopal. This gives them a ruling status unknown to their forerunners. Furthermore, most modern dioceses are so complicated that no single bishop, even if he is an ordinary, can govern without the help of at least one auxiliary. Larger dioceses have had as many as ten. In such circumstances an auxiliary bishop, given the right position, especially if he is Vicar General, can exercise for good or for ill more influence than the man empowered by the Pope with the diocesan pastoral office.

The fact that the Church is in the midst of a revolution calls for a different kind of bishop than would ordinarily be considered acceptable in times of ecclesiastical peace. A revolution calls for battle-wise generals with experience at least in war games, not simply business-as-usual types who are incapable of bold moves on behalf of whatever cause has been entrusted to them. One thinks immediately of men like Franklin Delano Roosevelt rather than Herbert Hoover, Winston Churchill rather than Neville Chamberlain. Was there anyone better qualified to lead American workers during the depression than John L. Lewis, or to turn a bankrupt Chrysler Corporation into a money machine than Lee Iacocca? Similarly, great bishops seem to rise to positions of leadership and historical prominence in Catholic Sees only when the Church is in deep trouble. Yugoslavia's Archbishop Alois Stepinac and Poland's Archbishop Stefan Wysyznski come to mind as heroic defenders of the Faith when the Church of Eastern Europe was overrun by the Stalins and Titos of the Communist World.

My point is a simple one: safe bishops serve the Church well during times of tranquility, but history proves time and time again that such types are incapable of doing battle, which is what a revolution is all about. During the contestations that followed Vatican II, the older bishops adopted a policy of appeasement of their internal enemies, which proved no more effective as an ecclesiastical defense, than it did for politicians a generation earlier.

The younger bishops who succeeded to stormy sees seemingly were provided with no guidance from higher authority, save to "cool it," as if negotiation from positions of weakness ever halted terrorism in its tracks. And terrorism is just about what academics and religious superiors were waging against Church authority from 1965 onward.

What kind of bishop, therefore, should be considered during this time of Catholic trial? Should it be a priest who never created or maintained a vibrant Catholic community, or one whose chief claim to fame is that he has been another bishop's secretary? What about the priest who was a silent collaborator with dissenters in the institution he headed, or the religious with a fairly consistent record of violating liturgical norms? What about the priest who does not believe in one or the other Catholic teaching, especially the doctrine contained in *Humanae Vitae?* Then there is a sitting bishop's favorite companion or workman, whose distinguishing attribute is his congeniality or his usefulness but who would not recognize a doctrinal problem if it knocked on his door.

In the naming of future bishops, there is still another obstacle to overcome—the unpopularity of the word "conservative." Here I am not thinking of Jansenists or right-wing Republicans, or a Marcel Lefebvre type. I have in mind simply the priest who believes "all that the Holy Catholic Church teaches" and is willing to die to conserve that message. But even to be that kind of conserver is a handicap, especially when the leadership of the NCCB has a deliberative voice in the choice. We have ambitious priests waiting in the wings today for any miter that might come their way, who read these signals quite well. They do not wish to be tagged as "too conservative" lest it be a mark against them in the selection process. So they adopt the voice of Jacob in their proclamations of fidelity to Magisterium, and develop hands of Esau for the purpose of giving away whatever is needed to establish their credentials as "moderate." The chances that these types will make it into hierarchy are good, but greatness rarely grows out of their kind.

Not long ago I asked a highly placed Vatican official, whose expertise in things Catholic-American can be taken for granted, what he thought of the chances of a certain bishop's rising to a position of influence within the higher councils of the U.S. hierarchy. He said: "I doubt it. He comes on too strong." The surprising thing about the answer was the favorable position already held by the bishop in question. Indeed, the bishop in his younger days was considered "a straddler," never saying anything seriously wrong, but placing his signature on studies, reports, or publications that were not quite right. Once in a position of real prominence, however, he began to say things people like me had not heard a bishop say publicly in a long time, even to the point of criticizing in a scholarly way some of the proposed actions of the NCCB. And although most Sunday Mass-attenders would hardly know his name, "he comes on too strong" in high circles to become a national leader of the Church.

I happen to know the bishop in question, and he is far from a firebrand, or New York's John Hughes (1842), or St. Paul's John Ireland (1884). If *he* does not qualify for a leadership role in the U.S. hierarchy then something is wrong with the norms for nominating bishops or the will to select relevant candidates. Two American prelates recently read Fr. Marvin O'Connell's sterling *John Ireland and the American Catholic Church.* At the end of his reading one archbishop concluded that this "consecrated blizzard of the West" was the very reason for a national conference of bishops today, if only to rein in Ireland's type of one-upmanship. Another prelate, reading the same book, opined that John Ireland, a great figure in U.S. Church history, would never make it into the hierarchy today. In 1979 I had occasion to suggest to an apostolic delegate far removed from the American scene that Karol Wojtyla would never have passed muster with the bishop-finding machinery of the United States. The delegate thought for a while and replied: "And if they knew the real Angelo Roncalli (John XXIII), he would not have made it either."

If Rome ever manages to get the norms for the selection of bishops in their proper order, there remains the consultative process, which is wider than it used to be but is still far from ideal. I used to say that Cardinal Spellman not only proposed the candidates he wanted made bishops but also provided the names of people to make the evaluations for the Holy See. It was almost a closed book from the start, although not even he got everyone he wanted. Still, it is a truism that bishops make bishops, and the process is very self-contained. I have no objections to that. Christ did not conduct a plebiscite to choose his Apostles. The election of bishops today by the populace would be a disaster, whatever its helpfulness in the early years of Christianity when communities were small. But there must be some better way to screen out potential troublemakers or nonperformers. It is not always possible to identify "the greats" in advance, but we ought to be able to exclude the unqualified or the dangerous. We have known how important prelates go to Rome to stamp their feet for special nominees that the Holy See has rejected or has placed on hold. And we know how often they win if they are sufficiently well placed. But higher authority should not have to find out after the fact that a newly consecrated bishop once had an undiscovered mental breakdown or that he is a critic of Magisterium.

3. Bishops, once appointed to govern a diocese or an important part of a diocese, must bishop.

By virtue of their office bishops are "teachers of doctrine, priests of sacred worship, and ministers of governance."

They may also be experts in *Wissenschaft,* famed orators, psychotherapists, television stars, Pulitzer Prize winners, and good friends. But in a few words Canon 375 defines their God-given roles and establishes the basis on which hopefully God will judge their work.

How many bishops do we know who have had the courage, or the wisdom, to speak so forcefully and decisively on a host of controverted matters pertaining to Catholic life as John Paul II? By comparison with him many seem timid, uncertain, or unable to address the issues with which the pope always deals forthrightly. Would not our Church in the United States benefit greatly if it had twenty-five bishops of his caliber? A handful of U.S. bishops, like

271

some bishops elsewhere, are publicly on a different doctrinal and disciplinary track than John Paul II (something he knows quite well). Probably also subversive are those bishops who in gatherings of priests and others, when questioned about the possibility of relaxed norms concerning contraception, homosexual activities, women's ordination, or general absolution (or the like), blithely evade their own teaching role by saying nothing new can be anticipated on those matters during *this* pontificate. Not only do these equivocations relativize the force of John Paul's teachings, these in most instances being mere reaffirmations in the twentieth century of what has been the constant teaching of Magisterium, but they raise questions about those bishops' own competence as the Church's "teachers of doctrine." This also sets a bad example for their priests and teachers.

It is not easy these days for a bishop to be an aggressive defender of the Faith, or even to be its pleasant conservator, in the so-called "open" Church. He may consider it his duty to correct an errant theologian running around his diocese, or he may insist that a particular Roman norm be observed, only to discover that one of his priests, trained at a "rebel" seminary under his predecessor, has leaked the story to the media, thus forcing the poor bishop to explain himself to the nation and, likely, to receive more abuse in return. One bishop walked into a troublesome diocese well-known for the widespread dissent extant during the previous administration. A diocesan official explained what happened in the ensuing years: "We rejoiced when we heard he was coming, because many of us were uncomfortable with the old bishop's policies. Roman norms were always stretched by him to their breaking point. The chancery crowd hated our new man because they recognized he would enforce universal norms. The bishop started well, but in short order he succumbed to the bureaucracy. His diocesan appointments today are hardly different from those of his predecessor. The dissenters still don't trust him, but we who expected so much do not think he has the courage to place the diocese on the right track." Another bishop was assured he had been given a fine diocese. But hardly inside the cathedral door, he ran into a buzzsaw of rebels. No one in high authority seemed to have evaluated the diocesan condition, at least enough to alert him, although this is a prerequisite of Church law.

About a dozen years ago, while touring the country for insights about how the Church was doing (my *Battle for the American Church* was then in process), I sat with a dozen priests of a large diocese for several hours one Sunday afternoon discussing priests' morale. The diocese was ruled by one of the nicest bishops it has been my privilege to know. He had succeeded a man of giant size, but chose instead to play the role of kindly pastor. To my surprise, the attending priests, some old enough to know, complained about the new man's indecisiveness, the delayed decisions, and his inability to restrain scandalmongers. When I pointed out that the priests upstate seemed to be less troubled, even though the bishop there was something of a taskmaster, really despised by the Catholic intelligentsia, a young priest in the group intervened to explain: "I went to the seminary there. Yes, he expects priests and religious to play by the rules, but he also runs a good diocese. A lot of us disagreed with some of his decisions, but he's a first-rate debater for the cause of the Church and he's afraid of no one. But he's very kind to those who need kindness most. Some of us looked upon him as a holy priest."

It is the responsibility of all diocesan bishops to insist firmly, with all due consideration for those who have been misled, that those who work under episcopal authority adhere to the doctrinal, liturgical, pastoral, and canonical norms of the Church. Officials in these households of the Faith who substitute their own contrary or evasive opinions for Church teaching cannot be permitted to hold positions of responsibility. Nor should bishops permit clergy or theologians to propagate teachings that are in open conflict with Magisterium, and perhaps heretical. Catholic institutions, certainly the Church's bishops, should not be subsidizing dissent teaching. Such advocates enjoy their own freedom to think and teach what and where they wish. But Church authorities ought not be paying them for undermining commitment to the faith.

Bishops must be careful especially about the seminary training of their future priests and the catechetical instruction of their young. This is a personal responsibility, one that is too frequently delegated to unsupervised underlings. Some seminaries are flourishing, some are not, some conform to Church directives, some do not. Does the bishop know which are which, and does he have input into places where his men attend, those who will be administering parishes long after he has gone to God? The same care must be exercised personally to strengthen what remains of the Catholic school system and to guarantee the authenticity of the teaching (of textbooks as well as classroom performance) and the good example given in these institutions. It is a matter of public record that over the last decade and more there have been tragic failures on both counts, defects often kept hidden from the bishop until public scandal erupts. Parents, those particularly who prize their own Catholic schooling, will not pay the costs presently being assessed for a training that they no longer consider authentically Catholic.

To be sure, friendly words about system, authority, and bishoping run against the grain of rugged individualists, creative types, and revolutionaries. These have a tendency to cry oppression, tyranny, and stifled initiative quite easily. But usually such shouts of outrage are little more than propaganda on behalf of their own self-will, perhaps an expression, too, of hostility toward all social restraints, except the ones they impose on others. I know very few people who like to live in a madhouse. A well-run house satisfies most well-behaved members of any community. I have lived with and under many bishops. It was not always easy, but by and large the arrangement worked well. I would rather live in a house where the only risk was the occasional heavy hand of a bishop. The chaos of everyone doing his own thing is frightening. Indeed, the cruelest form of tyranny in the Church today is exercised against those who dissent from the dissenting way.

Catholic teaching makes the Bishop "the Boss" of his diocese and the supervisor of all activity carried on there in the name of the Church. What has been stated in law for a long time must now be reasserted by those bishops who are one with the Pope in mind, heart, and soul.

The Council was just about over around Christmas 1965 when a handful of priests ran into their bishop and used the opportunity to ask whether they were now free to concelebrate, since the practice had been restored by Vatican II's Constitution on the Liturgy. The Bishop replied: "Soon. I just got home and I'm working on the guidelines." The group leader rejoined that they had scrutinized the document and felt that they could proceed with the innovation in good conscience. The Bishop had the last word: "I have spent twenty years of my life teaching future priests about conscience and have a high regard for it, even when it is improperly formed. But keep one thing in mind. My conscience is running this diocese. And until I issue new guidelines, you'll obey the existing law."

This is bishoping. No school can teach that. The Bishop has the talent. Or he does not.

4. The National Conference of Catholic Bishops must be democratized.

Two years ago, while corresponding with an archbishop about a forthcoming NCCB document, I received a note from him with the following sentence: "There was more freedom in the national assemblies of bishops when Cardinal Stritch and Cardinal Spellman were running things than there is today." A prominent Catholic layman, J. Peter Grace, who knows his way around the inner circles of State, as well as Church, is on public record with the opinion that ten or fifteen U.S. bishops run the other 350. His numbers may be inexact, but the stifling of the individual bishop has been one of the constant criticisms of national conferences by Cardinal Ratzinger. The record of the U.S. episcopal machinery, not only in its political trend, but in its tension with Rome, and in the one-sided ideology of appointments to the United States Catholic Conference, justifies the German prelate's fears. A hundred years ago (1889) the young "consecrated blizzard" made a point

275

relevant to contemporary politics, civil or ecclesiastical: "The timid walk in crowds, the brave in single file."

The only ones who can break the stranglehold by the few or the staff on that machinery, whatever their number, are the "silent majority," bishops all. There is more diversity among bishops on those "prudential judgments" than the literate Catholic laity have been led to believe.

5. The priest must be restored to his place of honor in the Church, especially as the pastor of souls.

Nothing in the Second Vatican Council, nor in the Revised Code of Canon Law, was intended to denigrate the status or role of priests within the Church, especially those charged with the care of souls. "Fathers" who share in the bishop's priesthood stand only a little lower than he as teacher of the faith, celebrant of the Eucharist and other sacraments, and minister of the Church's governing authority. In the lives of ordinary Catholics, parish priests are more important than the bishop, practically speaking. They are the ones who, when they are truly apostolic, create and maintain "the little Church," called the parish, who provide community and fraternity, sustenance for the faith and reinforcement of the Christian way of life. Within the active parish, ideally, Catholics find good teachers, support during stressful periods, spiritual enrichment, and forgiveness for their sins; and hopefully, they find God.

The Council and subsequent legislation may have directed priests to share their authority, to consult more widely, to open ministries to the laity, and to respect their competence in worldly matters. But not one of these instructions affects the priest's role as "Father" of the parish family, nor his role as the official link of Catholics with the Bishop, and through the Bishop with the Pope.

For some unfathomable reason, the importance of parish priests to the Church and to Catholic life has lately been underplayed. Efforts to enhance the status of others may have helped make them look like an endangered species, much as the family doctor has become. The transfer of "authority," traditionally exercised by pastors, to the religious, the laity, and the chancery may have clouded in others' eyes the dignity and special role of priests in the Church. Unwarranted assertions by so-called experts that Vatican II demoted the priest have not been constructive, either.

Origins, the USCC's documentary service, featured on its front page[1] an address which alleged that the decline in the number of priests and their present straits "are the natural and perhaps even inevitable result of the documents of the Second Vatican Council" and that "the Council demoted the priest from *Alter Christus* to *Alter Episcopus,*" i.e., sharer only of the priestly dignity fully represented by the bishop. Someone should have reminded *Origins'* editor that priests trained in an earlier generation understood full well that they shared in the fullness of the bishop's priesthood, but equally that each bishop and each priest is an *Alter Christus.* Today, some biblical critics, seemingly unable to find a letter signed, sealed, and dated by Christ Himself, have begun to doubt that the Lord ever intended or instituted a sacrificial priesthood at all. Still, the teaching Church knows better. John Paul II regularly reaffirms the *Alter Christus* nature of the priesthood,[2] the only reason in fact a young man should aspire to the burdens of this office. We ignore the Church's history when we forget that Christ took fishermen, tax collectors, tentmakers, and made them priests. Modern culture, personified by disenchanted elites of our time, would take priests and turn them into social workers, pop psychologists, and facilitators, anything that would disestablish "the Holy Rule" (hierarchy) of God over man, or of man over man in the name of God.

A great deal is said today about the low morale of priests, opinion-molders suggesting that more worldly benefits, more understanding or elbow-rubbing with bishops, more married or woman priests might solve the psychosocial problems of many. But the human happiness of priests has not been bettered by changes in Church structures, nor by shifting emphasis away from the importance of the work towards personal feelings of satisfaction. Depression among priests in our time is partly the result of a depressing of the religious significance of the priesthood itself. In the new dispensation, the priesthood is looked upon neither as a superior calling nor as an adequate response by the Church to people's contemporary needs. This new framework would make irrelevant not only the *Alter Christus* but the *Christus* Himself. Why should any man (or woman) wish to be that kind of priest? As refashioned, this is not the priesthood that sent Peter and Paul to Rome, Patrick to Ireland, Boniface to Germany, Francis Xavier to India, Charles Foucald to Africa or John Neumann to New York.

Unfortunately, contemporary bishops have been accused of contributing to the denigration of the priesthood by seeming to spend more time worrying about diocesan institutions and special interests within their jurisdictions, or occasionally by taking the sides of recalcitrant religious, for example, against pastors. If a given pastor proves himself incapable of following Church directives, he should be removed. Bishops should not allow the parish priest to be harassed, or consider him difficult, if he is the one who insists on observing the discipline of the Church. When a bishop undermines a pastor, he undermines his own authority.

I often think of how U.S. bishops, belatedly it is true, eventually strengthened and invigorated priestly status about the time the U.S. Church was moving towards its Catholic ascendancy. But enhance it they did. Perhaps the fact that large numbers of bishops then were once pastors themselves had something to do with the commonality of a parish-centered diocesan administration. The episcopal push for parochial schools was another contributing factor, making the local pastor a man with whom the Bishop would have to reckon. If the pastor would not, the Bishop often could not.

The "episcopal visitation" of every parish in the nineteenth and early twentieth centuries was a powerful force in the creation and maintenance of the unique U.S. parochial dynamism. The Bishop would spend a day and a night, sometimes two days, in

278

the neighborhood or town, survey the parochial scene, talk with the priests and the religious, conduct services for the laity, and repair to the rectory to meet any parishioner who wished to speak with his or her bishop. Whatever else it was designed to accomplish, this parochial visitation of the parish helped the Bishop place his personal stamp on the parish life of his time and gave him a first-hand look at the pastor's difficulties. How do you think the people felt when they knew they could walk into a rectory and talk to their bishop? Some of those visits might have made the pastor nervous, but by and large the Church benefited. Over all, the pastors could not claim they were ignored, and bishops developed a parochial sense.

The "episcopal visitation" was, of course, a device only as good as the use to which it was put. It worked best when there was advance preparation by the Bishop, who had to have his own priorities in order. In those days the instructions of the universal Church were high on the Bishop's checklist: the proper celebration of the liturgy and the administration of the sacraments, the Catholic catechesis of children and adults, personal outreach of priests to lukewarm and fallen-away Catholics, the visitation of homes (parish census), involvement of the parish in the neighborhood concerns, and the observance of diocesan norms. During these visitations bishops naturally came upon "bad news," but most of the time they had advance warning. Furthermore, those bishops knew how to deal with it, because they understood that wrongdoing, like disease, only grew to epidemic proportions by neglect.

By the time I was ordained (1942), the "episcopal visitation" was a joke, consisting mainly of a short conversation with the pastor, a quick scan of the parish registries, long enough for the Bishop to sign his name at the last entry, an early departure, but never an evaluation of the parish at all.

Perhaps the time has come for bishops to cancel meetings in central headquarters to spend time in every parish of their diocese week by week.

6. The place of fatherhood/motherhood must be reconstituted as central to the vocation of Catholic marriage, and after years of neglect by Catholic pastors, the family the "second little Church" must be reshaped into the centerpiece of the universal Church in the twenty-first century.

It is almost incredible that this suggestion need be made at all, a sign of the times perhaps. The modern generation of young Catholics almost have to be recatechized on the divine vocation of marriage, the central place of children, of fatherhood and motherhood in marriage, and the vital importance of the Church's sacred norms. If we neglect the foundation stone of the Church of the next century, perhaps because we cater unduly to special interests, we can no longer call the family a "little Church."

But this will require make-up work and for the task authentic teachers are required. Uncertain voices may have existed in the Church of St. Paul,[3] but after two millennia there is little reason why confused teaching on family life should exist under Catholic auspices. If the Church can appear countercultural on matters sociopolitical, why is John Paul II almost a voice crying in the wilderness on the morals of Catholic family life? In recent days political scientist George Weigel reminded bishops of St. Augustine's concept *tranquillitas ordinis,* a negative concept to be sure, but one without which sinful men cannot live in peace. As Weigel phrases it: "Order keeps things from getting worse than they would be under conditions of chaos and anarchy."[4] If the Church cannot reinforce its own teaching on marriage within its own infrastructure, then the universal catechism, the single significant by-product of the 1985 Extraordinary Synod, will turn out to be another Church document that is to be filed and forgotten.

To explicate in detail the need for a new "family crusade" within the Church goes beyond the scope of this book. Yet those of us who owe our faith to our parents as much as to anyone recognize the difficulties facing the young man and woman of today who wish to settle down and raise a real Catholic family. All around them they see homes which are places where beds are shared more than kinship and where temporary or disturbed relationships are commonplace, not the fulfillment of marriage vows. Because of their youth they may not realize how over a span of forty years the father's role as the one responsible for the family welfare has unraveled. They surely live under intense pressure to send mother out into the marketplace to make money, rather than have her create at home a nesting place for children and a haven on earth for herself and her husband. These neophytes may not know that birthrates of the married are down, but they cannot escape the knowledge that birthrates of the unmarried are up. Engaged couples are pelted with data about lonely children, battered children, sexually abused children, children with AIDS, children increasingly passed on to strangers or professionals because parental hands are no longer there to hold them. How can they not be affected by the cultural drift toward "rotating polygamy," toward sex without marriage, sex without children, sex of a man without a woman, of a woman without a man.

Such young people, if they are themselves products of a good Catholic family, have a right to ask: What is the Church doing about our nation's one-time chief civilizing institution? And more importantly about the Church in miniature? If they have a longer view than their years indicate, they might even wonder: What has happened to the large family, that phenomenon of the 1950s, which was then so dominantly Catholic? Prior to Vatican II, 20 percent of all Catholic households sheltered four or more children, a fact of our religious life which prompted Pius XII to call the large family "most blest by God and especially by the Church." What priest can or would speak in this fashion today? At the present parish level the modern Catholic lady who bears a third child is frequently looked upon as an anomaly, if not an abnormality. Many of her religious peers after the first or second have their tubes tied, sometimes in a Catholic hospital. These aberrations were unthinkable two generations ago.

The U.S. bishops missed a golden opportunity after World War II when a timely Catholic family apostolate was spontaneously generated by couples themselves. Today the bishops must deal with a formidable enemy within—the contraceptive mind of so many of their subordinates and coworkers and the contumacious unwillingness of that kind of Catholic to help reinforce the Church's family ethos, so eloquently articulated by John Paul II.

The Church should initiate a national crusade, long overdue considering *Humanae Vitae,* on behalf of *Natural* family planning —not only to teach our people how to be married and Catholic, when child-spacing is indicated, but to educate the vast body of religious Americans as to what authentic married love is and why marriages based on this kind of love are more meaningful, more perduring, and more fruitful for both Church and society. For the Catholic people alone, NFP promises this much at least—a married life in conformity with God's law. When such training reaches down to the parish level as Sunday Mass, regular confession, and the parochial school once did, the Church will have regained its place in the heart of the aspiring Catholic family. Failure to institutionalize NFP within the Church is one of our most culpable post-Vatican II defects.

7. Suitable defense mechanisms, organized and maintained by properly formed Catholic laity are a necessary component of the "aggiornamento" initiated by Vatican II.

Where are the apostolic lay movements that the Church has been talking about for three centuries? Clergy are not going to reform the social structures of civil society. Their preaching is important, and surely their condemnation of public sin and social crime. Citizenry everywhere accept this guidance, indeed look forward to it, even when the episcopal indictments strike too close to home. But when clerics, especially bishops, become too involved in the political process against the reigning but non-Christian mores, they foster the endemic anti-Catholicism of the nation's opinion molders. If the Church is to have an easier time evangelizing a hostile culture, it needs the effective lay movements.

This may be the Church's most arduous external task: to bring its corporate influence to bear on the public institutions of our society, if only indirectly, especially on the government, on the media, and on those who fashion the secular mind sets of the country's public leaders. We are not speaking here simply of overcoming pornography, condoms, and abortion, although we must not underestimate their importance as rallying points for religious activists of many persuasions. There is also the critical matter of freedom of religion in our free country. In the last forty years religionists have allowed themselves to be antiestablished out of public life, and religion to be reduced to the status of public oddity. So much so that the comfortable public role of an otherwise avowed religionist has become capsulated in a single formula: "I believe in Jesus Christ but . . ." And this has occurred at a moment in U.S. history when the most formidable adversary today of religious influence in American life is government and its various subdivisions or bureaucracies.

It is also something of a mystery why religious groups permit the media to trivialize or treat contemptuously the teachings and sacred authority of their churches. The 1987 pilgrimage of John Paul II to his American faithful occasioned what appeared at times to be an anti-papal crusade. The frequency with which dissident Catholics were called upon by media to explain away the Church and its pope was sinister. The media would not have dared treat the Jewish, black, or labor community with such cynicism. The religious forces of the nation, not excluding Catholics, need a well-supported league of some kind, or two or three, to defend the interests of our religious citizenry, as B'nai B'rith, the NAACP, and the AFL-CIO protect the rights of their constituents. Catholics have been pressured to hide from charges of censorship and to cower before accusations aimed at denying influence within the media to religionists. The Catholic Church does not have an effective role in the world of electronic communications, a puzzling fact of life in view of the success of Evangelical Protestants, who use television effectively to shore up the faith of their flocks.

As a final point, it is incumbent on the Catholic community to draw on that segment of the world of Catholic higher education which still is or wishes to be institutionally committed to the Catholic Church and its faith. A major tragedy for the Church is that the aspiring Catholic Harvards of our time have become more Harvard than Catholic and are of little use to the Church in confronting the neopagan and statist ideas that prevail in the higher regions of American society. It is time, perhaps, for bishops to acknowledge that, like Harvard, many Catholic colleges have sold their birthright. However, there are still a large number of Catholic scholars who believe in the truths of their faith and are quite willing to defend them. These are not the scholars quoted frequently on CBS or by the *New York Times*, oftentimes not even in *Origins*.

If we can speak of the Catholic lay apostolate any longer, and we can if we mean "Catholic" as well as "lay," then pastors must give their support to these kinds of faithful and permit them to take the Catholic cause into the marketplace, where they, not clergy, will demand respect and get it, after they first fight for recognition.[5]

With a fully developed alternative to the present secularized organs of opinion-molding, our Catholic people can hopefully once more take pride in their Church and the quality of their parish and family life, even if it is not mainstream secularized America.

There are still many other things that could be written in greater detail about *Keeping the Church Catholic with John Paul II*, enough perhaps that a good-sized library would be needed to contain them. But these are written to encourage the faithful to believe that Christ lives in His Church today and among His people as He did in Jerusalem, dying a little here, rising gloriously there; that He lives not only in the Eucharist, but in His Vicar John Paul II and the bishops in union with him, not only for the sake of their eternal salvation but to represent God's Word to this blessed country of ours. In the words of James Cardinal Gibbons, uttered as the Church of the United States was entering what may have been the period of its greatest piety (August 8, 1919): "Only from Christianity can America draw the blood that will give her life for the future and that strong nourishment will come to her from Christ through the Church." Amen.

NOTES

1. February 4, 1988.
2. *John Paul II in America*, p. 126.
3. 1 Corinthians 14:8.
4. *Tranquillitas Ordinis*, p. 31.
5. Richard John Neuhaus's *The Naked Public Square*, called "The book from which further debate about church-state relations should begin," calls for the development of a public philosophy grounded in values that are based in Judaeo-Christian religion.

Selected Bibliography

Benestad, Brian. *Pursuit of a Just Social Order.* Washington, D.C.: Ethics and Public Policy Center, 1982.

Bouyer, Louis. *The Decomposition of Catholicism.* Chicago: Franciscan Herald Press, 1969.

Brown, Harold, O.J. *Heresies.* Garden City, N.Y.: Doubleday & Co., 1984.

Brown, Raymond E. *Crises Facing the Church.* New York: Paulist Press, 1975.

Burke, Cormac. *Authority and Freedom in the Church.* San Francisco: Ignatius Press, 1987.

Castelli, Jim. *The Bishops and the Bomb.* Garden City, N.Y.: Doubleday/Image, 1983.

Clark, Stephen B. *Man and Woman in Christ.* Ann Arbor, Mich.: Servant Publications, 1980.

The Code of Canon Law. Washington, D.C.: Canon Law Society of America, 1983.

Cohalan, Florence. *A Popular History of the Archdiocese of New York.* New York: U.S. Catholic Historical Society, 1983.

Cooke, Bernard (ed.). *The Papacy and the Church in the United States.* New York: Paulist Press, 1989.

DeLeatapis, Stanislaus, S.J. *Family Planning and Modern Problems: A Catholic Analysis.* New York: Herder and Herder, 1967.

DeLubac, Henri, S.J. *Splendor of the Church.* San Francisco: Ignatius Press, 1984.

Dolan, Jay P. *The American Catholic Experience.* Garden City, N.Y.: Doubleday & Co., 1985.

Dulles, Avery, S.J. *The Reshaping of Catholicism.* San Francisco: Harper & Row, 1988.

Ellis, John T. *The Life of James Cardinal Gibbons* (2 vols.). Westminster, Md.: Christian Classics, 1987.

Flannery, Austin, O.P. *Vatican Council II: The Conciliar and Post-Conciliar Documents.* Northport, N.Y.: Costello Publishing Co., 1975.

Fogarty, Gerald P. *The Vatican and the American Hierarchy from 1870 to 1965.* Wilmington, Del.: Michael Glazier, 1985.

Gallup, George, and Jim Castelli. *The American Catholic People.* Garden City, N.Y.: Doubleday & Co., 1987.

Gleason, Philip. *Keeping the Faith: American Catholicism Past and Present.* Notre Dame: University of Notre Dame Press, 1987.

Gremellion, Joseph, and Jim Castelli. *The Emerging Parish.* San Francisco: Harper & Row, 1987.

Guilday, Peter. *History of the Councils of Baltimore.* New York: Macmillan, 1932.

Hitchcock, James. *Catholicism and Modernity: Confrontation or Capitulation.* New York: Crossroads, 1979.

Hoyt, Robert. *The Birth Control Debate.* Kansas City: NCR Press, 1968.

Human Sexuality (A Study Commissioned by the Catholic Theological Society of America). New York: Paulist Press, 1977.

John Paul II in America. Boston: St. Paul Books, 1987.

John Paul II, Reflections on Humanae Vitae. Boston: St. Paul Editions, 1984.

Kaiser, Robert B. *The Politics of Sex and Religion.* Kansas City: Leaven Press, 1985.

Kauffman, Christopher J. *Tradition and Transformation in Catholic Culture.* New York: Macmillan, 1988.

Kelly, George A. *Catholics and the Practice of the Faith: 1944.* New York: Paulist Press, 1946.

———. *The Lay Apostle.* Washington: National Catholic Welfare Conference, 1963.

———. *Catholics and the Practice of the Faith: 1967 and 1971.* New York: St. John's University Press, 1972.

———. *Why Should the Catholic University Survive?* New York: St. John's University Press, 1973.

———. *Who Should Run the Catholic Church?* Huntington: Our Sunday Visitor Press, 1976.

———. *The Battle for the American Church.* Garden City, N.Y.: Doubleday & Co., 1979.

———. *The Crisis of Authority: John Paul II and the American Bishops.* Chicago: Regnery Gateway, 1982.

———. *The New Biblical Theorists: Raymond E. Brown and Beyond.* Ann Arbor, Mich.: Servant Books, 1983.

———. *Inside My Father's House.* New York: Doubleday, 1989.

Küng, Hans, and Leonard Swidler. *The Church in Anguish.* San Francisco: Harper & Row, 1986.

Lawler, Philip. *How Bishops Decide: An American Catholic Case Study.* Washington, D.C.: Ethics and Public Policy Committee, 1988.

Martin, Malachi. *The Jesuits.* New York: Simon & Schuster, 1987.

McBrien, Richard. *Catholicism* (2 vols.). Minneapolis: Winston Press, 1980.

Muggeridge, Anne R. *The Desolate City.* San Francisco: Harper & Row, 1986.

Murphy, Matthew. *Betraying Bishops.* Washington, D.C.: Ethics and Public Policy Committee, 1987.

Neuhaus, Richard J. *The Naked Public Square.* Grand Rapids, Mich.: Eerdmans, 1984.

———. *The Catholic Moment.* San Francisco: Harper & Row, 1987.

Noonan, John. *Contraception.* Cambridge: Harvard University Press, 1965.

———. *A Private Choice: Abortion in the Seventies.* New York: Free Press, 1979.

O'Brien, David J. *The Renewal of American Catholicism.* New York: Oxford University Press, 1972.

O'Connell, Marvin R. *John Ireland and the American Catholic Church.* St. Paul: Minnesota Historical Society Press, 1988.

Rieff, Phillip. *The Triumph of the Therapeutic.* New York: Harper Torchbooks, 1968.

Shaw, Richard. *Dagger John: The Life of Archbishop John Hughes.* New York: Paulist Press, 1977.

Shea, John Gilmary. *The Catholic Church in the United States.* New York: D. H. McBride & Company, 1890.

Smith, John T. *The Catholic Church in New York* (2 vols.). New York: Hall & Locke Company, 1905.

Wakin, Edward, and Scheuer, Joseph F. *The De-Romanization of the American Catholic Church.* New York: Macmillan, 1966.

Watch, Timothy (ed.). *The Heritage of American Catholicism.* New York: Garland Publishing, 1988.

Weigel, George. *Tranquillitas Ordinis.* New York: Oxford University Press, 1987.

Index

291

INDEX

INDEX

INDEX

McBrien, Richard, 21, 46, 213
  on authoritarian bishops, 222
  on relationships with non-Catholic
    Christians, 241
McCarrick, Theodore, Archbishop, 158
McCloskey, John Cardinal, 236
McCormick, Richard A., Father, 135,
  201, 227
  on doubt, 42
  on sexuality, 43
McFarland, Norman, Bishop, 159
McInerney, Ralph, 75, 181, 191, 216
McIntyre, J. Francis A. Cardinal, 224
Macioce, Thomas M., 142–43
McManus, Frederick, Monsignor, 75
McManus, William, Bishop, 174
McShea, Joseph, Bishop, 79
Magisterium
  Birth Control Commission minority
    report, 45
  canon law regarding, 231–32
  Cardinal Wright on, 62–68
  current controversy, 58
  overextension, 257
  Pius XII teachings on, 16
Maguire, John, Archbishop
Mahony, Roger M., Archbishop
  on AIDS statement, 158, 172
  on NCCB, 143–44, 165
Man and Woman in Christ, 177
Mangan, Joseph, Father, 134
Many Faces of AIDS, 171, 172
Marriage
  annulment of. *See* Nullity
  church doctrine on, 98–100, 108
  corruption by contraception, 30
  encyclical (1930), 30
  internal forum solution, 108
  resurgence as a divine vocation, 280–
    81
Marriage tribunals, 99, 107, 198
Marshall, John, 13–14, 50
Martina, Giacomo, 17
Marxist political ideology, 245
May, John, Archbishop, 151

  on the doctrinal responsibilities
    statement, 190–91, 266
  as president of NCCB, 166–67
May, William, 134, 160–61, 181, 216
Menninger, Karl, on sin, 245
Merthaler, Bernard, 46
Missionaries of Charity, 155
Modernism, 62
Molloy, Edward, 74
Mooney, Christopher, 46
Moral absolutes
  binding power, 253–54
  importance of, 246–53
  on sexual behavior, 250–52
Moran, Gabriel, 46
Murphy, Matthew, 136, 257
Murphy, Roland, Father, 46
Murray, John Courtney, Father, 12
  on objective moral norms, 49

National Catechetical Directory, 70, 89,
  92–93
National Catholic Reporter, 13, 14, 70,
  184, 227
National Catholic Welfare Conference,
  12, 126
National Conference of Catholic Bishops
  democratization for, 275–76
  economic pastoral, 136–43
  establishment, 126
  exclusionary tactics, 167, 181
  future direction, 214
  General Secretary's powers 143–44
  meeting, 1987, 152–53
  meeting, 1988, 164–68, 173–75, 179
  meeting, 1989, 185–90
  meeting with John Paul II, 1989,
    192–203
  "Norms for Licit Theological
    Dissent", 47
  on population questions, 138–39
  proposals regarding doctrinal
    responsibilities, 152–53, 178–79,
    185–90

297

INDEX

publication procedures, 144
relationship with bishops, 143–45
staff actions on Ratzinger's letter, 168
staff appointments, 143–44
Unity, restoration, 219
Universal Catechism, 128
Urs von Balthasar, Hans, 201

Vagnozzi, Aegidio Cardinal, 109–10
Vatican document on episcopal
   conferences controversy, 167, 182–
   85
Vatican II (1962–65)
   change resulting from, 15, 18, 215,
      238
   on contraception, 35
   decentralization through, 125–26
   effect on American Catholicism, 199–
      201, 203, 238
   human problem focus, 218
   on infallibility, 255
   internal reforms, 16
   interpretations of its purpose, 218–19,
      238
   on other religions, 239
   reasons for, 16–17, 230, 262
   on special training centers, 64
   and the U. S. bishops, 117
   as the work of the Spirit, 219
Vaughan, Austin, Bishop, 170
   on the doctrinal responsibilities
      statement, 188

on religious pluralism, 81
on standards for confession, 174
on the Vatican document on episcopal
   conferences, 183
Villot, Jean Cardinal, 63, 66
Visser, Jan, Father, 39
Vitz, Paul, 81–82

Weakland, Rembert, Archbishop, 137–
   38, 146, 151, 174
Weigel, George, 280
Whatever Became of Sin?, 245
Whealon, John, Archbishop, 166, 174
Wiedner, Marie, Sister, 106
Willebrands, Johannes Cardinal, 241
Women
   apostolic letter on, 179
   ordination, 58, 163
   role in Church, 151, 163–64
Women for Faith and Family, 175
Women's pastoral, 175–78
Woodstock Letters, 13
Wrenn, Michael, Father, 65
Wright, John, Cardinal, 62–70
Wuerl, Donald, Bishop, 164–65, 166
Wysyznski, Stefan, Archbishop, 268

Young Catholics, Church ties, 217
Your Child and Sex, 13

Zalba, Marcellino, Father, 34

GEORGE A. KELLY, ordained a priest in 1942, holds a Ph.D. in Social Science from Catholic University of America. He was parish priest and pastor during the first half of his ministry. Later, he was director of the Institute for Advanced Studies at St. John's University, New York. Presently, he is a research professor there for Contemporary Catholic Problems. Founder of the Fellowship of Catholic Scholars, he was named a consultant to the Holy See in 1983.